T0214823

Lecture Notes in Computer Science 8429

Commenced Publication in 1973
Founding and Former Series Editors:
Gerhard Goos, Juris Hartmanis, and Jan van Leeuwen

For further volumes:
http://www.springer.com/series/7407

Narayan Desai · Walfredo Cirne (Eds.)

Job Scheduling Strategies for Parallel Processing

17th International Workshop, JSSPP 2013
Boston, MA, USA, May 24, 2013
Revised Selected Papers

 Springer

Editors
Narayan Desai
Mathematics and Computer Science
 Division
Argonne National Laboratory
Argonne, IL
USA

Walfredo Cirne
Google
Mountain View, CA
USA

ISSN 0302-9743   ISSN 1611-3349   (electronic)
ISBN 978-3-662-43778-0   ISBN 978-3-662-43779-7   (eBook)
DOI 10.1007/978-3-662-43779-7
Springer Heidelberg New York Dordrecht London

Library of Congress Control Number: 2014941592

LNCS Sublibrary: SL1 – Theoretical Computer Science and General Issues

Printed on acid-free paper

Springer is part of Springer Science+Business Media (www.springer.com)

Preface

This volume contains the papers presented at the 17th workshop on Job Scheduling Strategies for Parallel Processing that was held in Boston, USA, on May 24, 2013, in conjunction with the IEEE International Parallel Processing Symposium 2013.

This year 20 papers were submitted to the workshop. All submitted papers went through a complete review process, with the full version being read and evaluated by an average of four reviewers. We would like to especially thank the Program Committee members and additional reviewers for their willingness to participate in this effort and for their detailed, constructive reviews.

As a prime venue of the parallel scheduling community, the Job Scheduling Strategies for Parallel Processors workshop offers a vantage point for one to witness the evolution in the area. When it began in 1995, parallel job scheduling was in its infancy. The first large-scale parallel machines had emerged over the preceding few years, demonstrating the practical need for parallel schedulers. Early parallel systems, and even modern supercomputers, have a very static set of resources and configuration. More recently, cloud systems have emerged in much larger scale configurations. Such systems differ from traditional supercomputers due to the frequent failure of its constituent components and a highly dynamic workload. Each kind of system has unique challenges associated with scheduling, but it seems that the workloads may be converging somewhat; supercomputers are increasingly running so-called many task workloads, whereas cloud workloads are including more workloads with task coupling. While the workload targets of these classes of systems will likely remain distinct, it is quite likely that similar scheduling techniques will be needed in both cases over the next few years, marrying dynamism with parallelism.

Another change caused by the growing importance of cloud systems is the integration of scheduling into a larger landscape of business concerns. With the extreme level of investment in cloud infrastructure, management processes like capacity planning have become coupled with scheduling into a far richer resource management landscape than we have previously seen. Open challenges remain in many areas and are often increased due to the implications of on-demand workloads. There is also an increased need for richer interactions between workloads and resource management infrastructure, which could enable dynamically moldable jobs, or other novel models for variable resource occupancy.

At the same time, large-scale systems have become far more accessible than ever before, broadening the use of large-scale computational campaigns. As more resource are used in this way, the incentive to optimize this process has grown substantially. Complex techniques are now used to optimize for cost and time to solution. This adds an economic dimension that previously did not exist in large-scale systems.

All of these areas are complex and remain unsolved. JSSPP has evolved with the area and now fully covers parallel scheduling for commercial environments while still maintaining strong interest in its traditional areas: scientific computing, supercomputing, and cluster platforms.

The workshop began with a keynote talk by Stephen Elliot, from Amazon Web Services. Stephen gave an overview of the Amazon spot market for computing resources, and described some of the open issues in scheduling the spot market. The AWS spot market is particularly interesting in a few regards. It is built on functional economic principles, using dynamic pricing to minimize resource waste and maximize utilization. Another interesting characteristic of the spot market is the direct integration of capacity planning into the resource management process. This model is a departure from the traditional HPC systems where systems are built and then operated largely in steady state for several years. By contrast, cloud systems function in a continuous acquisition model, where hardware resources are added on a regular basis. This model has very different properties, and enables different strategies for resource management. We expect research in this area to grow in the coming years.

In addition to this topic, scheduling issues were discussed in a broader context in more established areas, from hardware scheduling, to scheduling within budget constraints, scheduling for performance, and analysis of scheduling tasks within resource management software. Adopting a broader basis for scheduling discussions was an explicit goal of the workshop this year, and will be continued in future workshops.

JSSPP has a long-standing tradition of covering workload modeling and metrics analysis. After all, optimizing for the wrong metric cannot produce the right result. The work of Emeras et al. examines how to enhance our understanding of the parallel system by combing the view of the scheduler (on which resources allocated are considered used) with instrumentation of what effectively happens at the machine level (on which not all allocated resources are indeed utilized). Krakov et al. explore heatmaps as an alternative to the long-standing problem that summarizing a parallel system's behavior with one-number statistics invariably leads to losing important information, and sometimes is downright misleading.

Scheduling fairness remains a topic of interest for the community. Klusáček et al. investigate the very definition of fairness when multiple resources are taken into account, describe the problems resulting from it, and propose solutions. Rajbhandary et al. work in the nut-and-blots of the fairness problem, proposing a new scheduling algorithm that beats the state-of-art one. We expect activity in fairness to be extended in the next few years to accommodate for the cloud reality, where consumers who pay more get better quality of service. We are likely to see research on which fairness is weighted (by price or otherwise).

How to schedule big data jobs was also actively debated during the workshop, a recognition of how important it has become in recent years. Cao et al. introduce a handful of scheduling algorithm that simultaneous target throughput and budget optimization for DAG applications, which are common in big data pipelines. Agosta et al. explore how to perform task placement of MapReduce applications to improve data locality and thus performance.

As the scale of parallel systems keep increasing, a centralized scheduler overseeing the entire system starts to become a bottleneck. Balasubramanian et al. address this issue introducing decentralized scheduling strategies that backfill jobs locally and dynamically migrate waiting jobs to leverage residual resources. Likewise, the scale of today's systems make energy consumption a major concern, both from an economic and an environmental viewpoint. Zhou et al. show how power-aware job scheduling can reduce the energy cost significantly by as much as 25% with minimal impact to system utilization.

As parallel systems grow in scale, they also grow in complexity. It is interesting to note that meta-heuristics are emerging as an effective way to deal with such complexity. Shai et al. introduce Max-Jobs, a meta-heuristic that combines simpler matching heuristics to improve the matching of jobs to machines. Deng et al. go a step further even and dynamically change the whole scheduling algorithm as to accommodate for changes in workload and conditions of the parallel system.

The proceedings of previous workshops are available from Springer as LNCS volumes 949, 1162, 1291, 1459, 1659, 1911, 2221, 2537, 2862, 3277, 3834, 4376, 4942, 5798, 6253, and 7698. Those volumes are also available online.

January 2014   Narayan Desai
                                                               Walfredo Cirne

Organization

Workshop Organizers

Narayan Desai   Argonne National Laboratory, USA
Walfredo Cirne   Google, USA

Program Committee

Henri Casanova	University of Hawaii at Manoa, USA
Julita Corbalan	Technical University of Catalunya, Spain
Dick Epema	Delft University of Technology, The Netherlands
Dror Feitelson	The Hebrew University, Israel
Ian Foster	Argonne National Laboratory, USA
Alfredo Goldman	University of Sao Paulo, Brazil
Allan Gottlieb	New York University, USA
Morris Jette	SchedMD, USA
Rajkumar Kettimuthu	Argonne National Laboratory, USA
Derrick Kondo	Inria, France
Zhiling Lan	Illinois Institute of Technology, USA
Virginia Lo	University of Oregon, USA
Satoshi Matsuoka	Tokyo Institute of Technology, Japan
Jose Moreira	IBM T.J. Watson Research Center, USA
Bill Nitzberg	Altair Engineering, USA
Mark Squillante	IBM T.J. Watson Research Center, USA
Dan Tsafrir	Technion, Israel
John Wilkes	Google, USA
Ramin Yahyapour	The University of Göttingen, Germany

Reviewers

Henri Casanova	Rajkumar Kettimuthu
Julita Corbalan	Dalibor Klusáček
Dick Epema	Zhiling Lan
Gilles Fedak	Bill Nitzberg
Dror Feitelson	David Oppenheimer
Liana Fong	Uwe Schwiegelshohn
Eitan Frachtenberg	Mark Squillante
Alfredo Goldman	Wei Tang
Allan Gottlieb	Dan Tsafrir
Alexandru Iosup	Ramin Yahyapour
Morris Jette	

Contents

Analysis of the Jobs Resource Utilization on a Production System

Joseph Emeras[(✉)], Cristian Ruiz, Jean-Marc Vincent, and Olivier Richard

LIG Laboratory, Grenoble, France
{Joseph.Emeras,Cristian.Ruiz,Jean-Marc.Vincent,Olivier.Richard}@imag.fr

Abstract. In *HPC* community the System Utilization metric enables to determine if the resources of the cluster are efficiently used by the batch scheduler. This metric considers that all the allocated resources (memory, disk, processors, etc.) are full-time utilized. To optimize the system performance, we have to consider the effective physical consumption by jobs regarding the resource allocations. This information gives an insight into whether the cluster resources are efficiently used by the jobs. In this work we propose an analysis of production clusters based on the jobs resource utilization. The principle is to collect simultaneously traces from the job scheduler (provided by logs) and jobs resource consumptions. The latter has been realized by developing a job monitoring tool, whose impact on the system has been measured as lightweight (0.35 % speed-down). The key point is to statistically analyze both traces to detect and explain underutilization of the resources. This could enable to detect abnormal behavior, bottlenecks in the cluster leading to a poor scalability, and justifying optimizations such as gang scheduling or best-effort scheduling. This method has been applied to two medium sized production clusters on a period of eight months.

Keywords: Workload traces · Monitoring · Performance evaluation · Optimization · High performance computing

1 General Context

High Performance Computing (HPC) platforms have appeared as a solution for solving advanced computation problems. Nowadays these systems have evolved passing from the shared memory multiprocessors to clusters which can have hundreds of thousands of processors. In these kind of systems a central component called the Resource and Job Management System (RJMS) is in charge of managing the users' tasks (jobs) on the system's computing resources.

Studying the RJMS workload has become a widely used method for HPC systems valuation. The workload in the RJMS context can be defined as the set of all individual jobs that are processed by the system during a specific period of time. With workload traces, one can reconstruct the scheduling, determine the system's computing resources utilization, compare different systems and their

N. Desai and W. Cirne (Eds.): JSSPP 2013, LNCS 8429, pp. 1–21, 2014.
DOI: 10.1007/978-3-662-43779-7_1, © Springer-Verlag Berlin Heidelberg 2014

workloads according to several metrics like *Average Weighted Wait Time* and *Average Weighted Response Time* as used in [1]. This study can lead to the construction of models as proposed in [2] and more generally described in [3]. However, looking only at the workload traces may not be sufficient. To get a better understanding of the use of such systems we need to look at both how the jobs interact with the RJMS but also how they consume the allocated resources. In other words, we need to look at both the workload and the jobs activity on the resources.

The idea of associating RJMS workload traces to the jobs resource consumptions has been mentioned in several works. Reference [4] points out the fact that the System Utilization metric, commonly used in system evaluation misses information about the computer sub-systems (network, memory, processor) usage. According to [5] it is also necessary to take into account other characteristics such as I/O activity which have a big impact on the global performance of HPC systems. However, the aforementioned association has never been fully achieved.

The System Utilization metric is the ratio of the computing resources allocated to the jobs over the available resources in the system. In fact, this metric corresponds more to the *System Resource Allocation* as it does not give information about the physical utilization of the resources. In this paper we will focus on the Resource Utilization metric which reflects the ratio of the consumption of a resource by a job over the amount of resource allocated by the system to this job. For each resource type: core, memory, IO, we will look at their utilization by the jobs on the clusters.

The following Section presents several works related to Workload and Jobs tracing. The first part presents briefly D. Feitelson et al. works on workload traces then several methods for retrieving information about the jobs consumptions are presented. Then in Sect. 3 we present the solution chosen to collect jobs resource consumptions data. Section 4 describes the clusters on which data was collected and the trace characteristics. Section 5 presents the analysis of the results of the different resources consumption metrics. Finally, Sect. 6 discusses the results and gives some perspectives.

2   State of the Art

2.1   Workload Traces

Workload traces are provided by the Resource and Job Management System, they contain information about the jobs arrivals, their resources request and allocation, their characteristics like runtime, wait time or execution information. Two workload traces format exist and are commonly used:

(a) Standard Workload Format (SWF)[1]. It is an initiative to make workloads data on parallel machines freely available and presented in a standard format [6]. This work is presented in the Parallel Workload Archive[2]. It provides

---

[1] SWF: http://www.cs.huji.ac.il/labs/parallel/workload/swf.html
[2] PWA: http://www.cs.huji.ac.il/labs/parallel/workload

several traces from real production systems and is a big step in the field of workload characterization. Many other works were based on this format, in particular for workload models generation. The SWF format gives information about the jobs requests, allocations, characteristics and consumptions. The jobs consumptions values provided by SWF are the average processor time and the average memory used by processor.

(b) Grid Workload Archive (GWA)[3]. The Grid Workload Archive constitutes an effort to build a data repository of grid workload traces for the scientific community. This format is based on SWF, it adds some grid specific aspects like sites, virtual organizations, co-allocations, workflows. This information contributes to the improvement of the middleware in charge of the scheduling process.

2.2   Jobs Consumption Traces

Two options are possible to produce a trace of the jobs consumptions. First, giving for each job, for each type of resource (memory, processor, disk, network), a single representative value of the resource consumption. The question is thus *"How representative of the real consumption this value is?"*. Or, for each job, giving a trace of the resource consumptions over time. This can be viewed as a monitoring of the jobs consumptions.

In [7], R. Jain proposes one possible classification of the different monitoring techniques. In this classification, the monitoring process can be *event-driven* or by *sampling*. The event-driven method is very efficient and there is no monitoring overhead if the event is rare. The sampling method as for it, is well adapted for frequent events but a loss of data captured is inevitable and a frequency resolution has to be chosen. This section presents the state of the art of the existing monitoring systems that can be adapted to our context.

Monitoring Provided by the Existing Batch Schedulers. Several RJMS provide an embedded system for monitoring the jobs consumptions.

SLURM [8][4]: uses different mechanisms to know which processes are members of a SLURM job, then monitors their consumptions. The cgroup isolation mechanism requires a very recent kernel version, the other one is based on the Linux process table.

OAR [9][5]: provides a mechanism that monitors the jobs consumptions in terms of processor, memory and network. As for SLURM, it uses different mechanisms to know which processes are members of an OAR job, these are the cpuset or cgroup features of the kernel and require a recent kernel version. This data collection is not automatic and is triggered at user request.

---

[3] GWA: http://gwa.ewi.tudelft.nl/pmwiki/
[4] SLURM. https://computing.llnl.gov/linux/slurm/
[5] OAR: http://oar.imag.fr

LoadLeveler[6]: allows the user to gather information about resource consumption. It offers different ways to consult this information and create different class of reports. As for OAR, this mechanism is not automatic.

All these approaches are linked to a particular batch scheduler system. For all of them, the traces generated give for each job a single value (generally the mean) for each type of resource consumption. This is problematic for several reasons. First for the memory consumption, the mean does not give valuable information. At least the maximum value and how many times this value was reached must be reported. Then for the IO consumption, the variance of the reads and writes can vary a lot and the mean is still not representative enough. We prefer to adopt a monitoring of the resources over time, that will give us all the details of the evolution of the consumptions and thus enable a deeper analysis of the cluster's resources utilization.

Monitoring and Profiling Tools. Many monitoring and profiling/tracing tools exist in the literature, but our approach needs specific requirements. First, we need to collect the jobs resource consumptions, this is a completely different process than machine monitoring. Then, we need to collect these data in a temporal way. This means that data has to be collected over time along with the jobs executions. Last, we want to collect jobs consumption data on production clusters which implies two constraints: the impact of the monitoring on the compute nodes has to be negligible; and the setup of the monitoring on the cluster has to be as simple as possible. On a running production cluster it is not acceptable to deeply modify the configuration of the nodes, nor install or update too many softwares; and the update or modification of the nodes' kernel is not possible.

Means and maximum values are not sufficient for analyzing the behavior of the applications over time, we need a more fine-grain view of their consumptions. Several systems like Ganglia [10] and Nagios [11] have been developed to monitor a system or a cluster infrastructure but are resource centric, they perform their monitoring at the machine level. Our approach needs to be job centric to enable us to extract the resource consumptions per job as proposed in [12]. Other approaches more application-oriented exist as [13] which gathers an application consumptions in an online manner taking advantage of two tools, TAU [14] as the data collector and Supermon [15] as the transport layer. Or [16] which monitors an application at runtime, with a low overhead, allowing it to study the overhead penalties incurred by Linux Systems in the execution of HPC applications. The difference between our approach and the systems mentioned above is the fact that we aim to monitor all the jobs executed in the cluster, generating a trace of the resource consumptions over time. This requires a very lightweight tool, capable of monitoring all the jobs with a low overhead and with an amount of data generated that can be easily stored and processed. These conditions were not respected by these tools.

---

[6] LoadLeveler: http://www-03.ibm.com/systems/software/loadleveler

Linux Kernel tools like Performance Counters[7] or CGroups[8] are not a possible option for our systems because they imply the update of the compute nodes kernel.

We also tested several event based tools like IPM [17], TAU [14], ltrace[9], but either their overhead was too high or the amount of data collected was too important (hundreds of MB for a single application run) to enable a global workload analysis. An event-driven approach would thus be too intrusive and the amount of data produced would have been too big.

The approach chosen was then a sampling monitoring, enabling us to restrict the amount of data collected and to set the precision required.

Because of the production constraints we chose to collect information about the consumptions from the */proc* subsystem (as in the OpenTSDB[10] approach). In this virtual file system (present on any Linux system), for each process is given its consumption of resources such as memory, processor, or IO on the Distributed File System (DFS). With this method, no modification nor software installation is needed on the compute nodes.

3   Resource Consumption Capture

This section presents the approach used in order to instrument the system, which allowed us to have more detailed information about jobs resources consumption during their execution. This monitoring process is divided into two parts:

- The monitoring of the jobs' processes execution in each compute node of the cluster. This is performed by a monitor daemon running on each node.
- The collection of all the traces generated by each job.

3.1   Monitor Daemon

It is important to understand that we do not want to depend on the synchronization of measures. A centralized clock that forces measure times would be too intrusive for the system. Instead, every node is responsible for measuring each job every minute and the clocks between the nodes are synced (this is a common requirement in HPC). Every measure is tagged with its timestamp.

The monitor daemon, written in Perl, gathers resource consumption information for a job that is running on the machine. This information includes every process involved in the job and their resource consumption values obtained from */proc* directory. We first validated this method by making several tests with jobs whose behavior were well-known to ensure that information given by */proc* was consistent with what we expected. Collected values and trace format are described in Tables 1 and 2. In order to know which processes belong to the job,

---

[7] https://perf.wiki.kernel.org
[8] http://www.kernel.org/doc/Documentation/cgroups/cgroups.txt
[9] A library call tracer. http://linux.die.net/man/1/ltrace
[10] http://opentsdb.net

the monitor looks into the cpuset directory, which is the interface to the *cpuset*[11] kernel mechanism to provide job isolation. Therefore with all this information collected, the monitor generates a trace file per job. The cpuset feature is supported by most of the RJMS as PBS, Loadleveler, Torque[12], Slurm[13], OAR[14], it is the most portable method for collecting the jobs processes.

We wanted the finest granularity possible without generating a big perturbation on the nodes and a minute step allowed us to have a perturbation under 1 % in the worst case. It is thus a good compromise information/intrusiveness as presented in Sect. 3.2.

As these traces will be mixed with RJMS traces, a 60 s granularity seems reasonable as the scheduling decisions and the resources allocations are in the order of the minute.

To be as lightweight as possible, the monitoring tool does not reformat or process data during the capture. Values taken from */proc* are written directly to the log for the overhead to be in the analysis process, not during traces capture.

Table 1. Trace format

Trace fields	
Name	Description
Time	Unix Time Stamp in seconds
JOB ID	Job id assigned by the batch scheduler
PID	PID of process that belongs to the job
Node ID	Provenance of the capture
Measure	Measure as presented in Table 2

Table 2. Data collected during a measure

Values captured	
Name	Description
command	Name of the binary executed
vmPeak	Peak virtual memory size (KB)
vmSize	Total program size (KB)
vmRss	Resident Memory (KB)
vmSwap	Size of swap usage (KB)
syscr	Number of read syscalls
syscw	Number of write syscalls
read_bytes	Bytes read from the DFS
write_bytes	Bytes written to the DFS
core	Core utilization percentage
receive	Bytes received from the network
transmit	Bytes transmitted to the network

3.2   Intrusiveness and Sampling Evaluation

This section presents the evaluation of our approach in terms of disruption in the system. The cost of retrieving information from the RJMS and converting it to SWF format is null as it is done post mortem. We will thus study the cost

---

[11] http://www.kernel.org/doc/man-pages/online/pages/man7/cpuset.7.html

[12] http://www.clusterresources.com/torquedocs21/3.5linuxcpusets.shtml

[13] https://computing.llnl.gov/linux/slurm/

[14] http://oar.imag.fr/sources/2.5/docs/documentation/OAR-DOCUMENTATION
-ADMIN/#cpuset-feature

to monitor the jobs. It is very important for the validity of the data collected that the monitoring process does not interfere with the jobs themselves. It is obviously also important for the validity of the jobs results. We chose that the job overhead should be strictly less than one percent. All the tests were performed over a machine Intel Xeon E5420, with 8 cores and 24 GB of main memory. We evaluated the implementation under a 100 % processor load of the machine, with one process per core and measured the monitor overhead by using the Sysbench multi-threaded benchmark tool. The evaluation ran 8 processes, each one checking a prime list up to 18000. Results are presented in Table 3.

Table 3. Overhead (in terms of perturbation in the application execution time) vs. sampling period. All values are in seconds

Sampling Freq.	Mean	Min	Max	Overhead (%)
No	573	573	573	0
60 s	573.6	573	574	0.10
30 s	574.4	574	575	0.24
10 s	577	576	578	0.69

Table 4. Overhead (in terms of perturbation in the application execution time) vs. number of processes monitored per job. All values are in seconds

Type	Mean	Min	Max	Overhead (%)
16 processes				
No moni-toring	513	513	513	0
monitoring	514.1	514	515	0.21
32 processes				
No moni-toring	512	512	512	0
monitoring	513.8	513	516	0.35

We also evaluated the noise for more than 8 processes with a 60 s frequency to have an idea of the scalability of the solution. The results are shown in Table 4. The disruption caused by the monitoring was found to be almost linear regarding the number of processes to monitor in these conditions. Given that there were four times more processes than cores in the 32 processes benchmark, the result of a 0.35 % overhead is acceptable.

The memory used by the daemon is very small (few MB) and it doesn't use the network during the capture. The reads and writes are a few KB every minute on the local disk and the Distributed File System is not solicited so the IO perturbation is negligible.

3.3   Collecting Mechanism

Data is gathered using dedicated jobs that collect the logs when the system is underloaded. This operation does not need to be frequent; week-ends, holidays, night-times or maintenance periods can be used for this. We used a special maintenance period during holidays for this purpose. Each job requests a whole node and is in charge of gathering and compressing the trace files generated so far by the jobs executed on that machine. Then it sends them to a dedicated node in charge of storing the trace data.

3.4 Off-Line Data Processing

Once we have collected data about jobs resources consumption we need to bind it to the RJMS log to be able to compute the resource utilization ratio. This ratio is at a given time, for a given job, the amount of resource consumed by the job over the amount of resource allocated by the system to this job. To make it simpler to use and redistributable, we first build the SWF file from the RJMS log. The SWF is an abstract view of the log, this format gives us the amount of resource allocated by the system for each job.

As measures are not guaranteed to be synchronized between nodes during the capture, a shift in the measures dates can appear. Thus we first re-sample the measures then bind them to the RJMS logs with R[15]. The whole re-sampling and binding process is available in a R script. See Sect. 5.3 for more information.

4 Experiment Environment

Data was collected from production clusters of the Ciment project[16]. This project aims at gathering several computational infrastructures to provide computing power to users in different disciplines like environment, chemistry, astrophysics, biology, health, physics. The CiGri project relies upon the OAR RJMS to submit the jobs on the clusters. All the Ciment clusters are managed by the CiGri[17] lightweight grid software that gathers clusters resources to make them available as a grid for the users.

The monitoring tool was implanted and run on two of the Ciment production clusters: *Foehn* and *Gofree*. As they come from the same grid, their respective workload should not be too different from each other. Their characteristics are detailed in Table 5. A short summary of data collected is presented in Table 6.

One particularity of the Ciment platform is that users can submit a particular type of job: the "besteffort" jobs. These jobs are scheduled in a dedicated queue. They have a very low priority and can be preempted whenever a "normal" job arrives and needs the resource. The goal of such jobs is to maximize the cluster utilization as they are plentiful. Generally, these jobs request one core to the RJMS. These special jobs are multiparametric sequential jobs. A user using these kind of jobs has generally several instances of the same application running in different jobs with different parameters.

---

[15] http://www.r-project.org/

[16] CIMENT Project. https://ciment.ujf-grenoble.fr/

[17] CiGri Project: http://cigri.imag.fr/

Table 5. Clusters characteristics

	Foehn	Gofree
Brand	SGI	Dell
CPU model	X5550	L5640
Nodes	16	28
CPU/node	2	2
Cores/cpu	4	6
Memory/node	48 GB	72 GB
Total storage	7 TB	30 TB
Network	IB DDR	IB QDR
Total Gflop/s	1367.04	3177.6
Buy date	2010-03-01	2011-01-01

Table 6. Trace summary for both clusters.

	Foehn	Gofree
Capture start	2011-06-01	2011-05-24
Capture months	8	7
Log size	2.6 GB	3.1 GB
Number of jobs	53662	20093
Besteffort jobs	50403	15596
Normal jobs	3259	4497
Active users	54	35

5   Analysis

In this section we analyze the consumption of the jobs from data collected during the capture regarding their requests. This analysis is done for the following metrics: core utilization, memory utilization and IO activity on the network file system. The two clusters although belonging to the same platform are located in two different laboratories. When submitting a job, the users of the platform can both choose on which cluster the job will run or don't specify anything. In this case it is the local cluster which is selected by default. As we know, most of the users don't request specifically a cluster or tend to prefer the local cluster. Thus we analyze separately the results from the two clusters. Moreover, jobs from the **normal class** and **besteffort class** have very different patterns. Besteffort jobs are multiparametric jobs that generally request only 1 core (although we know that some besteffort jobs request several cores). They are supposed to be processor intensive with few memory usage and few IO activity. Normal jobs are generally parallel jobs requesting several nodes/cores. Their consumption patterns are not really known and are probably more varied. Hence, the following analysis of the jobs consumptions is done on the two classes separately on each cluster.

To address the analysis of the consumptions in a global way for each class we look at the resources utilization distribution. This will give us an idea of the different existing patterns.

Squashed Area Ratio. Along with the distribution of the utilizations we will also consider the impact of a particular phenomenon into the global system activity. We present thus the Squashed Area metric (SA) that represents the jobs execution activity. Reference [18] defines SA as the total system's resource consumptions of a set of jobs, computed by:

$$SA = \sum_{j \in jobs} allocated\_cores_j \times run\_time_j.$$

Thus, for a job or a set of jobs, we look at the SA ratio of this set regarding the workload SA of its class (i.e. the proportion of this set area over the total class area). This enables us to determine if a particular phenomenon is significant enough regarding the rest of the workload.

Core. In data collected we have for each job j, for each core c allocated to j, the proportion of core consumed by the processes running on c and belonging to j along its execution. We denote this value: $core\_consumption_j^c(t_i)$. With t_i being the date of the measure i. Thus, we can compute for each measure date t_i the total amount of core consumed by a job with:

$$core\_consumption_j(t_i) = \sum_{c \in allocated\_cores_j} core\_consumption_j^c(t_i).$$

Then, with n being the number of consumption measures taken for j, we can compute per job its core utilization mean by:

$$core\_utilization\_mean_j = \frac{\sum_{i \in [1,n]} core\_consumption_j(t_i)}{allocated\_cores_j \times n}.$$

In the following analysis we consider the distribution of these values to identify different utilization patterns.

Memory. The OAR version managing Foehn and Gofree clusters doesn't provide a memory isolation of the jobs on the nodes. This feature in OAR is only available with the Cgroup feature of the kernel enabled which is not the case. Thus it is interesting to look whether jobs use a lot of memory or not. Indeed, a job which uses intensively the memory could disturb other jobs sharing the same node.

We introduce the *theoretical_memory_per_core* value which is equal to a node memory over the number of cores on the node. As each cluster has an homogeneous architecture, this value is the same for all the nodes in a cluster. Foehn and Gofree doesn't have the same number of cores and memory per node but their *theoretical_memory_per_core* is the same and is equal to 6GB. We consider thus that a job which consumes less than this value per allocated core is not disturbing for the other jobs.

Then, for a given job we know its theoretical maximum memory. This value is equal to *theoretical_memory_per_core* × *allocated_cores_j*. Thus we know that jobs that consume more than 100 % of this value are potentially disturbing other jobs by using too much memory on at least one node.

For the analysis of the memory utilization we will look at two sub-metrics:

- The mean memory used by a job (computed by the same method than the core utilization mean) vs. its theoretical maximum memory. This tells us how the job behaves on average regarding its theoretical maximum memory.
- The maximum memory used on the cores allocated to this job. This will tell us if the job used more than the *theoretical_memory_per_core* on one of its allocated cores or not.

File System IO. As the Distributed File System (DFS) is a central component of a cluster we are also interested into its usage patterns. On Gofree no user has complained about slow IO on the DFS. This is not the case for Foehn where users have reported several IO problems. Unfortunately we could only monitor the IO utilization on the Distributed File System on the Gofree cluster and this for only two months and a half. Gofree DFS consists in an NFS server that serves the users' home directories through the GigaBit Ethernet network. We tested its capabilities in terms of bandwidth with the IOR[18] benchmark [19]. We used IOR in a single file/single client mode with file sizes of 64 MB and blocks of 4 KB. 4 KB is the default block size. 64 MB and 64 KB are the most frequent write sizes in Gofree (see Fig. 15). We chose 64 MB instead of 64 KB because this last value is too small (only 16 physical writes) to have a correct idea of the bandwidth. We repeated the test 10000 times and got a max speed of 103 MB/s for the writes and 4030 MB/s for the reads. The mean write speed was 98 MB/s with a standard deviation of 5. Several other tests with higher values of file sizes gave us similar results. For concurrent sequential tests IOR showed that the bandwidth was more or less fairly divided between the different writing processes. For parallel tests (with MPIIO API, one file per process, up to 48 processes) IOR showed a maximum value close to 96 MB/s which is a little less than with the single process mode but still in the same bandwidth range than the mean speed of sequential writes. This gives us an approximative idea of the global bandwidth of Gofree DFS.

The read bandwidth is quite high (close to a local file system bandwidth) and generally the type of IO which are problematic are the writes, thus we will focus on the analysis of the writes patterns.

5.1   Foehn Cluster

Normal Class Jobs. Figure 1 presents the distribution of the core utilization means for normal class jobs on Foehn cluster. We observe a peak in the distribution corresponding to a core utilization near 100 %. An other peak, less important corresponds to a low core utilization (between 0 % and 25 %). However when looking at the SA ratio of these two peaks the tendency reverts. The SA ratio of the high utilization peak is only 12.7 % of the total workload SA and the SA ratio of the low utilization peak is of 53.7 %. For these jobs, very few of

---

[18] http://sourceforge.net/projects/ior-sio/

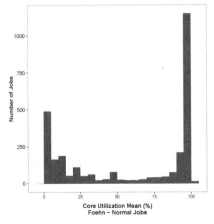

Fig. 1. Distribution of the jobs' core utilization means.

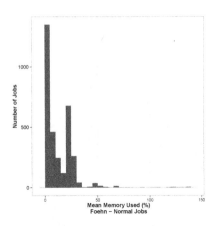

Fig. 2. Distribution of the mean memory used by job.

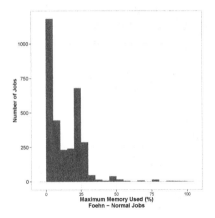

Fig. 3. Distribution of the maximum memory used per job by an allocated core to this job, values ≤100 %.

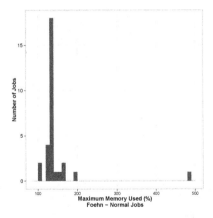

Fig. 4. Distribution of the maximum memory used per job by an allocated core to this job, values >100 %.

them consume a lot of memory (only 22 jobs). Among them only 5 consume more than their theoretical maximum memory. For these memory intensive jobs, the maximum memory used per core is 125 % of the *theoretical_memory_per_core*. Figure 2 presents the distribution of the mean memory used per job. We can observe that memory intensive jobs are very rare on Foehn but exist.

Figures 3 and 4 present the maximum memory used on a core per job. We split the representation of the distribution in two groups for more clarity: up to 100 % and more than 100 %.

There are 31 jobs whose mean memory usage is over 100 %. Unsurprisingly, jobs that have a mean memory usage over 100 % are the same than the jobs that have a peak memory usage on an allocated core over 100 %. These jobs have a peak value grouped around 140 %. Only 1 job has a very high peak memory usage of 480 %, it is a job that requested 2 cores and lasted for 18 min then was canceled by its user.

In Foehn, we observe that many jobs are using the cores computing power very efficiently and don't use a lot of memory. These jobs seem to be cpu bound. However their weight in the workload is counterbalanced by larger and shorter jobs (larger number of resources but with a runtime being a little shorter on average). Regarding the memory usage distribution, we can think that these jobs suffered from something else than memory problems. But when we look at the number of cores allocated to the jobs of the two groups (jobs with average core utilization under 25 % and jobs with average core utilization near 100 %) we remark something very particular. The mean number of allocated cores is 4 times bigger for the jobs that have a core utilization in the lower peak. This can be an IO scalability issue with jobs waiting on IO, as we know that Foehn DFS has bandwidth problems, this having been reported several times by the users. However this can also come from an over-reservation of cores by the users. Sadly, we currently miss information to explain the reason of this phenomenon.

Besteffort Class Jobs. Figure 5 presents the distribution of core utilization for besteffort jobs on Foehn cluster. We observe two peaks, one corresponding to a core utilization mean around 25 %, the other around 100 %. For the lower utilization peak (from 0 to 25 %), its SA ratio is 55.5 %. The SA ratio for the jobs exactly in the 25 % peak is 42.4 %. For the jobs involved in the higher distribution peak, even though there are fewer, their SA ratio is about the same (40.8 %). 99.2 % of these jobs reserve only 1 core. These jobs never use more than the theoretical memory per core. 99.5 % of them actually use less than 1/3 of this theoretical memory per core.

Only 6 users are involved in the low core utilization peak, but 5 of them are also involved in the high utilization peak. The user only present in the low utilization peak accounts for 41.9 % of the besteffort SA and has a core utilization less than 25 % in 99.4 % of the cases. He reserves 4 cores in all his besteffort jobs. In almost all the cases his processes consume less than 310 MB and never higher than 620 MB.

After contacting the user, he explained that he noticed that if two of his jobs were running on the same node, the performances of the two jobs were very bad. After investigating the cause of this it was found that the application was memory intensive in terms of bandwidth. The maximum memory used was small compared to the amount of memory available on the node but when two jobs were accessing the memory at same time, there was a bottleneck in the access to the memory. The solution adopted by the user to avoid this performance loss was to reserve the whole socket (corresponding thus to 4 cores) even though the application only used 1 core. As Foehn nodes are NUMA, reserving the whole

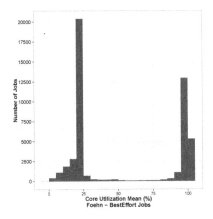

Fig. 5. Distribution of the jobs' core utilization means.

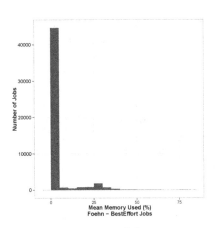

Fig. 6. Distribution of the mean memory used by job.

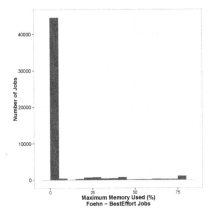

Fig. 7. Distribution of the maximum memory used per job by an allocated core to this job, values ⩽100 %.

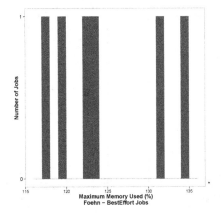

Fig. 8. Distribution of the maximum memory used per job by an allocated core to this job, values >100 %.

socket enabled the jobs to have their own memory slot and thereby not being disturbed. The problem here was not a misconfiguration of the job or a bad reservation request but a lack in the RJMS constraint description that forced the user to over-reserve.

Figure 6 shows that besteffort jobs don't consume a lot of memory on average. Only 6 jobs (not represented on the figure for clarity) have a mean memory utilization greater than their theoretical available memory. Their mean memory use is between 7 and 8 GB.

In Figs. 7 and 8 we observe that besteffort jobs don't have big memory peaks. Only 6 jobs have peaks between 115 and 135 %. these jobs are all 1 core jobs and five of them belong to the same user.

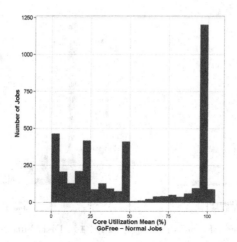

Fig. 9. Distribution of the jobs' core utilization means.

Except the singularity of the user reserving one entire socket and few jobs with memory usage peaks, besteffort jobs on Foehn tend to be cpu bound.

5.2   Gofree Cluster

Normal Class Jobs. Figure 9 shows the distribution of the core utilization means for jobs in the normal class in Gofree. We observe a very particular distribution with four peaks around 0, 1/4, 1/2 and 1 of core utilization mean. The most surprising is when we look at the number of cores allocated to these jobs vs their core utilization. The higher peak has a core allocation of 1 node in 50 % of the cases (with a maximum of 1 node). The peak around 1/2 has a core allocation of 2 nodes in 85 % of the cases (with a maximum of 2 nodes). The peak around 1/4 has a core allocation of 3 nodes in 48 % of the cases and 4 nodes in 35 % of the cases (with a maximum of 4 nodes). The jobs below 50 % of core utilization are not an isolated phenomenon, 2/3 of the users are involved in these jobs and their presence is distributed all along the trace. These users are also involved in the high utilization peak. The memory used for these jobs is low (less than 1/3 of theoretical memory) for 89 % of them. Only 7 jobs use up to 100 % of their theoretical available memory. Figures 10 and 11 show us a memory utilization quite low for most of the jobs of this class.

This behavior of core utilization vs core allocation is very noteworthy and we suspect a scalability problem although we can't say where is the bottleneck (results of IO consumption on data collected during the IO capture period showed the DFS is usually not very stressed, see 5.2). However, as for Foehn, this can also come from an over-reservation of cores by the users. These two phenomena of low core utilization on both clusters will need further investigations and the jobs' knowledge of the users involved.

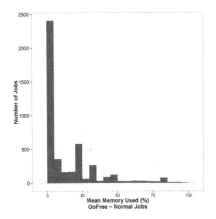

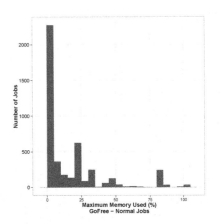

Fig. 10. Distribution of the mean memory used by job.

Fig. 11. Distribution of the maximum memory used per job by an allocated core to this job.

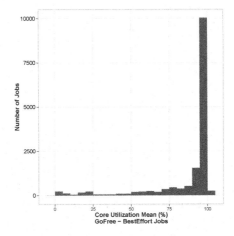

Fig. 12. Distribution of the jobs' core utilization means.

Besteffort Class Jobs. Figure 12 shows that besteffort jobs in Gofree have a high core utilization. Jobs below 75 % of core utilization represent 0.37 % of the normal jobs SA and jobs below 90 % account for 7 % of the class' SA. Core allocation for besteffort jobs in 85 % of the cases is 1 with other values being 4 and 6 (1 cpu socket). Figures 13 and 14 show us a low memory utilization on average and on maximum. Regarding these results we can say that besteffort jobs in Gofree are cpu bound.

Global IO Activity. Figure 15 shows the distribution of the size of the files written by the jobs. We can observe a big peak at 64 KB. This comes from many

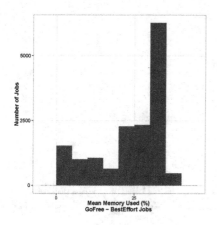

Fig. 13. Distribution of the mean memory used by job.

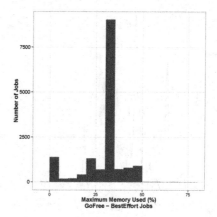

Fig. 14. Distribution of the maximum memory used per job by an allocated core to this job.

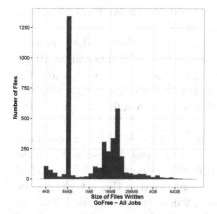

Fig. 15. Size of files writes on the DFS on Gofree cluster for all jobs.

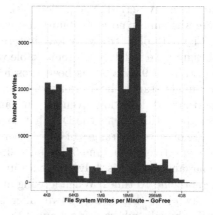

Fig. 16. Distribution of the aggregated file system writes sizes (per Minute) on Gofree cluster.

besteffort jobs that write small files. Generally, besteffort jobs tend to write either files of 64 KB or 32 MB. Normal jobs tend to write files of 4 KB and 16 MB.

Figure 16 presents the distribution of the aggregated writes by the jobs on the File System. We can observe that the most frequent sizes the DFS has to write in a minute is either small (between 4 KB and 16 KB) or medium (between 8 MB and 64 MB). It seems that the DFS is not really overloaded. Very few values are high (up to 6 GB in a minute).

In order to see how the load is distributed along the time we plot Figs. 17 and 18. Figure 17 presents the aggregated writes per day on the DFS. We can observe that the daily IO write activity is very irregular with intense periods

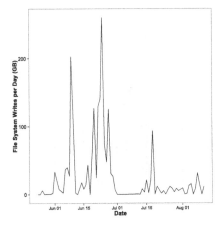

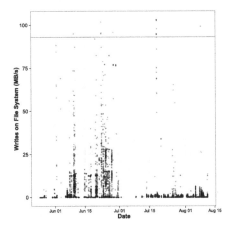

Fig. 17. Daily aggregated writes on the DFS.

Fig. 18. DFS load (write speed) on Gofree cluster.

and an empty period. The period with no IO activity occurred during holidays, there was almost no job submitted during this time.

Figure 18 plots the write load in terms of speed on the Gofree DFS server. In this figure, we isolate some remarkable values above the vertical line at 93 MB/s. The value of 93 MB/s has been chosen because it reflects the speed where the DFS might start to be overloaded. It corresponds to the mean write speed minus the standard deviation given by our bandwidth tests with IOR. We refer at the area above this line as the DFS hot zone.

We observe five ranges of dates where the DFS is in the hot zone. These dates are respectively the June 9, June 22, June 28, July 18 and August 8. The most remarkable period is July 18 where in a period of two hours the DFS reached the hot zone 10 times. When looking at the jobs involved in this activity we see that two jobs (belonging to two different users) where competing for IO on the DFS. The jobs where using 4 and 12 nodes. They didn't use much memory and their mean core utilization was quite low. The job using 4 nodes was canceled by the user before its end. This particular scenario let's us think that this job that was canceled was suffering for slow IO and thus killed by its owner. The scenario is about the same during June 22 where four jobs where competing on IO. One ended, canceled by the user and one had an IO write pattern alternating big writes with periods of inactivity (few memory used, no core activity) probably being blocked on IO. However this event lasted for only 10 min. The other periods are less remarkable as the presence of the DFS in the hot zone was brief (only one peak) with few jobs involved in IO activity.

5.3 Reproducibility

All the tools, traces and R-Sweave documents used to process this analysis are available on a Git repository[19] for the sake of reproducibility and sharing.

---

[19] Git clone https://forge.imag.fr/anonscm/git/evalys-tools/evalys-tools.git

6 Discussion and Perspectives

Monitoring the jobs resource consumptions and linking it to their resource allocation enabled us to detect some particular behaviors on the clusters. Moreover, the monitoring over time allowed us to have a more precise view of the resources utilization, particularly it enabled us to reconstruct the Distributed File System (DFS) write load along time. The study of the utilization for the different resource types gave us a better comprehension of our users' usage of the clusters. We are now able to propose some enhancements in our future scheduling strategies based on the observed usage of the system.

The problem of memory bandwidth risen in the analysis is very interesting because we can encounter the same lack of constraint description for memory, IO or network in most current RJMS. As the Squashed Area ratio of the user involved in this phenomenon weights a lot regarding the rest of the workload, the core computing power loss is important. Here it is not a resource quantity problem, but a problem concerning the bandwidth to access the resource. We cannot try strategies like scheduling other besteffort jobs on the same socket since we don't know their bandwidth usage patterns. A possible solution would be to define memory, IO and network bandwidths as resources in the RJMS in the same way cores are defined as resources. Thus we enable the user to reserve not only a set of cores but an amount of bandwidth on the node depending his/her need. However, this kind of guarantee is not possible nowadays.

It is also noteworthy that besteffort jobs on both clusters are core efficient with a low memory usage. This will be used as a scheduling tweak; besteffort jobs, whenever it is possible, should be scheduled on the same nodes. As we now are sure that they will not disturb with one another, we will pack these jobs on the same set of nodes to improve their efficiency. Besteffort jobs are killed whenever a normal job needs the resource they are running on. By packing them we reduce the fragmentation and thus the probability for them to be killed.

The problem of the DFS overload is also interesting. We observed that generally the DFS is not too loaded but when it happens and there are jobs competing for IO it ends with the cancellation of one of these IO intensive jobs. Giving the users the possibility to tag their jobs (e.g. as IO intensive) at the submission to the RJMS might prevent such situations, the RJMS will simply not schedule two IO intensive jobs at the same time.

Monitoring jobs resource consumptions revealed problems that were not visible with the sole System Utilization metric. Coupling jobs consumptions and RJMS logs enabled us to exhibit and quantify significant particular cases. On mid-sized computing centers, the study of the jobs resource utilization will become a necessary way to a deeper understanding of the users needs and their jobs consumption patterns. Particular patterns discovered by the analysis of the jobs resource utilization will lead to dedicated system setup and optimizations to improve both users and administrators satisfaction.

References

1. Ernemann, C., Song, B., Yahyapour, R.: Scaling of workload traces. In: Feitelson, D.G., Rudolph, L., Schwiegelshohn, U. (eds.) JSSPP 2003. LNCS, vol. 2862, pp. 166–182. Springer, Heidelberg (2003)
2. Lublin, U., Feitelson, D.G.: The workload on parallel supercomputers: modeling the characteristics of rigid jobs. J. Parallel Distrib. Comput. **63**, 2003 (2001)
3. Feitelson, D.G.: Workload modeling for performance evaluation. In: Calzarossa, M.C., Tucci, S. (eds.) Performance 2002. LNCS, vol. 2459, pp. 114–141. Springer, Heidelberg (2002)
4. Rudolph, L., Smith, P.H.: Valuation of ultra-scale computing systems. In: Feitelson, D.G., Rudolph, L. (eds.) JSSPP 2000. LNCS, vol. 1911, pp. 39–55. Springer, Heidelberg (2000)
5. Zhang, Y., Sivasubramaniam, A., Moreira, J., Franke, H.: Impact of workload and system parameters on next generation cluster scheduling mechanisms. IEEE Trans. Parallel Distrib. Syst. **12**, 967–985 (2001)
6. Chapin, S.J., Cirne, W., Feitelson, D.G., Jones, J.P., Leutenegger, S.T., Schwiegelshohn, U., Smith, W., Talby, D.: Benchmarks and standards for the evaluation of parallel job schedulers. In: Feitelson, D.G., Rudolph, L. (eds.) JSSPP 1999. LNCS, vol. 1659, pp. 67–90. Springer, Heidelberg (1999)
7. Jain, R.: The Art of Computer Systems Performance Analysis: Techniques for Experimental Design, Measurement, Simulation, and Modeling. Wiley, New York (1991)
8. Yoo, A.B., Jette, M.A., Grondona, M.: SLURM: simple linux utility for resource management. In: Feitelson, D.G., Rudolph, L., Schwiegelshohn, U. (eds.) JSSPP 2003. LNCS, vol. 2862, pp. 44–60. Springer, Heidelberg (2003)
9. Capit, N., Costa, G.D., Georgiou, Y., Huard, G., Martin, C., Mounie, G., Neyron, P., Richard, O.: A batch scheduler with high level components. In: Cluster Computing and the Grid, pp. 776–783 (2005)
10. Massie, M.L., Chun, B.N., Culler, D.E.: The ganglia distributed monitoring system: design, implementation and experience. Parallel Comput. **30**, 817–840 (2004)
11. Imamagic, E., Dobrenic, D.: Grid infrastructure monitoring system based on nagios. In: Proceedings of the 2007 Workshop on Grid Monitoring. GMW '07, pp. 23–28. ACM, New York (2007)
12. Curry, R., Simmonds, R.: Job centric cluster monitoring. In: 12th International Conference on Parallel and Distributed Systems, ICPADS 2006. vol. 1, 8 p., 25 September 2006
13. Nataraj, A., Sottile, M.J., Morris, A., Malony, A.D., Shende, S.S.: *TAUoverSupermon*: low-overhead online parallel performance monitoring. In: Kermarrec, A.-M., Bougé, L., Priol, T. (eds.) Euro-Par 2007. LNCS, vol. 4641, pp. 85–96. Springer, Heidelberg (2007)
14. Shende, S.S., Malony, A.D.: The tau parallel performance system. Int. J. High Perform. Comput. Appl. **20**, 287–331 (2006)
15. Sottile, M.J., Minnich, R.G.: Supermon: A high-speed cluster monitoring system. In: Proceedings of the IEEE International Conference on Cluster Computing, CLUSTER '02. IEEE Computer Society, Washington, DC (2002)
16. Sharma, S., Bridges, P.G., Maccabe, A.B.: A framework for analyzing linux system overheads on hpc applications. In: Proceedings of the 2005 Los Alamos Computer Science Institute Symposium, October 2005

17. Fuerlinger, K., Wright, N.J., Skinner, D.: Effective performance measurement at petascale using IPM. In: Proceedings of the Sixteenth IEEE International Conference on Parallel and Distributed Systems (ICPADS 2010), Shanghai, China, December 2010
18. Song, B., Ernemann, C., Yahyapour, R.: Parallel computer workload modeling with markov chains. In: Feitelson, D.G., Rudolph, L., Schwiegelshohn, U. (eds.) JSSPP 2004. LNCS, vol. 3277, pp. 47–62. Springer, Heidelberg (2005)
19. Shan, H., Antypas, K., Shalf, J.: Characterizing and predicting the I/O performance of HPC applications using a parameterized synthetic benchmark. In: Proceedings of the 2008 ACM/IEEE conference on Supercomputing. SC '08, pp. 42:1–42:12. IEEE Press, Piscataway (2008)

Decentralized Preemptive Scheduling Across Heterogeneous Multi-core Grid Resources

Arun Balasubramanian[1]([⊠]), Alan Sussman[2], and Norman Sadeh[1]

[1] Institute for Software Research, Carnegie Mellon University,
5000 Forbes Avenue, Pittsburgh, PA 15213, USA
arunb.umd@gmail.com, sadeh@cs.cmu.edu
[2] Department of Computer Science, University of Maryland,
College Park, MD 20742, USA
als@cs.umd.edu

Abstract. The recent advent of multi-core computing environments increases the heterogeneity of grid resources and the complexity of managing them, making efficient load balancing challenging. In an environment where jobs are submitted regularly into a grid which is already executing several jobs, it becomes important to provide low job turn-around times and high throughput for the users. Typically, the grids employ a First Come First Serve (FCFS) method of executing the jobs in the queue which results in suboptimal turn-around times and wait times for most jobs. Hence a conventional FCFS scheduling strategy does not suffice to reduce the average wait times across all jobs. In this paper, we propose new decentralized preemptive scheduling strategies that backfill jobs locally and dynamically migrate waiting jobs across nodes to leverage residual resources, while guaranteeing (on a best effort basis) bounded turn-around and waiting times for all jobs. The methods attempt to maximize total throughput and minimize average waiting time while balancing load across available grid resources. Experimental results for both intra-node and internode scheduling via simulation show that our scheduling schemes perform considerably better than the conventional FCFS approach of a distributed or a centralized scheduler.

Keywords: Distributed systems · Scheduling · Preemptive scheduling · Performance · Load balancing · Heterogeneous processors · Grid computing

1 Introduction

Modern machines use multi-core CPUs to enable improved performance. In a multi-core environment, it has been a challenging problem to schedule multiple jobs that can run simultaneously without oversubscribing resources (including cores). Contention or shared resources can make it hard to exploit multiple computing resources efficiently and so, achieving high performance on multi-core machines without optimized software support is still difficult [15]. Moreover,

N. Desai and W. Cirne (Eds.): JSSPP 2013, LNCS 8429, pp. 22–41, 2014.
DOI: 10.1007/978-3-662-43779-7_2, © Springer-Verlag Berlin Heidelberg 2014

grids that contain multi-core machines are becoming increasingly diverse and heterogeneous [10], so that efficient load balancing and scheduling for the overall system is becoming a very challenging problem [4,5] even with global status information and a centralized scheduler [21].

Previous research [9] on decentralized dynamic scheduling improves the performance of distributed scheduling by starting jobs capable of running immediately (backfilling), through use of residual resources on other nodes (when the job is moved) or on the same node. However, the scheduling strategy is non-preemptive and follows a first come first serve approach to schedule the jobs. This results in suboptimal wait times and turnaround times for most jobs in the queue. It also results in suboptimal overall job throughput rate in the grid.

The performance of distributed scheduling and overall job throughput in such multicore environments can be improved by following a preemptive scheduling strategy where jobs that have lower estimated running times in the queue are scheduled to run immediately. The techniques of migrating jobs to use residual resources on neighboring nodes can also be used to increase the overall CPU utilization. However, because of limited and/or stale global state information, efficient decentralized job migration can be difficult to achieve. Moreover, a job profile often has multiple resource requirements; a simple job migration mechanism considering only CPU usage cannot be applied to in such situations. In addition, guarantee of progress for all jobs is also desired, i.e., no job starvation.

The contribution of this paper is a novel dynamic preemptive scheduling scheme for multi-core grids. The scheme includes (1) local preemptive scheduling, with backfilling on a single node and (2) internode scheduling, for backfilling across multiple nodes. The approach is inspired by ideas from the preemptive schedulers in the context of operating systems, and schedules jobs at regular intervals based on its priorities. The priorities of the jobs are determined according to their remaining time for completion and the amount of time the job has spent waiting in the queue. It is a completely decentralized scheme that balances load and improves throughput when scheduling jobs with multiple constraints across a distributed system. We demonstrate the effectiveness of these algorithms via simulations that show that the decentralized preemptive scheduling approach outperforms the non-preemptive scheduler that follows a first-come-first-serve strategy.

The rest of this paper is organized as follows. Section 2 discusses the related work on various preemptive scheduling strategies in literature. Section 3 discusses the distributed scheduling strategies and describes the basic architecture of the peer-to-peer grid systems and the resource management schemes for multi-core machines. The term definitions related to the scheduling algorithm are presented in Sect. 4. The preemptive scheduling approach is discussed in Sect. 5. The simulation results are presented in Sect. 6. Conclusions and future work are presented in Sects. 7 and 8, respectively.

2   Related Work

Various scheduling algorithms (both preemptive and non-preemptive) have been described in the literature, especially in the contexts of Operating Systems, Batch Processing and Real time scheduling environments. First-come first serve (also termed as FCFS), Round-Robin, shortest-remaining time, fixed priority preemptive scheduling are some of the scheduling algorithms that are widely in use. In classical UNIX systems [2,20], if a higher priority process became runnable, the current process was preempted even if the process did not finish its time quantum. This resulted in higher priority processes starving low-priority ones. To avoid this, a 'usage' factor was introduced to calculate process priority. This factor allowed the kernel to vary processes priorities dynamically. When a process was not running, the kernel periodically increased its priority. When a process received some CPU time, the kernel reduced its priority. This scheme could potentially prevent the starvation of any process, since eventually the priority of any waiting process would rise high enough to be scheduled. While operating system schedulers usually act on the basis of information obtained from the processes executed so far and the priority of processes, batch processing and real time schedulers have added information, such as estimated job completion times and job deadlines, respectively. Our environment closely resembles that of the Batch Processing scenario since it is reasonable to obtain estimates of the job completion times.

Previous research [9] on distributed scheduling scheduled jobs in a FCFS fashion. Although this approach had minimal scheduling overhead, the turnaround times, waiting times and response times were high for many jobs since the long running jobs hogged the CPU. Also, no prioritization resulted in the system having trouble meeting the process deadlines. The work done by Snell et al. [16] on preemption based backfill addresses the problem of inefficient resource utilization by backfilling lower priority jobs. The preemptive backfill technique used in the paper allows the scheduler to schedule lower priority jobs even if they cannot finish execution before the next higher priority job is scheduled. We use a similar technique for our strategies. The work on checkpoint based preemption [13] discusses employing checkpoints for preemption and improves the job scheduling performance in waiting time by addressing the inaccuracies in user-provided runtime estimates.

Shortest remaining time [6] is a scheduling method that is a preemptive version of shortest job next [18] scheduling. In this algorithm, the process with the smallest amount of time remaining until completion is selected to execute. Since the executing process is the one with the shortest amount of time remaining (by definition), processes always run until they complete or a new process is added that requires a smaller amount of time. This leads to higher wait times for long running jobs. Highest Response Ratio Next (HRRN) [19] scheduling is a preemptive discipline, in which the priority of each job is dependent on its estimated run time, and also the amount of time it has spent waiting. Jobs gain higher priority the longer they wait, which prevents indefinite postponement (process starvation). i.e. the jobs that have spent a long time waiting compete against those estimated to have short run times. In this paper, we use the idea of 'Higher Response Ratio Next' in a distributed environment to ensure that long running jobs are not starved of CPU usage while at the same time guaranteeing that shorter jobs finish early. This contributes to the overall high throughput in the system.

3   Background

Several scheduling strategies have been studied in the context of distributed computing ranging from cluster computing to the now-prevalent heterogeneous computing grids. Most of the distributed scheduling strategies in the heterogeneous environments are focused on application level scheduling [3] (i.e. they focus on how to efficiently break down and schedule the sub-tasks of the application) so as to maximize the use of the heterogeneous components like GPUs, CPUs and memory. Some research has also been done to address the issue of dynamically scheduling each incoming job by learning through past performance histories [7] and migrating jobs [9]. However, they all schedule the incoming jobs in a non-preemptive or FCFS order. Though studies have been carried out on the pre-emptive strategies (as discussed in related work) for scheduling jobs submitted onto the grid, a considerable scope still exists for further studies.

Al-Azzoni and Down [1] proposes a scheduling strategy which consists of policies that utilizes the solution to a linear programming problem which maximizes system capacity. This however is a centralized approach and hence has the limitations of a centralized scheduler. The paper on computational models and heuristic methods on grid scheduling by Xhafa and Abraham [23] exceptionally summarizes the scheduling problems involved in grid computing. It also gives good insight on the different scheduling strategies that can be used and presents heuristic methods for scheduling in grids. However, they fail to discuss in detail the benefits of the opportunities presented by a preemptive scheduling model. We then date back as early as Condor [12]; a system that employs a preemptive strategy. Although Condor does not have a centralized/decentralized preemptive scheduler, the local scheduler enforces preemption of the job whenever the user resumes activity. Our scenario can be compared to this in the sense that a higher priority job (a user process in case of Condor) may be ready to run at any given instant.

A pivotal aspect to be considered before scheduling is finding the right node to run the job. Various resource discovery techniques exist in the literature that assign the incoming jobs to chosen nodes. The Classified Advertisement (ClassAd) [14] and the CAN [17] approaches are examples of distributed matchmaking algorithms that match incoming jobs to lightly loaded nodes. Matchmaking is the initial job assignment to a node that satisfies all the resource requirements of the job, and also does load balancing to find a (relatively) lightly loaded node. A good matchmaking algorithm has several desirable properties:

expressiveness, load balance, parsimony, completeness, and low overhead. The matchmaking framework should be expressive enough to specify the essential resource requirements of the job as well as the capabilities of the nodes. It should balance load across nodes to maximize total throughput and to obtain the lowest job turnaround time. However, over-provisioning can decrease total system throughput, therefore the matchmaking should be parsimonious so as not to waste resources. Completeness means that as long as the system contains a node that satisfies a job's requirements, the matchmaker should find that node to run the job. Finally, the overall matchmaking process should not incur significant costs, to minimize overhead.

The ClassAd matchmaking framework is a flexible and general method of resource management in pools of resources which exhibit physical and ownership distribution. Aspects of the framework include a semi-structured data model to represent entities, folding the query language into the data model, allowing entities (resource providers and requestors) to publish queries as attributes. The paradigm also distinguishes between matching and claiming as two distinct operations in resource management: A match is an introduction between two compatible entities, whereas a claim is the establishment of a working relationship between the entities. The representation and protocols facilitate both static and dynamic heterogeneity of resources, which results in a robust and scalable framework that can evolve with changing resources.

The Content Addressable Network (CAN) is a distributed, decentralized P2P infrastructure that provides hash table functionality. The architectural design is a virtual multi-dimensional Cartesian coordinate space, a type of overlay network, on a multi-torus. Points within the space are identified with coordinates. The entire coordinate space is dynamically partitioned among all the nodes in the system such that every node possesses at least one distinct zone within the overall space.

A job in our system is the data and associated profile that describes a computation to be performed. The grid system may contain heterogeneous nodes with different resource types and capabilities, e.g. CPU speed, memory size, disk space, number of cores. Jobs submitted to the grid also can have multiple resource requirements, limiting the set of nodes on which they can be run. We assume that every job is independent, meaning that there is no communication between jobs. To build the P2P grid system, a variant of the CAN [17] distributed hash table (DHT) is employed, which represents a node's resource capabilities (and a job's resource requirements) as coordinates in the d-dimensional space. Each dimension of the CAN represents the amount of that resource, so that nodes can be sorted according to the values for each resource. A node occupies a hyper-rectangular zone that does not overlap with any other nodes zone, and the zone contains the nodes coordinates within the d-dimensional space. Nodes exchange load and other information with nodes whose zones abut its own (called neighbors). The following steps describe how jobs are submitted and executed in the grid system.

(1) A client (user) inserts a job into the system through an arbitrary node called the injection node.
(2) The injection node initiates CAN routing of the job to the owner node.
(3) The owner node initiates the process to find a lightly loaded node (runnode) that meets all of the job's resource requirements (called matchmaking). (For more details on the owner node and matchmaking, refer to Kim et al. [8])
(4) The run node inserts the job into an internal FIFO queue for job execution. Periodic heartbeat messages between the run node and the owner node ensure that both are still alive. Missing multiple consecutive heartbeats invokes a (distributed) failure recovery procedure.
(5) After the job completes, the run node delivers the results to the client and informs the owner node that the job has completed.

The owner node monitors a job's execution status until the job finishes and the result is delivered to the client. To enable failure recovery, the owner node and the run node periodically exchange soft-state heartbeat messages to detect node failures (or a graceful exit from the system). More details about the basic system architecture can be found in Kim et al. [8]. The studies conducted in this paper can be used in any of the contexts discussed above or even any arbitrary network. Also, the waiting time is calculated as the non-executing time spent by the jobs after the job has migrated to the node where it would be scheduled for execution i.e. we do not account for the time spent by the job between the job submission and job migration in the network. This is in contrast to the waiting times usually computed in a distributed environment where it is the non-executing time spent by the job from the time it was submitted in the network until it completes execution. More on this is discussed in the 'Experiment and Results' section. The neighbors of the node are arbitrarily generated. We produce results for nodes with neighbors having similar resource constraints and nodes with larger number of neighbors in order to show the effectiveness of our algorithms in the CAN-like and other highly interconnected networks.

4   Term Representations

(1) J_a = An arbitrary job in queue (Non executing job)
(2) J'_a = Currently Running (or executing) Job
(3) J_h = Job at head of queue
(4) J'_{Pmin} = Minimum Priority Job running currently in a given set
(5) J'_{Rmin} = Minimum Resource consuming Job running currently in a given set
(6) $J'_{running}$ = A set comprising jobs that are currently running
(7) $J'_{covered}$ = A set comprising jobs covered so far for preemption analysis
(8) J'_{rem} = The remaining jobs (those yet to be examined for preemption)
(9) P_{j_a} = Priority of Job J_a waiting in queue
(10) $P_{j'_a}$ = Priority of currently running job

(11) P_{j_h} = Priority of Job at head of queue J_H

(12) $P_{max}(J'_{covered})$ = Priority of the Highest priority job that is covered so far

(13) $P_{min}(J'_{covered})$ = Priority of the Lowest priority job that is covered so far

(14) $P_{max}(J'_{rem})$ = Priority of the Highest priority job from the remaining jobs (those yet to be examined for preemption)

(15) $P_{min}(J'_{rem})$ = Priority of the Lowest priority job from the remaining jobs (those yet to be examined for preemption)

(16) R_{J_a} = Resource requirements for Job J_a. The algorithm treats all resource types (CPU's, GPU's, memory and disk space) as a set R.

(17) R_f = Current free residual resources

(18) $R_f(temp)$ = Residual resources that would be available when some current running jobs are preempted

(19) R_{j_h} = Resource requirements of Job at head of queue

(20) $R_{j'_i}$ = Resource requirements of Job currently running

(21) $R_{j'_{Pmin}}$ = Resource requirements of J'_{Pmin}

(22) $R_{j'_{Rmin}}$ = Resource requirements of J'_{Rmin}

(23) $T_{rem}(J_a)$ = Remaining Time for Job J_a

(24) W_{J_a} = Waiting time of Job J_a defined as the non-executing time spent by the job after it has migrated to the node where it would be scheduled for execution.

5   Preemptive Scheduling

5.1   Local Scheduling

This section deals with the scheduling criteria for a single node. As mentioned in Sect. 2, we combine the ideas of 'shortest remaining time next' and the 'higher response ratio next' to come up with a preemptive scheduling algorithm for the grids. The 'shortest remaining time next' ensures that jobs that have the smaller remaining time are run, so they end sooner. However, this could lead to starvation for long running jobs and hence we increase the priority for jobs that wait longer in the queue. Thus, the jobs waiting in the node's queue have their priorities calculated as

$$P_{j_a} = ((\alpha * W_{J_a}) - (\beta * T_{rem}(J_a)))$$

i.e. the priority for a job is directly proportional to its wait time W_{J_a} and negatively proportional to its estimated time for completion $T_{rem}(J_a)$. α is the weight factor associated with the wait time. β is the weight associated with the remaining time for completion. Typically, the β value is set to 1. The section on 'Experimental Results' provides more details on the values of α.

The job queue is sorted according to the order of their priorities calculated as above. Initially, the jobs in the head of the queue are scheduled until the available resources are insufficient for the next job to run. Next, those jobs that can run in the available residual resources are scheduled to run (Backfilling). Since the backfilled jobs have priorities associated with them, they are also prone to preemption and therefore do not starve jobs waiting in the queue. The scheduler is invoked at the following 3 phases in the system:

(1) After every periodic scheduling interval δ.
(2) As a new job enters the queue.
(3) A job completes its execution.

The periodic interval δ is much higher when compared to the scheduling intervals for schedulers in the OS. This is because in a heterogeneous environment we expect the time taken for context switches to be more expensive. And so, frequent context switches would result in low overall CPU utilization. More details regarding the values of δ are discussed in the Results section.

The scheduler is invoked when a new job enters the queue because the newly arrived job could be backfilled. And, when a job completes execution, it frees up some resources which allows new jobs to run. At every scheduling turn, the priority of the job in the head of queue is compared with that of the least priority job that is currently running. This is done because the queued job cannot run currently if its priority is lower than the lowest priority job that is currently running. This also addresses the backfilled jobs immediately since backfilled jobs have the lowest priority among the running jobs. Figure 1 demonstrates the scenario where the scheduler preempts a lower priority job with a higher priority job and backfills another job in its residual resources.

If the priority of the job at head of queue (P_{j_h}) is greater, the scheduler checks if the current running job J'_{Pmin} frees up enough resources for the new job to run. If yes, the job J'_{Pmin} is preempted and J_h is scheduled. Otherwise,

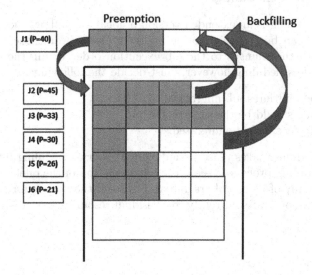

Fig. 1. Local preemptive scheduling

the scheduler compares the priority of the second lowest priority job (J'_a) with J_h. This is carried out until the scheduler appropriately preempts jobs that free up just the right amount of resources for the job J_h to run. If the scheduler is unable to free up sufficient resources for the job to run, the job J_h is not scheduled in this interval and has to wait until the next scheduling turn. The scheduling (at every scheduling turn) is carried out for all jobs in the queue that have a higher priority than the lowest priority job that is currently running. The details are described in the 'Preemptive scheduling algorithm' below.

5.2 Context Switching and Its Impact

The cost of a context switch is well quantified in [11] and in (http://blog. tsunanet.net/2010/11/how-long-does-it-take-to-make-context.html). Although the paper talks about context switching time of up to 1.5 ms for large working sets, the article in the blog gives a good worst case approximation for context switches (about 40 μs) for current Intel processors. Even if we assume a worst case value of 1 ms for each context switch, that results in less than 0.02 % error for scheduling interval $\delta = 5$ s in our calculations of wait times. In fact, we only have context switches when there is preemption and so not every scheduling interval would have a context switch. The time taken for context switches can be further reduced if jobs are pinned to a particular core since this would avoid cache pollution (i.e. reduce the effect of thrashing). Due to these reasons, we believe it is safe to ignore the time taken for context switches in our experiments.

5.3 Internode Scheduling

Internode scheduling is an extended version of local scheduling; the target node for backfilling can be the neighboring nodes in the network. Local scheduling deals only with the changes to the job execution order within the queue on a node. Internode scheduling however, must decide the following:

(1) Which node initiates job migration,
(2) Which node should be the sender of a job,
(3) and which job should be migrated.

Internode scheduling takes place periodically at every scheduling interval after the local scheduling process to see if the job at the top of the queue in the node can be run on any of its neighbors and also to see if the node can run the job of any of its neighbors in its currently free residual resources.

Algorithm 1. Preemptive Scheduling Algorithm

---

procedure
ScheduleJobs(JobQueue)
 1: UpdateWaittimes()
 2: CalculatePriorities()
 3: **while** $R_f \neq 0$ **do**
 4:     $J_h = $ nextHighPriorityJobInQueue()
 5:     If $R_{j_h} < R_f$.
 6:     $R_f = R_f - R_{j_a}$
 7: **end while**
 8: $J_h = $ nextHighPriorityJobInQueue()
 9: **while** $(P_{j_h} > P_{min}(J'_{running}) || P_{j_h} \neq 0)$ **do**
10:     $J'_{covered} = 0$
11:     $J'_{rem} = 0$
12:     $R_f(temp) = R_f$
13:     $J'_{covered} = J'_{Pmin}$
14:     **if** $R_{j_h} <= (R_{j'_{Pmin}} + R_f(temp))$ **then**
15:         Preempt(J'_{Pmin})
16:         Run(J_h)
17:     **else**
18:         $R_f(temp) = R_f(temp) + R_{j'_{Pmin}}$
19:         FindJobstoPreempt()
20:     **end if**
21:     $J_h = $ nextJobInQueue()
22: **end while**
end procedure
procedure
UpdateWaittimes()
 1: $W_{J_a} = CurrentTime - EntryTime(J_a) - TotalRuntime(J_a)$
end procedure
procedure
CalculatePriorities()
 1: $P_{j_a} = ((\alpha * W_{J_a}) - (\beta * T_{rem}(J_a))$
end procedure
procedure
FindJobstoPreempt( )
 1: **while** $(J'_{rem} \neq 0)$ **do**
 2:     Select J'_a such that $P_{j'_a} > P_{max}(J'_{covered})$ and $P_{j'_a} = P_{min}(J'_{rem})$
 3:     $J'_{covered} += J'_a$
 4:     $J'_{rem} = J'_{running} - J'_{covered}$
 5:     **if** $P_{j'_a} > P_{j'_h}$ **then**
 6:         break {cannot preempt jobs}
 7:     **else**
 8:         **if** $R_{j_h} <= R_{j'_a}$ **then**
 9:             Preempt(J'_a)
10:             Run(J_h)
11:             break

```
12:      else
13:         FindOptimal(J'_covered, J_h)
14:      end if
15:   end if
16: end while
end procedure
procedure
FindOptimal(J'_covered, J_h)
 1: if R_{j_h} <= (R_{j_{a'}} + R_f(temp))  then
 2:    for each J'[i] in J'_covered with P_{j'_i} < P_{j'_a} and R_{j'[i]} = R_{J'_{Rmin}}
 3:    if R_{j'_a} + R_{j'[i]} >= R_{j_h}  then
 4:       Preempt J'[i], J'_a
 5:       Run J_h
 6:       break
 7:    else
 8:       searchCombinationsforOptimalPreemption(J'[i], J'_covered)
 9:    end if
10:    end for
11: else
12:    R_f(temp) = R_f(temp) + R_{j'_a}
13: end if
end procedure
```

In the PUSH scheduling model the job sender initiates the migration process. First, the sender node tries to match priority of the job at the head of the queue with the neighboring node's queue. If the priority of the job at head of the queue in its neighbor node is less than the job at the sender node, a PUSH message for the job is sent to its neighbor containing the job's priority (of sender node) and the resource requirements. If the job can be backfilled at the neighbor node, the PUSH message is accepted. Otherwise, a PUSH-reject message is sent back to the sender node. If a job can be run on multiple neighbors, the sender sends it to the node that has minimum objective function value as follows. Figure 2 shows the case where a job at the head of queue on one node is pushed to run on the neighboring node.

$$f_{Inter-PUSH} = BM * FM * (1/CPU_{speed})$$

where BM and FM are defined as follows:

$$BM = \frac{max_k(S^k + R^k_j)}{\frac{(\sum_{k=1}^{K}(S^k + R^k_j))}{K}} = \frac{MaximumUtilization}{AverageUtilization}$$

$$FM = 1 - \frac{(\sum_{k=1}^{K}(S^k + R^k_j))}{K} = 1 - AverageUtilization$$

where K is the number of resources (or requirements), S^k is normalized utilization for resource $k(1 < k < K, 0 < S^k < 1)$, and R^k_j is job j's normalized

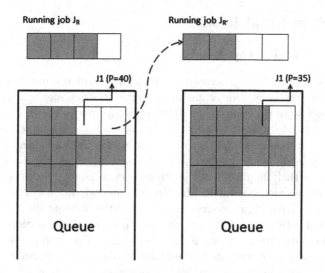

Fig. 2. Internode scheduling

requirement for resource $k(0 < R_j^k < 1)$. BM measures unevenness across utilization of multiple resources, and FM measures how much resources are underutilized on average. Therefore, lower BM and FM imply better balanced resource utilization and better average utilization, respectively.

To prefer the fastest node among neighbors, the objective function also includes an inverse term for CPU speed. Before sending a job profile, there is a simple confirming handshake process between a sender and a potential receiver to avoid inappropriate job migration because the potential receiver information may not be up-to-date at the sender.

In the PULL model, a receiver node tries to obtain a job from its CAN neighbors so as not to waste its available resources. However, the node does not have all information on the queued jobs resource requirements in its neighbors to minimize neighbor update message sizes, so the node invokes a PULL-Request message to the node having the closest priority job at the head of queue that is higher than the priority of job at the head of the queue in the current node. If there are multiple such nodes, the request is sent to the node with maximum queue size among its neighbors. If there are multiple candidate jobs in the waiting queue, then the job that has minimum objective function value (BM * FM, as above), is selected. If there is no candidate job, then the requesting node gets a PULL-Reject message and continues to look for another potential sender having the appropriate priority along with maximum queue length not contacted recently.

6   Experiment and Results

6.1   Experimental Setup

A synthetic workload was generated to model the grid resource configuration containing heterogeneous nodes capable of executing a heterogeneous set of jobs. The simulation scenario consists of 1000 multi-core nodes (having 1, 2, 4 or 8 cores), and 5000 jobs submitted to run on those nodes. Each node has multiple resource capabilities such as CPU speed, memory size, disk space and the number of cores. The jobs are also modeled similarly having the heterogeneous resource configuration as their requirements. A high percentage of the nodes (and jobs) have relatively low resource capabilities (requirements), and a low percentage of nodes (and jobs) have high resource capabilities (requirements).

The interval between job submissions follow a Poisson distribution, with varying average job inter arrival times in the experiments. Each job has an estimated running time associated with it. The estimated times are uniformly distributed between 0.5T and 1.5T, with T = 3600 s, running on a canonical node with a normalized CPU speed of 1. The simulated job running time is then scaled up or down by the CPU speed relative to the canonical node.

We compare our schemes to the FCFS scheduler with backfilling which schedules jobs in the order they arrive and also performs backfilling of jobs on residual resources. To measure the performance of the long running grid system, we run the simulations in a steady state environment. By steady state, its implied that the job arrival and departure rates are similar, so that the system achieves a dynamic equilibrium state during the simulation period, with the system neither highly overloaded nor underutilized. Hence, the average total system load is determined by the inter-job arrival rate. However, very lightly loaded systems were not tested, because they are not very interesting for measuring dynamic scheduling performance.

The total waiting time for a job is usually calculated as the non-executing time spent by the job from the time it was submitted in the network till it completes execution. However, in this paper we do not account for the time spent by the job between the job submission and job migration process in the network. Instead we consider the job arrival time as the time at which the job arrives at the node where it can be executed. Thus, the wait times are redefined as the non-executing time spent by the jobs after the job has migrated to the node where it would be scheduled for execution.

The neighbors of the node are arbitrarily generated. We produce results for nodes with neighbors having similar resource constraints and nodes with varying neighbors in order to show the effectiveness of our algorithms in the CAN and other interconnected networks. Specifically, we produce results for a network where each node is connected to exactly two other nodes (abbreviated as 2-NN) and a CAN-like network with 3–4 neighbors. We say CAN-like because the network constructed does not strictly adhere to CAN specifications though each node is connected to 4 other nodes that have similar resource capabilities. For simplicity we refer to the CAN-like network as CAN' in the following sections.

6.2   Experimental Results

Figure 3 lists and compares the median wait times across all jobs for each job inter-arrival time. The median wait times are plotted for the four scenarios FCFS with Backfilling, Local preemptive scheduling with Backfilling and Internode scheduling (in both CAN' and 2-NN). We experimented with different values for α. However, setting $\alpha = 0$ yielded the lowest median wait times across all jobs and so, we use this value to plot our graphs. This is essentially a Shortest Job First preemptive strategy i.e. at any time, the job with the smallest remaining executing time is chosen to run irrespective of its waiting time in the queue.

When the jobs have low inter-arrival times, jobs arrive quickly onto the node and spend more time waiting in the queue. In contrast, when jobs have higher inter-arrival times, they arrive considerably later than its previous job and end up with comparatively lower wait times. It is clear from Fig. 3 that local preemptive scheduling algorithm results in significantly lower wait times when compared to the FCFS strategy for all cases of job inter-arrival times. Significant differences can also be observed between waiting times of local preemptive and internode scheduling proving the effectiveness of the internode scheduling algorithm. The differences in wait times for CAN' and 2-NN internode scheduling algorithms is low for low job inter-arrival times (1.5 and 2.0) and increases with increase in job inter-arrival times. This shows that the internode scheduling is more effective for more neighbors especially when the job inter-arrival time is high. This is because for low job inter-arrival times, job migrations to neighboring nodes are rare since those nodes are already executing many jobs.

We also conducted experiments for values $\alpha = 0.5$ and $\beta = 1$ so that jobs that have been waiting in the queue for a while get a chance to run. In this scenario, the jobs that have waited in the queue for a long time compete against the shorter running jobs. The intuition behind this experiment was to prevent the long waiting jobs from being starved of CPU and to reduce their total waiting time. Figure 4a shows the gain achieved in the wait times for the top 10 % of long waiting jobs in CAN'. We also observed similar results for the 2-NN and

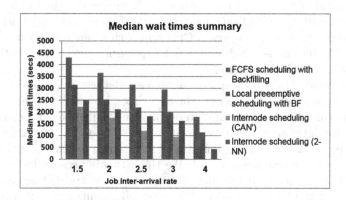

Fig. 3. Median wait times for different job inter-arrival times

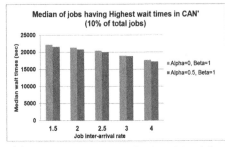 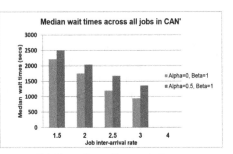

(a) Median waittimes in long waiting jobs   (b) Overall median waittimes

Fig. 4. Median wait time comparisons in CAN'

local preemptive scheduling scenarios. Figure 4b shows the median wait time comparisons of the two approaches. The choice of picking the appropriate value of alpha depends on what type of service we intend to provide the end-users (i.e. bounded wait times for all jobs vs. highest throughput for most jobs). We believe the values of the wait times to be dependent on the type of load (jobs) being submitted to the nodes and the network environment.

Figure 5a–c illustrates the distribution of the wait times for jobs in all the environments, i.e. preemptive scheduling (both local and internode scheduling) and non-preemptive FCFS scheduling. The first 2000 jobs having the lowest wait times have been omitted in plotting the graphs. We did this because so many jobs wait for very little time and so cutting off the part where all the lines completely overlap doesn't lose any information. The plots show that the waiting times of jobs decreases with increasing job inter-arrival times in the FCFS environment. The curves in Fig. 5a show improvement in the percentage of jobs completed with low wait times for local and internode scheduling as compared to the FCFS scheduling. We can also observe that the curves for local preemptive scheduling and internode scheduling (for 2-NN) are almost overlapping. However, the distinction between these curves becomes more apparent with higher job inter-arrival times. We can see a marked improvement (in Fig. 5c) on the percentage of jobs completed with low wait times for our preemptive scheduling strategies over the non-preemptive FCFS approach when the job inter-arrival rate is 4.0. The internode scheduling in CAN' performs significantly better than the non-preemptive FCFS strategy.

We also repeated the same experiment for a smaller scheduling interval of 2.5 s to observe any significant variances in the wait times. However, the improvements in the median and average wait times were almost negligible except for Internode-scheduling for inter-arrival rate of 4 s in CAN'. The CAN' (for inter arrival time = 4 s) responded very well (almost 50 % decrease in median wait time) with the change in the scheduling interval. We think this is because the CAN' has more neighboring nodes with similar resource requirements that are capable of running the job and thus succeeds with a higher probability of scheduling the job when compared to the 2-NN topology. Also, due to high job inter-arrival time

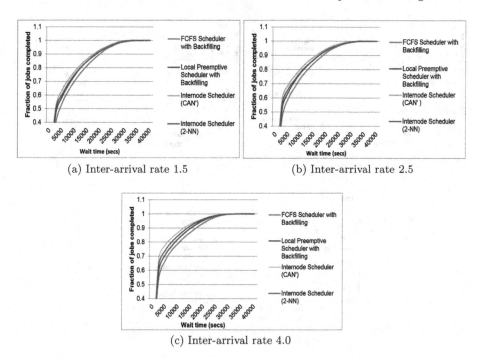

(a) Inter-arrival rate 1.5   (b) Inter-arrival rate 2.5

(c) Inter-arrival rate 4.0

Fig. 5. Fraction of jobs completed in the four schedulers

the scheduler is able to find more such nodes because the neighboring nodes have more likelihood of having empty cores. We believe that factors such as the order in which the jobs are submitted, their execution times and the resource requirements for these jobs, all play a critical role in determining the optimal scheduling interval. More on this is discussed in the Future Work section.

Another important scheduling criterion is reducing the maximum wait time, so that no (or fewer) jobs wait a very long time to run. Figure 6a–c focuses on the tails of the job distributions of Fig. 5a–c (the last 100–200 jobs having the highest wait times). Figure 6a shows that the local preemptive scheduler does better than internode scheduler when the job inter-arrival rate is 1.5. We believe this is because since a large number of jobs arrive in a short span of time, the jobs migrated to neighboring nodes would result in longer job queues for some nodes; thus increasing the wait times for jobs further down the queue. In other words, there is a load imbalance. We can see a similar trend in Fig. 6b though there are fewer such jobs. As the job inter-arrival time increases, this effect is reduced. In Fig. 6c we observe an interesting trend where Internode-2NN does better than both local preemptive and Internode CAN' schedulers.

The total number of preemptions for shortest-job first strategy in the Local preemptive scheduling (for scheduling interval of 5 s) scenario varied from 556 (for Inter-arrival times = 1.5 s) to 471 (for IAT = 4 s) while that for Internode scheduling varied between 570 to 480. This was approximately equal to 1/8th the

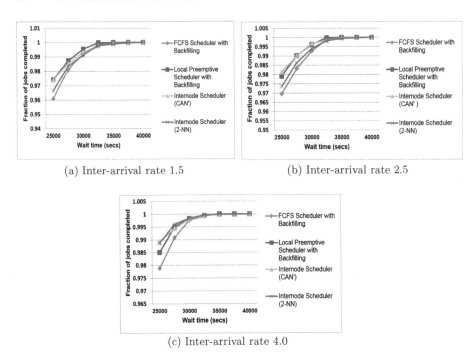

(a) Inter-arrival rate 1.5   (b) Inter-arrival rate 2.5

(c) Inter-arrival rate 4.0

Fig. 6. Fraction of jobs completed in the four schedulers (towards the end)

total number of jobs submitted in the system. As mentioned before, we believe that factors such as the order in which the jobs are submitted, their execution times, resource requirements and load balancing of these jobs all play a critical role in determining these numbers. For scheduling interval (δ) of 2.5 s, we didn't notice any significant differences in these values. The number of preemptions started to increase considerably only when the value of alpha was set to 1 or higher. But this resulted in high median and average wait times across the network.

7   Conclusion

A preemptive scheduling algorithm (with backfilling) for multi-core grid resources was designed and implemented. As part of local scheduling, jobs that are estimated to complete sooner were given higher priority compared to long running jobs while at the same time ensuring that the long running jobs get their fair share of the CPU. The results show that our algorithm yields lower average and median wait times when compared to the FCFS approach. In particular, the shortest-job first algorithm yields the lowest median wait-times for the system compared to cases where long running jobs compete for the CPU. The Internode scheduling ensures that those jobs that cannot be immediately scheduled are PUSHED to a neighboring node if it can run in their residual resources. It also allows a node to PULL jobs from neighboring nodes to utilize its local residual resources. An appropriate value for α, the weight for the waiting time for a job, ensures to lower the wait times for long waiting jobs. In addition, the median wait times for CAN-like systems can be further lowered by choosing the appropriate value for the scheduling interval δ.

8   Future Work

The local scheduling and internode scheduling algorithms find and execute a job using residual free resources in a node. This means that only jobs that can start running immediately will be moved. However, if the load across nodes is skewed, the job queue lengths vary greatly, and hence a more pro-active queue balancing scheme would improve load distribution and overall throughput across heterogeneous nodes. To address this, we illustrate the same technique used in [9] here. Firstly, the maximally loaded resource among the K available resources is set as the Load of a node, and the algorithm minimizes the total sum of the Loads among neighbors, and also balances Load across the nodes [22]. The term W_i^k is defined, normalized load for Resource k of Node i by:

$$W_i^k = \sum_{J_j \in Queue_i} (R_j^k), 1 \leq k \leq K$$

where J_j is Job j, R_j^k is the kth normalized resource requirement for J_j, and $Queue_i$ is the job queue for node i. The normalized load of Node i, L_i is given by

$$L_i = Max(W_k^i), 1 \leq k \leq K$$

The PUSH and PULL job migration models can be used for queue balancing, as they were for internode scheduling. For PUSH, a node i computes normalized load (L_i) for itself and for its neighbors. If L_i is the locally maximum value among all its neighbors, then node i checks its queue to find candidate jobs for migration that reduce L_i if the (candidate) job is moved. Among these jobs, those jobs that satisfy the priority constraints in the neighboring node are considered. When there are multiple candidate jobs, the algorithm selects the job and the receiver node that minimize an objective function if the job is moved to the neighbor.

The PULL model is similar to the PUSH model, except that the node with a locally non-zero minimum normalized load among equal or less capable neighbors will initiate the PULL process from the most loaded node among its neighbors. The Queue Balancing technique may further improve the performance of the desktop grid system.

Further research can be done by experimenting with different sets of workloads for different types of networks. We could then observe what values of δ and α give optimal values for the median wait times across the nodes.

Acknowledgements. We appreciate the comments received from anonymous reviewers of the JSSPP 2013 workshop. They pointed out some key issues that has led us to do further research on this topic. We thank Manjunath Gopinath, Bin Liu, Sarat Babu Eruvuru, Bhavani Bhaskar and Abhishek Prasad for their participation in discussions and their feedback on this idea.

References

1. Al-Azzoni, I., Down, D.G.: Dynamic scheduling for heterogeneous desktop grids. J. Parallel Distrib. Comput. **70**(12), 1231–1240 (2010)
2. Bach, M.J.: The Design of the UNIX Operating System, Chapter 8 - Process Scheduling and Time. Prentice Hall, Upper Saddle River (1986)
3. Berman, F., Wolski, R., Figueira, S., Schopf, J., Shao, G.: Application level scheduling on distributed heterogenous networks. In: Proceedings of the 1996 ACM/IEEE Conference on Supercomputing. ACM/IEEE (1996)
4. Zhou, D., Lo, V.: Wave scheduler: scheduling for faster turnaround time in peer-based desktop grid systems. In: Feitelson, D.G., Frachtenberg, E., Rudolph, L., Schwiegelshohn, U. (eds.) JSSPP 2005. LNCS, vol. 3834, pp. 194–218. Springer, Heidelberg (2005)
5. Zhou, D., Lo, V.: Wavegrid: a scalable fast-turnaround heterogeneous peer-based desktop grid system. In: Proceedings of the 20th International Parallel and Distributed Processing Symposium (IPDPS2006), April 2006. IEEE Computer Society Press (2006)
6. Harchol-Balter, M., Schroeder, B., Bansal, N., Agrawal, M.: Size-based scheduling to improve web performance. ACM Trans. Comput. Syst. **21**(2), 207–233 (2003)
7. Jiménez, V.J., Vilanova, L., Gelado, I., Gil, M., Fursin, G.G., Navarro, N.: Predictive runtime code scheduling for heterogeneous architectures. In: Seznec, A., Emer, J., O'Boyle, M., Martonosi, M., Ungerer, T. (eds.) HiPEAC 2009. LNCS, vol. 5409, pp. 19–33. Springer, Heidelberg (2009)
8. Kim, J.S., Keleher, P., Marsh, M., Bhattacharjee, B., Sussman, A.: Using content-addressable networks for load balancing in desktop grids. In: Proceedings of the 16th IEEE International Symposium on High Performance, Distributed Computing (HPDC-16), June 2007 (2007)
9. Lee, J., Keleher, P., Sussman, A.: Decentralized dynamic scheduling across heterogeneous multi-core desktop grids. In: Proceedings of the 19th International Heterogeneity in Computing Workshop (HCW2010), April 2010. IEEE Computer Society Press (2010)
10. Lee, J., Keleher, P., Sussman, A.: Supporting computing element heterogeneity in p2p grids. In: Proceedings of the IEEE Cluster 2011 Conference, September 2011. IEEE Computer Society Press (2011)
11. Li, C., Ding, C., Shen, K.: Quantifying the cost of context switch. In: Proceedings of the 2007 Workshop on Experimental Computer Science ExpCS '07. ACM, New York (2007)
12. Litzkow, M., Livny, M., Mutka, M.: Condor-a hunter of idle workstations. In: 8th International Conference on Distributed, Computing Systems, pp. 104–111 (1988)
13. Niu, S., Zhai, J., Ma, X., Liu, M., Zhai, Y., Chen, W., Zheng, W.: Employing checkpoint to improve job scheduling in large-scale systems. In: Cirne, W., Desai, N., Frachtenberg, E., Schwiegelshohn, U. (eds.) JSSPP 2012. LNCS, vol. 7698, pp. 36–55. Springer, Heidelberg (2013)
14. Raman, R., Livny, M., Solomon, M.: Matchmaking: distributed resource management for high throughput computing. In: Proceedings of the 7th International Symposium on High Performance, Distributed Computing, July 1998, pp. 140–146 (1998)

15. Moore, S.: Multicore is bad news for super computers. IEEE Spectrum. **45**(11), 15 (2008)
16. Snell, Q.O., Clement, M.J., Jackson, D.B.: Preemption based backfill. In: Feitelson, D.G., Rudolph, L., Schwiegelshohn, U. (eds.) JSSPP 2002. LNCS, vol. 2537, pp. 24–37. Springer, Heidelberg (2002)
17. Ratnasamy, S., Francis, P., Handley, M., Karp, R., Shenker, S.: A scalable content addressable network. In: Proceedings of the ACM SIGCOMM Conference, August 2001 (2001)
18. Stallings, W.: Operating Systems: Internals and Design Principles, 4th edn. Prentice Hall, Upper Saddle River (2001). ISBN: 0-13-031999-6
19. Tanenbaum, A.S.: Modern Operating Systems, 3rd edn. Pearson Education, Upper Saddle River (2008). ISBN: 0-13-600663-9
20. Thompson, K.: UNIX implementation. Bell Syst. Tech. J. **57**, 1931–1946 (1978)
21. Leinberger, W., Karypis, G., Kumar, V.: Job scheduling in the presence of multiple resource requirements. In: Supercomputing '99: Proceedings of the 1999 ACM/IEEE Conference on Supercomputing (CDROM), p. 47. ACM, NewYork (1999)
22. Leinberger, W., Karypis, G., Kumar, V., Biswas, R.: Load balancing across near-homogeneous multi-resource servers. In: Proceedings of the 9th Heterogeneous Computing Workshop, appears with the Proceedings of IPDPS 2000, pp. 60–71 (2000)
23. Xhafa, F., Abraham, A.: Computational models and heuristic methods for grid scheduling problems. Future Gener. Comput. Syst. **26**(4), 608–621 (2010)

Comparing Performance Heatmaps

David Krakov and Dror G. Feitelson[(✉)]

School of Computer Science and Engineering,
The Hebrew University of Jerusalem,
91904 Jerusalem, Israel
feit@cs.huji.ac.il

Abstract. The performance of parallel job schedulers is often expressed as an average metric value (e.g. response time) for a given average load. An alternative is to acknowledge the wide variability that exists in real systems, and use a heatmap that portrays the distribution of jobs across the performance × load space. Such heatmaps expose a wealth of details regarding the conditions that occurred in production use or during a simulation. However, heatmaps are a visual tool, lending itself to high-resolution analysis of a single system but not conducive for a direct comparison between different schedulers or environments. We propose a number of techniques that allow to compare heatmaps. The first two treat the heatmaps as images, and focus on the differences between them. Two other techniques are based on tracking how specific jobs fare under the compared scenarios, and drawing underlying trends. This enables a detailed analysis of how different schedulers affect the workload, and what leads to the observed average results.

1   Introduction

Graphs and visualizations are generally acknowledged to be important tools for understanding complex systems. But as Anscombe [1] noted, few of us escape the notion that graphs are rough, and when dealing with large amounts of data numerical computations are the "real" analysis. Such analysis assumes that we are able to find a numerical formula that is congenial to the data. However, numerical recipes typically entail an abstraction and simplification, while in many real-world examples it is best to first look at the data in all its complexity and observe its behavior, perhaps forgoing more formal analysis altogether [2].

Parallel job scheduler performance evaluation is no exception to this rule. The conventional approach for performance evaluation of parallel jobs schedulers tries to condense the varied information about scheduling behavior into few representative metrics such as the *mean response time* (the time between job submittal and completion) or the *mean slowdown* (the ratio between the actual runtime and the response time, which includes the wait time). However, using the mean fails miserably on asymmetrical distributions [4]. Slowdown is especially problematic, as short jobs may have disproportionately high slowdowns. Downey [5] calls the tendency to report summary statistics for non-symmetric distributions

N. Desai and W. Cirne (Eds.): JSSPP 2013, LNCS 8429, pp. 42–61, 2014.
DOI: 10.1007/978-3-662-43779-7_3, © Springer-Verlag Berlin Heidelberg 2014

that exist in real workload data a "bad habit"; Frachtenberg [7] mentions using the mean for asymmetrically distributed (skewed) results as one of the pitfalls of parallel job scheduling evaluation.

A major reason for using simple condensed metrics is the need to compare different job scheduling strategies applied to the same workload, or to show how performance depends on some parameter (e.g. how simulation results change with load conditions). But if our metrics (and specifically, their averages) mis-represent reality, any comparison based on them becomes questionable. As research of parallel job scheduling strategies commonly revolves around comparison of alternatives, finding a good comparison tool becomes an important problem.

Heatmaps are a powerful tool to visualize large amounts of data, and are gaining hold in various areas as an analysis tool for complex information. When applied to parallel job schedulers performance evaluations they can help to visualize how various job metrics distribute relative to different load conditions [8], in contrast to the traditional approach of using the average metric as a single data point for evaluation. Thus heatmaps can help avoid the pitfall of misleading performance metrics.

However, it is difficult to visually compare different runs. Such comparisons are important to identify odd patterns and find better behavior. But — as the examples we explore will show — heatmaps may "look the same" despite having important but subtle differences. Naturally, since heatmaps visualize a job distribution over the load × performance space (as recorded from some scheduler and workload), one can use statistical analysis tools to compare different job distributions and obtain numerical results. But as we will show, this approach can be misleading as well.

As an alternative, we suggest to stay in the visual domain. We therefore need ways to highlight changes in behavior and allow high resolution analysis of the differences between heatmaps representing different scheduling algorithms or conditions. We present a number of such techniques in this paper. The first is simple image subtraction. The second is based on ratios, and is similar in spirit to the Kullback-Leibler divergence. Two additional schemes are based on tracking how individual jobs move across the load × performance space.

2   Heatmaps Applied to Evaluation of Parallel Job Schedulers

The performance of a computer system obviously depends on the workload it handles. Reliable performance evaluations therefore require the use of representative workloads. The workload used for the evaluation should represent real job distributions, including internal correlations and structure emerging from user feedback and system boundaries. As a result, evaluations of new schedulers often use workload logs obtained from real production systems to drive a simulation. Many real world traces are available at the Parallel Workloads Archive [11], converted into the Standard Workload Format (SWF) [3].

Heatmaps were recently proposed as a tool that allows high resolution analysis of a job trace or of simulation results [8]. This is based on the observation that a single trace or simulation contains a wealth of information about behavior under different load conditions, which can be exploited to zoom in on different conditions [12].

Specifically, a heatmap is like a scatter-plot showing the distribution of the jobs in the log. In our heatmaps the X axis is the load experienced by each job, and the Y axis is the job's performance, as measured per-job by common metrics such as slowdown or response time. The heatmap image is based on a fine grid where each bin shows how many jobs experienced the load and performance represented by the bin's coordinates. "Hot" (dark) bins mean lots of jobs and "cold" (light) bins are few jobs.

We use the same engine for heatmap calculation as was used in our previous work [8], and have made its code available online [13]. The load experienced by a job is computed as the weighted average of the utilizations of the system during the job's lifetime. During a job's lifetime the utilization changes at discrete points when some other job either starts or terminates. Assume this happens n times, and denote the job's arrival time by t_0, its termination by t_n, and the utilization at interval i by $U(t_i, ti + 1)$. The load experienced by the job is then

$$\text{load} = \sum_{i=1}^{n} \frac{t_i - t_{i-1}}{t_n - t_0} U(t_{i-1}, t_i)$$

Since the distribution of most metrics is very skewed (for example for wait time, there are very few jobs that wait a lot and many jobs that wait a little, covering times from few seconds to days), the Y axis is plotted in logarithmic scale. Bin shades are also log scaled — there are many bins with very few jobs (typically 1–2) and few bins with a lot of jobs (hundreds). The bins are hexagonal and use a 50×50 grid with approximately 2,500 bins.

As an example, consider the behavior of the job scheduler of the CTC-SP2 system based on a year-long trace. Figure 1 shows a heatmap of the wait time jobs experienced in the original trace as a function of the load. The blue X marks the spot of the average wait time and load. Few observations are evident:

1. The mean wait time is not very representative of the distribution.
2. There is a distinct blob of jobs at the left side that seems to reflect a set of jobs that suffered from some congestion condition.
3. Wait times follow a bimodal distribution, with many jobs concentrated around low wait times and many more around a higher wait time. The short wait times may reflect some minimal granularity of activating the scheduler, meaning that it only runs say once a minute and therefore does not schedule newly arrived jobs immediately.
4. There are many jobs in the "background", showing no distinct relation between load level and experienced wait time.

Moreover, compare this with an EASY simulation based on same job arrivals as the original trace, shown in Fig. 2. The simulation is quite different from

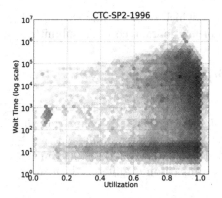

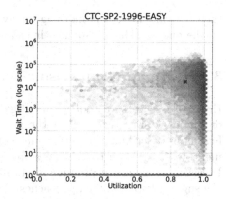

Fig. 1. Heatmap of the original log from the CTC-SP2 computer, showing asymmetrical job distribution.

Fig. 2. Heatmap of EASY simulation based on the CTC-SP2 log.

the original log, notably in the spread of jobs and in the maximal wait times observed. Generally, looking into heatmaps of many real world systems, it has been shown that both real world traces and simulation results exhibit distributions for which the traditional mean-based comparison metrics are ill-suited [8].

For our comparison evaluation we use FCFS, EASY backfilling, and conservative backfilling (CONS) schedulers. In FCFS (First-Come-First-Serve) jobs are kept in order of arrival and whenever there are enough resources (free processors) for the first queued job, it is allocated its required resources and starts to run. If sufficient resources are not available, jobs are queued waiting for them to become available. Jobs never jump each other in the queue.

EASY [9] is a popular backfilling algorithm, and the most commonly used method for batch scheduling [6]. It approaches the problem of idle resources in the FCFS setting using the following optimization: when a job arrives or terminates the scheduler scans the queue of waiting jobs by order of arrival, running them as available processors allow. Once it reaches a job it can't run (requires more processors than available) the scheduler makes a *reservation* for the job. A reservation guarantees enough processors at the earliest time when the job will be able to run, based on current knowledge of when enough processors will become available after termination of currently running jobs. The scheduler then continues to scan the queue for smaller jobs that can be started without interfering with the reservation, and executes them. This action is called *backfilling*. Since the scheduler can not know when the jobs will end, it relies on run time estimates provided by the user. Once a running backfilled jobs exceed its user estimation it is killed by the scheduler to ensure waiting jobs with reservations start on time. "EASY_P", a hypothetical EASY with "perfect" exact user estimations, is also used as a reference for comparison.

CONS [10] is the "vanilla" backfilling algorithm, in which no job can delay any previous job in the queue. All jobs in the queue receive reservations upon their arrival (unlike the more aggressive EASY which reserves only the top job on the queue). Thus, response times and order are guaranteed upon submittal.

3   Heatmap Comparison Techniques

Heatmaps serve as a tool to investigate the whole population of jobs instead of summary statistics such as the average slowdown. Thus, by comparing the heatmaps describing the performance of a certain log under two different schedulers, we may hope to achieve a fine-grained comparison of these schedulers. However, no common practice exists for the comparison of different heatmaps. We suggest two possible approaches:

- **Visual heatmap comparison:** Visual (image) comparison can help identify changed areas between two job distributions. Since it is image based, such a visual approach can be used to compare vastly different populations. The input of this approach is a set of two heatmaps (two matrices of same size), and the output is an image that highlights differences between these heatmaps. Uses include (1) comparison of different schedulers on the same workload, especially powerful for comparing similar schedulers to highlight small changes in the resulting performance distribution; and (2) comparison of scheduling of different job sets, and observation of the behavior of the same scheduler over different workloads.
- **Job aware comparison:** If the compared heatmaps portray performance distribution of the same workload, that is the same set of jobs but under different schedulers, it is interesting to compare the performance experienced by individual jobs. Visual comparisons as described above do not use this information. The aim of this approach is to identify trends in the behavior of specific classes of jobs, such as what happens to high slowdown jobs, or how jobs with low run time are affected. This approach does not directly compare heatmaps — instead it shows how sets of jobs that created one heatmap moved in order to create the second heatmap.

The next two sections detail these two approaches.

4   Visual Heatmap Comparison

The visual approach is completely general, and can be applied to any pair of heatmaps. In its simplicity and applicability lies its greatest advantage.

A naive image comparison is employed. Each heatmap is actually a rendering of a 2D histogram, showing the number of jobs in each bin. The bins in the heatmaps correspond to each other, with a bin for each combination of load and performance. Denote bin i in the two heatmaps by A_i and B_i. Then, calculate the difference between the values for each bin, and determine the color based on whether is it less or greater than zero. We use two different differences:

Simple difference $D_i = B_i - A_i$

Ratio difference $D_i = \dfrac{B_i}{A_i}$

In both cases, we assign colors to differences using a logarithmic scale. Thus successively darker shades indicate growth in the order of magnitude of the difference. This approach helps to identify subtle differences between possibly very similar distributions of results. For example, see Fig. 3, which compares two very similar runs of the EASY scheduler. The second simulation (with somewhat better backfilling due to using perfect runtime estimates) has less jobs with high wait times across all utilization levels. The visual produces even more pronounced results when simulations are different enough — for example, Fig. 4 shows unsurprisingly clear advantage of EASY over FCFS.

In the above examples we use red and blue shading to distinguish whether the first or second heatmap dominates. This shows up prominently in color displays, but is not suitable for black and white printing. In a black and white version, equality can be gray, with advantages for one heatmap shown in darker shades and advantages for the other shown in lighter shades.

Figure 5 shows side-by-side comparisons between simple and ratio differences. Ratio differences sometimes create wider boundaries between areas where either heatmap dominates — as the SDSC-SP2 EASY vs. EASY_P comparison. This happens because in the boundary areas the advantage of one heatmap over the other is usually small in relative terms, even if it is large in absolute terms. On the other hand ratios are more susceptible to noise, as the noisy SDSC-SP2 CONS vs EASY ratio comparison shows, while simple difference clearly shows the advantage of EASY over conservative backfilling for that workload.

Relation to Kullback-Leibler Divergence

A comparison of two heatmaps is essentially just a comparison of two histograms, or distributions. Thus an alternative to our visual approach is to use statistical tools that compute the difference between two distributions. Applying this to our context, we can compute the difference between how two sets of jobs distribute over the performance × load space.

One commonly used tool to measure difference between distributions is the Kullback-Leibler divergence D_{KL}. This comes from information theory, and is typically used to compare a model distribution with the underlying "true" theoretical distribution. Specifically, given a base distribution P and an approximation Q, the divergence is defined as

$$D_{KL} = \sum_{i=1}^{n} P(i) log \frac{P(i)}{Q(i)}$$

If we're just interested in comparing distributions, this expression can be interpreted as follows. First, for each possible value i, find the ratio of the probabilities to observe i under P and Q. Then take the log of this ratio, to find its order of magnitude. Next, weight these values by $P(i)$, meaning that more weight is assigned to the more probable values. Finally sum it all up to obtain a measure

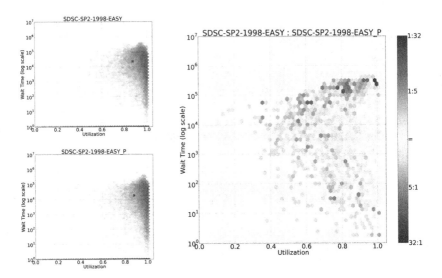

Fig. 3. Ratio comparison of two simulations based on the SDSC SP2 workload: EASY and "perfect" EASY (EASY_P). The original heatmaps are very similar. The darkest blue indicates that EASY_P had 32 times as many jobs in this bin as EASY (Color figure online).

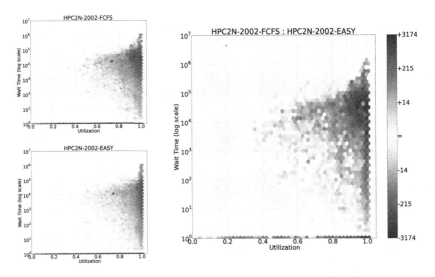

Fig. 4. Simple difference comparison of two different simulations (FCFS and EASY) based on the HPC2N workload. The darkest blue indicates that EASY had 3174 more jobs in this bin than FCFS (Color figure online).

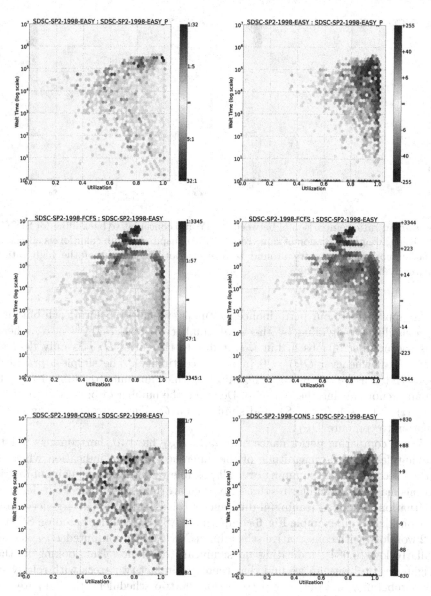

Fig. 5. Comparison of ratio differences (on the left) and simple differences (on the right) for the same pairs of heatmaps. Ratios show that some of the large absolute differences are actually small in relative terms.

of the overall divergence. A small divergence signifies similar distributions, or a good model. Note that the first steps are the same as in our ratio difference: we assign colors based on the log of the ratio.

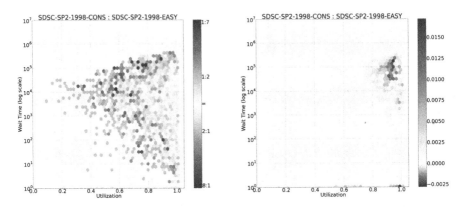

Fig. 6. Left: ratio comparison of between EASY and conservative backfilling for SDSC-SP2. Right: weighted version of same results (D_{KL} inspired). Note color levels adjusted to accommodate asymmetry around zero level. Note that most of the high ratios apparently have low weights.

To apply this to our performance heatmaps, we can transform each bin into a probability by dividing by the total number of jobs: $P(i) = j_i/N$, where j_i is the number of jobs in bin i. But due to the ratio, D_{KL} is only defined if $P(i) = 0$ whenever $Q(i) = 0$ (absolute continuity). The simplest practical approach to ensure this uses a uniform prior, which amounts to adding 1 to each bin and renormalizing the heatmap. Denoting the number of bins by S we then get $P(i) = (j_i + 1)/(N + S)$, and similarly for Q. These are plugged into the equation to compute D_{KL}.

When comparing performance heatmaps, D_{KL} has two shortcomings. First, it quantifies only the magnitude of the difference, with no indication which is better. Second, due to summing over all possible values, different pairs of distributions may lead to similar results. In particular, things may cancel out, leading to situations where a meaningful difference receives a very low divergence score.

Consider as an example Fig. 6 comparing EASY scheduling based on SDSC-SP2 workload with conservative scheduling (CONS). The computed D_{KL} is particularly low (0.084), indicating no significant difference. But looking at the weighted ratio heatmap we find that there are in fact two areas with relatively high probability and different patterns for the two schedulers, that apparently cancel out:

- With CONS the odds are higher than EASY for jobs experiencing higher wait time and slightly lower load. This combination results from using more reservations, more waiting in queue, and thus overall lower utilization.
- With CONS there is considerably less chance of a job to experience no slowdown with full utilization. One possible explanation is that these bins may represent small jobs that are executed under EASY due to aggressive backfilling.

5   Job-Aware Heatmap Comparison

Job aware comparisons use heatmaps as a tool to map what happened to certain classes of jobs by creating a heatmap of those jobs only and trying to generate a "before" and "after" view. It relies on domain specific understanding and especially the fact that the compared heatmaps show distributions of the same jobs. Thus this can't be used to compare arbitrary heatmaps or even the results of simulations using different logs.

Two approaches are explored: per-area comparison, where we plot heatmaps of jobs from select areas only in the original heatmap, and quiver plots, where we plot the trends of all jobs by creating a "stream flow" plot.

5.1   Area Plots

To compare performance results A and B for the same workload, we split the heatmap of A into a mesh sized $N \times M$, and plot a separate heatmap based on B for jobs that come from every square of the A mesh.

We use a 3×3 mesh in the figures below. Thus we partition the A heatmap into 9 squares, and partition the jobs in the workload into 9 sets, such that the jobs in each set contributed to one square of the heatmap. The sets correspond to all possible combinations of low, medium, and high load with low, medium, and high performance. In other words, we get 9 sets of jobs based on how they fared in the A evaluation: those jobs that experienced high load and low wait times will be in one set, those that experienced high load and medium wait times in a second set, those that experienced high loads and high wait times in a third set, and so on. Then we use the second evaluation to draw a separate heatmap showing the load and performance of the jobs in each of these sets.

Note that the sets need not be of equal size. Usually there are very few jobs that enjoy a low load but still suffer from high wait time or slowdown values, and sometimes there may even be no such jobs. On the other hand there are many jobs that experienced high loads, both with high and low performance.

The advantages of this approach are that it allows to keep the high resolution analysis (a heatmap) for classes of jobs. It can easily be extended to plotting any groups of jobs (such as jobs by a specific user) instead of basing classes on performance areas in A.

Results. When comparing different simulations using the same workload data set, the area plots allow to see differences in behavior:

- Figure 7 shows EASY vs. EASY_P ("perfect EASY", same as EASY but uses actual job runtimes instead of user estimates to determine reservations). Perfect EASY clearly performs better — all jobs with high wait times experienced lower wait times and moved "down" on the plot. Surprisingly, the class of few jobs with low wait times and high utilization (lower right) saw a substantial increase in wait times. Better packing comes at the expense of the jobs that did not previously wait in high load conditions.

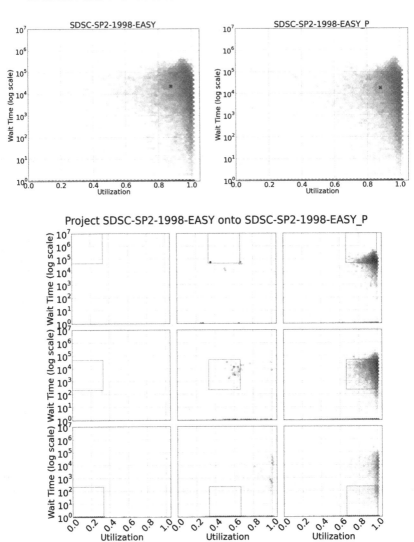

Fig. 7. Comparison of SDSC SP2 EASY and EASY_P simulations. The heatmaps derived from the two simulations are shown on top. The array of 9 heatmaps below show disjoint areas in the EASY heatmap (blue outline), and how the jobs in these areas were mapped to the EASY_P heatmap (Color figure online).

– Figure 8 shows FCFS vs. EASY, based on the HPC2N workload, which produced rather similar plots. Jobs in upper right were strongly affected, experiencing much lower wait times. Jobs in the center and middle right were affected as well: many jobs moved to the bottom zero wait-time line, probably because other jobs were packed better and left more processors free.

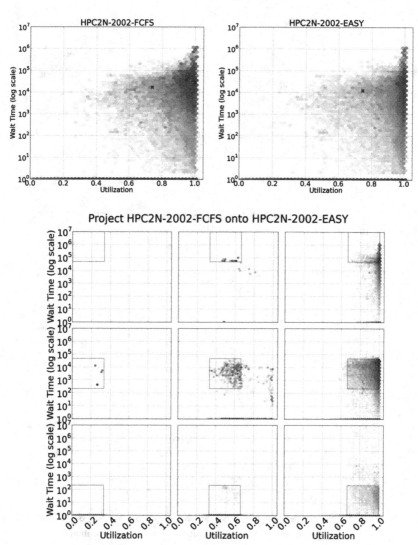

Fig. 8. Comparison of HPC2N FCFS and EASY simulations.

On the other hand, comparison of original schedulers versus simulations (Fig. 9) shows that there was very little relation between the job distribution in the original log and what these jobs experienced in the simulation. No matter where the jobs were originally, the distribution of each subset in the simulation is essentially the same.

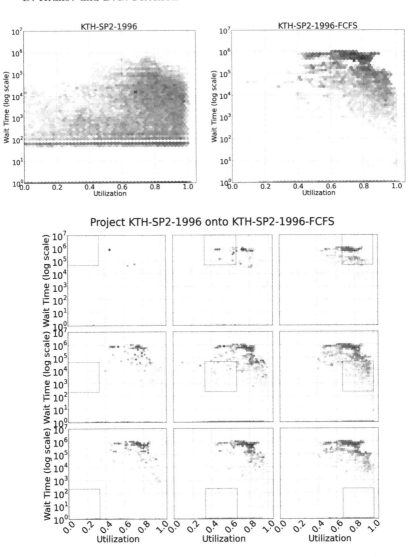

Fig. 9. Comparison of original KTH workload and FCFS simulation.

5.2   Quiver Plots

In this approach we split the A heatmap into a grid of relatively high resolution (a 40×40 grid with 1,600 cells is used). For each cell we potentially draw a quiver as follows:

1. Let J be the set of jobs in that cell of A. Look at the subset of jobs $J_{out} \subset J$ that leave the cell, that is that either the load they experienced (their x coordinate) or their performance level (their y coordinate) are out of the cell boundary in the B heatmap.

2. A quiver (vector) is plotted only for cells with more that a minimal number of leaving jobs ($|J_{out}| > 25$). This is done to reduce the amount of "noise" from changes in insignificant cells. The minimal number (25) is tuned for the logs analyzed, but an adaptive approach based on the average cell size can be employed.

3. Compute the placement of the quiver. The quiver's tail is placed at the mean location of the jobs in the A heatmap (by definition this is within the cell). Its head is placed at the mean location of the J_{out} jobs in the B heatmap:

$$tail.d = \tfrac{1}{|J_{out}|} \sum_{j \in J_{out}} j^A.d \quad \text{for } d \in \{x, y\}$$

$$head.d = \tfrac{1}{|J_{out}|} \sum_{j \in J_{out}} j^B.d \quad \text{for } d \in \{x, y\}$$

4. The quivers are based on only the leaving jobs to allow for a visually meaningful vector even when only a small percentage of the jobs are leaving, and so the mean of *all* the jobs is close to the cell or even within the cell. The color of the quiver is based on the percentage of the jobs moved, making it easy to distinguish cases where only a small fraction of the jobs moved from cases where most of the jobs moved.

Results. We first look at behavior of similar schedulers to check if trends can be identified, and whether there is symmetry between them. Consider the comparison EASY and EASY_P based on the SDSC SP2 data trace, Fig. 10.

- Top, EASY → EASY_P: jobs move towards a new "center" with higher load and lower wait time. Some percentage of the jobs with low wait time along the high load 1.0 axis may experience higher wait times in result. Jobs that experienced no wait time at all load levels may experience high wait times — the "picket fence" on the bottom. Zooming in on bottom cells shows a very uneven distribution: most of the jobs move right or left in terms of experienced load, but stays at zero wait time, while a small group (up to 40 %) "enters the game" and experiences higher (10^3) wait time closer to the average.
- Bottom, reversed plot of the same two simulations. A new center of weight draws jobs to it, with higher wait time and lower load. Interestingly, two trends are very similar to the previous plot. First, the "picket fence" at the bottom is present in both plots, as there are distinct jobs that had to wait in one scheme but not in the other. Second, Jobs that had an almost perfect packing (100 % experienced load) and low wait time move to the left, now experiencing higher delay. It seems that for the EASY scheduler both these effects are common to any run.

A similar center of weight shift can be seen when comparing EASY vs. Conservative backfilling, based on a number of different workload traces (Fig. 11).

When comparing the non backfilling FCFS to EASY (HPC2N workload based simulation in Fig. 12), EASY clearly helps lower wait times of jobs in all load levels and create a denser packing, resulting in higher achieved load. There are

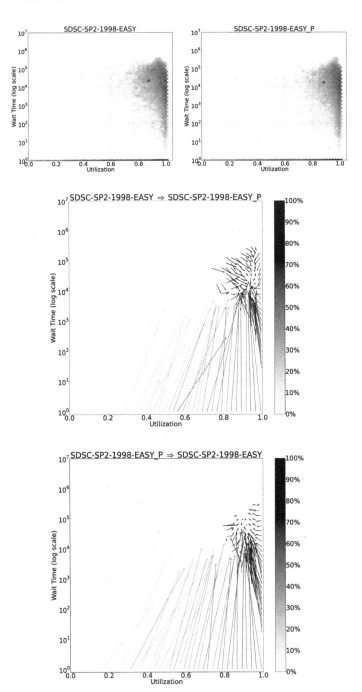

Fig. 10. Quiver plot comparison of SDSC SP2 EASY and EASY_P simulations. On the top the changes in job performance when moving from EASY to EASY_P, and on the bottom the other way around.

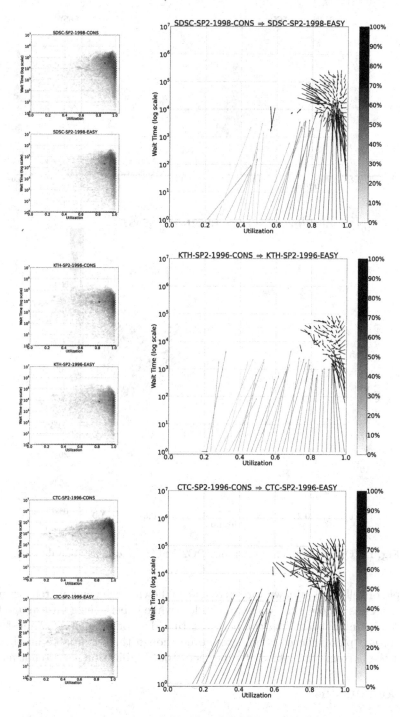

Fig. 11. Quiver plot comparison of CONS and EASY simulations on three workload traces.

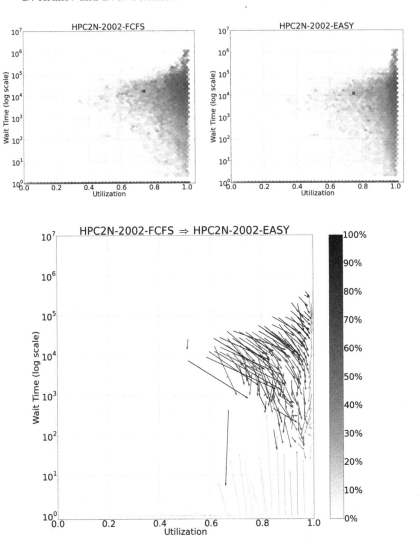

Fig. 12. Quiver plot comparison of HPC2N FCFS and EASY simulations.

a couple of cells with a downward arrow not following the general trend, representing a class of jobs that waited much less while experiencing on average the same load. Unlike backfilling comparisons, the edges of the plot are almost not affected: no "picket fence" is observed, even though there is a large number of jobs at the bottom, and jobs that experience 100 % utilization also do not move.

6   Conclusions

We suggested several different heatmap comparison techniques, some general image-based that are usable for any heatmaps (and in particular for performance heatmaps), and others that use specific domain knowledge on the underlying data and are only suitable for comparison of simulations based on the same underlying workload. *These techniques visualize how the whole distribution of performance results changes between the compared systems.* Thus they are significantly different from the common approach of comparing average performance values.

In some cases, looking at the whole distribution is crucial for reaching the correct conclusions. When conventional techniques are used, all the details are ultimately lost in favor of a single summary statistic. Thus a low Kullback-Leibler divergence (for example) is taken to mean that the compared distributions are similar. But this is not necessarily the case. It is also possible that some differences existed, but they canceled out. When looking at the whole distribution, these differences would be seen.

The image-based (**visual**) comparisons can be applied to any heatmaps, not only of parallel job scheduling evaluations. Moreover, they can even compare different job populations. In the context of job scheduling, such comparisons retain the ability of heatmaps to overcome the limitation of conventional average metrics, and provide a tool for comparing skewed distributions where average metrics are misleading.

Major advantages over the other methods are simplicity to compute and conciseness — a single heatmap is produced. Ratio difference visual comparison highlights more clearly acute differences between very similar job distributions, while simple difference is more representative of the overall changes. One disadvantage of using two colors is the inappropriateness for B&W printing or color-blind researchers. Gray levels may be used as a remedy.

A second group of methods is job aware plots. These can only be applied to the same job population. They are not applicable when the underlying data is different — e.g. to compare simulations based on a model that generates new jobs on each run. **Area plots** offer a high resolution view into different classes of jobs and can be used to dive in into edge cases. They do not allow for a single comparison representation, as each class is visualized separately. Thus area plots are complicated both to compute and to analyze.

Quiver plots employ averaging to plot trends of change. They create a single-image concise result, but as with any averaging, can be misleading when the average is not representative due to the presence of skewed distributions, as is the case with cells on the zero wait time axis. Quiver plots also suffer from noise in some of the logs checked. One possible remedy might be employing a low pass filter as a preliminary step.

For many cases the naive image difference comparison might be good enough, given its simplicity in computation and in visual understanding. For example, in the comparison of SDSC-SP2 EASY vs. EASY_P the visual comparison (Fig. 3) plainly shows that EASY_P reduces the number of high wait time jobs, which is exactly the basic result seen in the job-aware area plot and quiver comparisons (Figs. 7 and 10).

The job-aware comparisons allow for more advanced observations, at the possible expense of obscuring the general picture. In particular they can serve to understand some deeper behaviors:

- Looking into a job-aware comparison of a log's original scheduler versus a simulated one shows that the distribution of jobs remains similar in any large sub class of jobs. This shows that the simulation completely mixes the jobs and does not retain any relations with how they were treated in reality. This is a much stronger conclusion than can be derived based on the plainly visible difference between the heatmaps.
- Quiver plots show a "center of weight" that exists in backfilling based schedulers (both EASY and conservative backfilling). Jobs are drawn to it from all sides. This is a similar result to the postulation Rudolph and Smith made that schedulers have a "Desired Operating Range" (DOR) [12].
- Looking in both directions of comparison allows to highlight invariants in scheduler behavior. For EASY those are jobs with zero wait time or with 100 % experienced load. This might allow to distinguish more "interesting" jobs in the evaluation.

This paper is only a first try at heatmap comparison, which may serve as a basis for development of more advanced scheduler evaluation and comparison tools. Naturally, it would be interesting to apply the same techniques to a wider class of schedulers and environments. The techniques used can be extended, both in usability (how good is the visual representation) and applicability for different scenarios. One possible development of another type of comparison would be to compare time frames instead of comparing what happens to jobs: the change in a particular time window between two different scheduling runs. Another would be to group the jobs by different properties, such as the users who submitted them. As further research, heatmaps can also be drawn for different axes, for example wait time vs. job duration or job parallelism, allowing to observe correlations between performance effects and different job attributes.

Acknowledgements. Many thanks to all those who have made their workload data available through the Parallel Workloads Archive.

References

1. Anscombe, F.J.: Graphs in Statistical Analysis. Am. Stat. **27**(1), 17–21 (1973)
2. Feitelson, D.G.: Looking at data. In: 22nd International Parallel & Distributed Processing Symposium (IPDPS), April 2008
3. Chapin, S.J., Cirne, W., Feitelson, D.G., Jones, J.P., Leutenegger, S.T., Schwiegelshohn, U., Smith, W., Talby, D.: Benchmarks and standards for the evaluation of parallel job schedulers. In: Feitelson, D.G., Rudolph, L. (eds.) JSSPP 1999, IPPS-WS 1999, and SPDP-WS 1999. LNCS, vol. 1659, pp. 67–90. Springer, Heidelberg (1999)
4. Crovella, M.E.: Performance evaluation with heavy tailed distributions. In: Feitelson, D.G., Rudolph, L. (eds.) JSSPP 2001. LNCS, vol. 2221, pp. 1–9. Springer, Heidelberg (2001)

5. Downey, A.B., Feitelson, D.G.: The elusive goal of workload characterization. Perform. Eval. Rev. **26**(4), 14–29 (1999)
6. Etsion, Y., Tsafrir, D., Feitelson, D.G.: Process prioritization using output production: scheduling for multimedia. ACM Trans. Multimed. Comput. Commun. Appl. **2**(4), 318–342 (2006)
7. Frachtenberg, E., Feitelson, D.G., Petrini, F., Fernandez, J.: Adaptive parallel job scheduling with flexible coscheduling. IEEE Trans. Parallel Distrib. Syst. **16**(11), 1066–1077 (2005)
8. Krakov, D., Feitelson, D.G.: High-resolution analysis of parallel job workloads. In: Cirne, W., Desai, N., Frachtenberg, E., Schwiegelshohn, U. (eds.) JSSPP 2012. LNCS, vol. 7698, pp. 178–195. Springer, Heidelberg (2013)
9. Lifka, D.: The ANL/IBM SP scheduling system. In: Feitelson, D.G., Rudolph, L. (eds.) JSSPP 1995. LNCS, vol. 949, pp. 295–303. Springer, Heidelberg (1995)
10. Feitelson, D.G., Rudoplh, L., Schwiegelshohn, U., Sevcik, K.C., Wong, P.: Theory and practice in parallel job scheduling. JSSPP 1997. LNCS, vol. 1291, pp. 1–34. Springer, Heidelberg (1997)
11. Parallel Workloads Archive. http://www.cs.huji.ac.il/labs/parallel/workload/
12. Rudolph, L., Smith, P.H.: Valuation of ultra-scale computing systems. In: Feitelson, D.G., Rudolph, L. (eds.) IPDPS-WS 2000 and JSSPP 2000. LNCS, vol. 1911, pp. 39–55. Springer, Heidelberg (2000)
13. Performance Heatmap Utilities. https://bitbucket.org/krakov/heatmaps

Distributed Workflow Scheduling Under Throughput and Budget Constraints in Grid Environments

Fei Cao[✉], Michelle M. Zhu, and Dabin Ding

Department of Computer Science,
Southern Illinois University Carbondale,
Carbondale, IL 62901, USA
vicky@siu.edu

Abstract. Grids enable sharing, selection and aggregation of geographically distributed resources among various organizations. They are emerging as promising computing paradigms for resource and compute-intensive scientific workflow applications modeled as Directed Acyclic Graph (DAG) with intricate inter-task dependencies. With the growing popularity of real-time applications, streaming workflows continuously produce large quantity of experimental or simulation datasets, which need to be processed in a timely manner subject to certain performance and resource constraints. However, the heterogeneity and dynamics of Grid resources complicate the scheduling of streaming applications. In addition, the commercialization of Grids as a future trend is calling for policies to take resource cost into account while striving to satisfy the users' Quality of Service (QoS) requirements. In this paper, streaming workflow applications are modeled as DAGs. We formulate scheduling problems with two different objectives in mind, namely either maximize the throughput under a budget/cost constraint or minimize the execution cost under a minimum throughput constraint. Two different algorithms named as Budget constrained RATE (B-RATE) and Budget constrained SWAP (B-SWAP) are developed and evaluated under the first objective; Another two algorithms named as Throughput constrained RATE (TP-RATE) and Throughput constrained SWAP (TP-SWAP) are evaluated under the second objective. Experimental results based on GridSim showed that our algorithms either achieved much lower cost with similar throughput, or higher throughput with similar cost compared with other comparable existing algorithms.

Keywords: Streaming workflow · Task scheduling · Grid computing · Throughput and budget

1 Introduction

Grid computing has emerged as a promising solution for large-scale resource and compute-intensive applications. A wide range of scientific applications can be represented as complex workflows comprised of many computing tasks with

N. Desai and W. Cirne (Eds.): JSSPP 2013, LNCS 8429, pp. 62–80, 2014.
DOI: 10.1007/978-3-662-43779-7_4, © Springer-Verlag Berlin Heidelberg 2014

inter-task dependencies. Many of the scientific jobs can be modeled as Directed Acyclic Graphs (DAGs) where each vertex represents a computing task and each directed edge represents the execution dependency between adjacent tasks. Scheduling tasks onto heterogeneous and dynamically changing Grid resources needs to respect the precedence constraints and optimize certain criteria based on various user and system situations. We consider the Grid environment as an overlay network consisting of a number of heterogeneous computer nodes interconnected by network links. The network can be modeled as a directed weighted graph which can be complete or not due to network types.

A number of Grid workflow management systems such as Condor DAG-Man [1], Pegasus [2], and GridFlow [3], etc. have been developed. These systems provide middleware tools to control the mapping and execution of workflow modules by strategically considering the availability and capacities of the underling Grid resources. However, managing Grid environment to run various jobs is a complex task which requires scheduling policies to reach certain tradeoff due to different requirements from the perspectives of users and various Grid providers usually from different organizations. Existing Grid resource management systems are mainly driven by system-centric policies which aim to optimize a system-wide standard of performance, whereas future Grid environments need to guarantee certain level of Quality of Service (QoS) requirements as well as meet user-centric economic concerns [4]. A number of Grid systems such as Globus [5] have considered some of these multi-objective issues by using resource trading and QoS-based scheduling [4].

In recent years, execution costs on the Grid are being considered by more and more scientists due to the fact that different resources belonging to different organizations may have different allocation/pricing policies on resource usage [4]. The user computing cycle quote/allocation policy can be translated into certain pricing scheme which will be utilized by the scheduler to balance the workload. Such pricing mechanism is widely used by Cloud computing and could be converted to virtual dollars and utilized in the future Grid environment. Therefore, users with budget or quota constraint may not always desire the highest possible QoS such as throughput, i.e., the data production rate at the last task, for a smooth flow in streaming applications with multiple instances of input datasets [6]. Typical examples of these applications include video-based real-time monitoring systems that perform feature extraction and detection, facial reconstruction, pattern recognition, and data mining, etc.

In order to build some theoretical foundations for the future generation of paid Grid, we focus on developing workflow scheduling algorithms considering both budget and throughput constraints. In particular, we consider two different objectives of user requirements. One is to maximize throughput under a budget constraint while another one is to minimize the execution cost under the minimum throughput constraint.

In our approach, we strategically select an appropriate set of heterogeneous Grid resources in an arbitrarily connected network and map each computing task from the workflow to the most appropriate Grid nodes for certain performance criteria. If multiple tasks are mapped onto the same node (i.e., node reuse), the node's computing resource is shared in a fair manner by concurrent tasks executing on that node. Similarly, the bandwidth of a network link is also shared by concurrent data transfers. For budget constrained objective, the B-RATE algorithm adopts a layer-based mapping scheme and assigns partial cost constraint for each layer, then chooses the maximum partial throughput from the first layer to current mapping layer; The B-SWAP algorithm starts with a schedule that is optimized for throughput, and keeps swapping tasks between nodes by choosing those tasks whose cost savings result in the smallest loss in throughput under the budget constraint. To our best knowledge, there is currently no algorithm to maximize the throughput for streaming applications under budget constraint or minimize execution cost under throughput constraint in the Grid. The superiority of these two algorithms are demonstrated in comparison with some representative workflow scheduling algorithms to maximize the throughput including Streamline [7] and LDP [6] in a set of different scales of simulation cases. For throughput constrained objective, the TP-RATE algorithm also follows layer-based scheduling scheme and chooses the minimum partial cost whose partial throughput is larger or equal to the throughput constraint for each layer; the TP-SWAP algorithm starts with the cheapest schedule of tasks onto resources, and keeps swapping tasks that can lead to higher throughput with low cost increase.

This paper is organized as follows: Sect. 2 gives an overview of related works. Section 3 conducts analytical models and formulates the scheduling problem. In Sect. 4, the algorithms are described in details. Section 5 presents the performance evaluations. Conclusion can be found in Sect. 6.

2   Related Works

The optimization problem of scheduling DAG-structured tasks with complex execution dependencies has been studied for years and is known to be NP-complete [7]. Over the years, workflow scheduling problems in heterogeneous environments have attracted many research efforts, among which a significant amount of efforts have been devoted to workflow scheduling in Grid environments under different scheduling and resource constraints. For example, a number of DAG-structured Grid workflow management systems such as Condor DAGMan [1,8,9], Globus [5,10], Pegasus [2,11] and GridFlow [3] provide tools and infrastructure to control the execution of various workflow applications on the Grid. Condor is a specialized workload management system for compute-intensive jobs [8] and it can be used to serve Grid environment such as Globus Grid [10]. Directed Acyclic Graph Manager (DAGMan) [9] is a meta-scheduler for Condor jobs and manages dependencies between jobs at a higher level than the Condor Scheduler. Pegasus Workflow Management System [11] bridges the scientific domain with the execution environment (e.g., Clusters, Grids, Clouds, etc.) by automatically scheduling and monitoring high-level workflow onto underlying distributed resources. GridFlow includes a user portal and services of both global Grid workflow management and local Grid sub-workflow scheduling. Simulation, execution and monitoring functionalities are provided at the global Grid level, which work on the top of an existing agent-based Grid resource management system [3].

Meanwhile, many performance-driven workflow scheduling algorithms aim to achieve optimal execution performances [12] including the minimum overall execution time, the maximum reliability and throughput for streaming applications. Streamline [7], a workflow scheduler for streaming data, takes dynamic nature of the Grid into account and takes application requirements, constraints, and resource availability into consideration for scheduling decisions. To achieve the reduced overall execution time, Heterogeneous Earliest Finish Time (HEFT) heuristic algorithm [13] was proposed to initially order all the tasks of a workflow in descending order of their upward rank values calculated as the sum of the execution time and the communication time of the tasks. This algorithm is a commonly cited list-scheduling heuristic [14]. In [15], Dongarra et al. discussed the fundamental properties of a good bi-objective scheduling algorithm, and proposed an approximation algorithm namely RHEFT, which is extended from HEFT algorithm [13] by considering the reliability and allows the user to subjectively choose a trade-off between high reliability and low overall execution time. Recursive Critical Path (RCP) algorithm utilizes the dynamic programming strategy and iteratively find critical path to minimize the overall execution time [16]. This algorithm is used as the mapping scheme for the Scientific Workflow Automation and Management Platform (SWAMP) [17] which is a Condor/DAGMan-based workflow system that enables scientists to conveniently assemble, execute, monitor, control, and steer computing workflows in distributed environments via a unified web-based user interface. Experiments show that RCP provides a better mapping performance than the mapping scheme currently employed by the Condor Scheduler [17,18]. In [19], a new non-critical task mapping approach using A* and Beam Search (BS) algorithms to improve the RCP algorithm was proposed. For high workflow throughput, Gu et al. designed a greedy layer-oriented heuristic workflow mapping scheme (LDP) to identify and minimize the global bottleneck [6]. In [20], the same authors extended the LDP algorithm by taking reliability into account, and further developed a decentralized mapping procedure.

However, the commercialization of Grids requires market-driven strategies while considering users' QoS constraints like deadline and computation cost (budget). Such a guarantee of service is hard to provide in a Grid environment due to its shared, heterogeneous and distributed resources owned by different organizations with their own policies and pricing mechanisms [4]. Many algorithms for deadline and budget constrained scheduling have been proposed [21–27]. In [25], Sakellariou et al. proposed two different approaches, namely the LOSS approach and the GAIN approach to find the schedule for a given DAG-structured workflow and a given set of resources without exceeding the budget and is still optimized for overall execution time. The LOSS approach starts with a schedule that is optimized for overall execution time by using HEFT [14] or

HBMCT [28] and keeps re-mapping as long as the budget is not exceeded. The GAIN approach starts with the cheapest schedule and conducts re-mapping to minimize the overall execution time as long as the budget is still available. In [27], Yu et al. proposed a cost-based workflow scheduling algorithm that minimizes the execution cost for time-critical workflow applications by partitioning workflow tasks and generating schedules based on optimal task partition. It also allows the scheduler to re-compute some partial workflows during execution when their initial schedules are violated. A deadline assignment strategy was developed to distribute the overall deadline over each task partition. Abrishami et al. proposed a QoS-based workflow scheduling algorithm [23] based on the partial critical paths which first tries to map the overall critical path of the workflow such that it completes before the deadline and execution cost can be minimized, then it finds the partial critical path for each mapped task on the critical path and executes the same procedure recursively.

Our work differs from the above mentioned works in several aspects: (i) we consider both throughput and budget requirements; (ii) we consider incomplete Grid environment due to network connectivity and facility accessibility; (iii) we consider resource sharing among multiple concurrent computing tasks on computing nodes or concurrent data transfers over network links.

3   Problem Overview

3.1   Analytical Models

The left side of Fig. 1 shows a workflow of a distributed computing application constructed as directed acyclic graph (DAG) $G_T = (V_T, E_T)$ with $|V_T| = m$. Vertices are used to represent the set of computing tasks $V_T = \{T_1, T_2, ... T_m\}$: T_1 is the starting task and T_m denotes the ending task. The weight w_{ij} on edge e_{ij} represents the size of data transferred from task T_i to task T_j. The dependency between a pair of tasks is shown as a directed edge. Task T_j receives a data input w_{ij} from each of its preceding tasks T_i and performs a predefined computing routine whose complexity is modeled as a function $\zeta_j(\cdot)$ of the total aggregated input data size z_j. However, in real scenario, the complexity of a task is an abstract quantity which not only depends on the computational complexity of its own function but also on the implementation details realized in its algorithm. Upon completion of execution of task T_j, data output w_{jk} will be sent to each

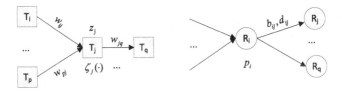

Fig. 1. Workflow model (left), Grid network model (right).

of its succeeding tasks T_k. A task cannot start its execution until all input data required by this task arrive. To generalize our model, if an application task has multiple starting or ending tasks, a virtual starting or ending task of complexity zero can be created and connected to all starting or ending tasks without any data transfer along the edges.

The right side of Fig. 1 shows a heterogeneous Grid network environment and is represented as an arbitrary weighted network graph $G_R = (V_R, E_R)$ with $|V_R| = n$, consisting of a set of computing nodes $V_R = \{R_1, R_2, ...R_n\}$. Depending on the network infrastructure, the topology of a computer network may be complete or not due to network connectivity and facility accessibility. Resource R_j is featured by its computing power p_j. The network link l_{ij} between resources R_i and R_j is featured by bandwidth b_{ij}, and the minimum link delay d_{ij}. Both nodes and links are considered as Grid resources. The parameters of a workflow are given in Table 1.

Inspired by previous work [20], executing a workflow will require the following time and cost:

(1) Execution time of task T_i on node $R_{i'}$

$$t_{exec}(T_i, R_{i'}) = \sum \frac{\alpha(t) \cdot \delta_i(t)}{p_{i'}} \tag{1}$$

where $\alpha(t)$ denotes the number of concurrent tasks executing on node $R_{i'}$ during Δt, $\delta_i(t) = \frac{p_{i'}}{\alpha(t)}\Delta t$ is the amount of partial task execution completed during time interval $[t, t+\Delta t]$ when $\alpha(t)$ remains unchanged, and $\zeta_i(z_i) = \sum \delta_i(t)$ is the total computational requirement of task T_i.

Table 1. Parameter of workflow and Grid network model

Parameters	Definitions
$G_T = (V_T, E_T)$	The computation workflow
m	Number of tasks in the workflow
T_i	The i-th computing task
e_{ij}	Dependency edge from task T_i to T_j
w_{ij}	Data size transferred over dependency edge e_{ij}
z_i	Aggregated input data size of task T_i
$\zeta_i(\cdot)$	Computational complexity of task T_i
$G_R = (V_R, E_R)$	The Grid network environment
n	Number of computing nodes in the Grid environment
R_j	The j-th node
p_j	Computing power of node R_j
l_{ij}	Network link between nodes R_i and R_j
b_{ij}	Bandwidth of link $l_{i,j}$
d_{ij}	The minimum link delay of link $l_{i,j}$
ξ_j	Unit executing price of node j (G\$/s)
λ_{ij}	Unit executing price of network link l_{ij} (G\$/s)

(2) Data transfer time of dependency edge e_{jk} over network link $l_{j'k'}$

$$t_{tran}(e_{jk}, l_{j'k'}) = \sum \frac{\beta(t) \cdot \delta_{jk}(t)}{b_{j'k'}} + d_{j'k'} \tag{2}$$

where $\beta(t)$ denotes the number of concurrent data transfer over link $l_{j'k'}$ during Δt, $\delta_{jk}(t) = \frac{b_{j'k'}}{\beta(t)} \Delta t$ is the amount of partial data transfer execution completed during time interval $[t, t+\Delta t]$ when $\beta(t)$ remains unchanged, and $w_{jk} = \sum \delta_{jk}(t)$ is the total data transfer size of dependency edge e_{jk}.

(3) Bottleneck time

$$BT = \max_{\substack{T_i \in V_T, e_{jk} \in E_T \\ R_{i'} \in V_R, l_{j'k'} \in E_R}} \left(\begin{matrix} t_{exec}(T_i, R'_i), \\ t_{tran}(e_{jk}, l_{j'k'}) \end{matrix} \right) \tag{3}$$

(4) Throughput

Throughput is the inverse of the global bottleneck of a mapped workflow in streaming applications where multiple instances of input datasets are continuously generated and fed into the workflow.

$$TP = \frac{1}{BT} \tag{4}$$

(5) Cost of executing task T_i on node R_j

$$C_j(T_i) = \xi_j \times t_{exec}(T_i, R_j) \tag{5}$$

(6) Cost of transfer data of dependency edge e_{jk} over network link $l_{j'k'}$

$$C_{j'k'}(e_{jk}) = \lambda_{jk} \times t_{tran}(e_{jk}, l_{j'k'}) \tag{6}$$

(7) Total execution cost (i.e. user charge) of scheduling a workflow

$$Cost = \sum_{i=1}^{m} C_j(T_i) + \sum_{\forall e_{jk} \in E_T} C_{j'k'}(e_{jk}) \tag{7}$$

3.2   Problem Formulation

The scheduling problem is defined as follows:

Definition 1. *Grid users can submit DAG-structured workflow applications modeled as $G_T = (V_T, E_T)$ that process streaming datasets with both budget and throughput requirements. The budget constrained user aims to maximize the application throughput within their specific budgets:*

$$\max_{all\ possible\ schedules} (TP),\ such\ that\ Cost \leq Budget \tag{8}$$

The throughput constrained user aims to minimize the execution cost while the minimum throughput is guaranteed:

$$\min_{all\ possible\ schedules} (Cost),\ such\ that\ TP \geq TPConst \tag{9}$$

where TP is the throughput, $Cost$ is the user charge, $Budget$ is the budget constraint, and $TPConst$ is the minimum throughput constraint.

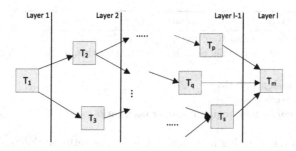

Fig. 2. Layer based sorting of the DAG-structured workflow.

4 Algorithm Design

The following notations are introduced to facilitate the description of our algorithms:

- $pre(T_i)$: the set of preceding tasks of task T_i;
- $V_{one-schedule}(pre(T_i))$: the set of nodes for possible mapping of those tasks in $pre(T_i)$;
- $suc(R_j)$: the set of succeeding nodes of node R_j;
- $\bigcap_{\forall R \in V_{one-schedule}(pre(T_i))}(suc(R))$: an intersection operation that finds the set of common succeeding nodes for $V_{one-schedule}(pre(T_i))$;
- $\bigcap_{\forall R \in V_{one-schedule}(pre(T_i))}(suc(R)) \cup R$, as the candidate mapping node set for task T_i, denoted as $V_{candidate}(T_i)$;
- $V_{Loss-candidate}(T_i)$: $V_{pre(T_i)} \cap V_{suc(T_i)}$, an intersection operation that casts on the set of nodes that task T_i's predecessor tasks are mapped onto, and the set of nodes that task T_i's successor tasks are mapped onto;
- $V_{Gain-candidate}(T_i)$: $V_{pre(T_i)} \cap V_{suc(T_i)}$, an intersection operation that casts on the set of nodes that task T_i's predecessor tasks are mapped onto, and the set of nodes that task T_i's successor tasks are mapped onto;

4.1 Budget Constrained Approaches

We develop two algorithms, namely B-RATE, B-SWAP for budget constrained users. The purpose of these two algorithms is to find the affordable resources to map workflow tasks in order to achieve the maximum throughput under certain budget constraint.

The B-RATE Algorithm. The B-RATE algorithm in Algorithm 1 first separates DAG-structured workflow tasks into ordered layers based on task dependency and node connectivity in the Grid environment as shown in Fig. 2. For each layer k ($k \in [1, MaxLayer]$), we calculate a cost constraint $CostConst_k$ using Eq. 10 where CR is the total computing requirement (i.e., number of

---

Algorithm 1. B-RATE(G_t,G_n,$Budget$)

Input: Task graph G_t, Grid Resource graph G_n, $Budget$
Output: A workflow schedule that maximizes the throughput under budget constraint.

1: **for all** $T_i \in$ task graph **do**
2:     Apply layer-based sorting;
3:     Calculate computing requirement for each task;
4: **end for**
5: Calculate total computing requirement CR for the entire workflow;
6: $MaxLayer =$ the number of total layers in G_t;
7: **for** $k =$ layer 1 to $MaxLayer$ **do**
8:     Calculate computing requirement CR_k for current layer;
9:     Calculate cost constraint $CostConst_k$ for current layer;
10:     **for all** task $T_i \in$ current layer **do**
11:         Find $pre(T_i)$ and $V_{one-schedule}(pre(T_i))$;
12:         Find $V_{candidate}(T_i)$;
13:     **end for**
14:     Find all possible mapping combinations of $V_{candidate}(T_i)$ for all tasks T_i in current layer;
15:     **for all** possible mapping combinations **do**
16:         Calculate $curCost$ for current layer;
17:         **if** $curCost \leq CostConst_k$ **then**
18:             Calculate $partialTP$;
19:         **else**
20:             Continue;
21:         **end if**
22:     **end for**
23:     Select the schedule(s) with the maximum $partialTP$, if there're several schedules with the same $partialTP$, choose the one with the minimum $curCost$;
24: **end for**
25: Calculate total $Cost$;
26: **return** TP, $Cost$;

---

instructions) for the entire workflow, and CR_k denotes the partial computing requirement for tasks in layer k:

$$CostConst_k = \frac{CR_k}{CR} * Budget \qquad (10)$$

In lines 10–14, for each task T_i in the current layer, we find its preceding tasks $pre(T_i)$ and possible set of their mapping nodes $V_{one-schedule}(pre(T_i))$, then determine the candidate node set $V_{candidate}(T_i)$ for mapping. In lines 15–22, we consider all possible combinations of $V_{candidate}(T_i)$ for all tasks T_i in current layer and calculate their costs. For those possible mapping combinations whose costs are within the cost constraint of current layer, the partial throughput $partialTP$ from the first layer to the current layer is calculated. In line 23, the schedule with the maximum $partialTP$ is selected. There might exist several possible schedules with the same throughput, we simply choose the one with the minimum $curCost$. Lines 8–23 are repeated until tasks from the last level are mapped, then we get the throughput and total execution cost. The complexity of this algorithm is $O(mn)$.

Algorithm 2. B-SWAP$(G_t,G_n,Budget)$

Input: Task graph G_t, Grid Resource graph G_n, $Budget$
Output: A workflow schedule that maximizes the throughput under budget constraint.

1: **for all** $T_i \in$ task graph **do**
2:     Apply layer-based sorting;
3:     Calculate computing requirement for each task;
4: **end for**
5: $MaxLayer =$ the number of total layers in G_t;
6: **for** $k =$ layer 1 to $MaxLayer$ **do**
7:     **for all** task $T_i \in$ current layer **do**
8:         Find $pre(T_i)$ and $V_{one-schedule}(pre(T_i))$;
9:         Find $V_{candidate}(T_i)$;
10:     **end for**
11:     Find all possible mapping combinations of $V_{candidate}(T_i)$ for all tasks T_i in current layer;
12:     **for all** possible mapping combinations **do**
13:         Calculate $partialTP$;
14:         Select the schedule(s) with the maximum $partialTP$, if there're several schedules with the same $partialTP$, choose the one with the minimum $partialCost$;
15:     **end for**
16: **end for**
17: Calculate total $Cost$;
18: **while** $Cost_{new} > Budget$ && $Cost_{cur} > Cost_{new}$ **do**
19:     **for all** $T_i \in$ task graph **do**
20:         $GenerateLossCandidateSetForEachTask()$;
21:     **end for**
22:     **for all** $R_j \in V_{Loss-candidate}(T_i)$ **do**
23:         Calculate $LossWeight(j)$;
24:     **end for**
25:     Select the task with the minimum $LossWeight$ to re-map;
26: **end while**
27: Calculate total $Cost$;
28: **return** TP, $Cost$;

The B-SWAP Algorithm. The B-SWAP algorithm in Algorithm 2 starts with identifying an initial schedule (in lines 1–16) which produces the maximum throughput of the entire workflow regardless of the budget (e.g., by using LDP [6]). In lines 18–26, if the available budget is larger or equal to the cost required for this schedule, this schedule can be used right away. However, if the budget is less than the cost of this schedule, swapping operations are invoked. The objective of this algorithm is to re-map those tasks to achieve the minimum loss in throughput for the largest cost savings. Each iteration ends with a reduced total cost with similar throughput. To determine the swapping strategy, $LossWeight$ for task T_i as the iteration loss between the current and new possible mapping schemes onto its candidate nodes in $V_{Loss-candidate}(T_i)$ are computed in Eq. 11:

$$LossWeight(j) = \frac{TP_{Cur} - TP_{New}}{Cost_{Cur} - Cost_{New}} \tag{11}$$

where TP_{Cur} and $Cost_{Cur}$ are the throughput and cost of current schedule, respectively; TP_{New} and $Cost_{New}$ are the throughput and cost of T_i re-mapped onto node R_j which is a candidate node from $V_{Loss-candidate}(T_i)$, respectively. If $Cost_{New}$ is larger than $Cost_{Cur}$, we ignore this candidate node. The algorithm keeps re-mapping by considering the smallest values of $LossWeight$. Our selection criteria of having large cost saving and small throughput loss will result in small value of $LossWeight$. The complexity of this algorithm is $O(mns)$, where s is the number of swaps.

4.2 Throughput Constrained Approaches

We develop two algorithms, namely TP-RATE, TP-SWAP for throughput constrained users. The purpose of this set of algorithms is to satisfy the minimum throughput constraint by finding the best resources that minimizes the execution cost.

The TP-RATE Algorithm. The TP-RATE algorithm (provided in Algorithm 3) applies layer-based sorting to the DAG-structured workflow and then schedule computing tasks to network nodes layer-by-layer. In line 9–17, for each layer, we consider all possible combinations of $V_{candidate}(T_i)$ for all tasks T_i in current layer, calculate their $partialTP$, and calculate $partialCost$ if their $partialTP$ is larger or equal to the throughput constraint $TPConst$. In line 18, the schedule with the minimum $partialCost$ is selected. If there are several possible schedules with the same $partialCost$, we simply choose the one with the minimum $partialTP$. Line 5–19 is repeated until the last task is reached, then we compute the total Cost. The complexity of this algorithm is $O(mn)$.

The TP-SWAP Algorithm. The TP-SWAP algorithm (provided in Algorithm 4) first schedules all the tasks to the cheapest node, there might be several nodes with the same unit cost, then choose the one with the maximum computing power. If the throughput is bigger or equal to required throughput constraint, then this schedule can be used straightaway. In other cases that the throughput is smaller than the constraint, swap is invoked. The objective of this algorithm is to achieve the maximum gain in throughput for the least increase in cost via module re-mapping. It means that for each re-map, the new schedule's throughput is close to the current schedule but with less increase in cost. To determine such re-map, $GainWeight$ values for each task T_i scheduled to each of its candidate nodes in $V_{Gain-candidate}(T_i)$ are computed as Eq. 12:

Algorithm 3. TP-RATE(G_t,G_n,$TPConst$)

1: **for all** $T_i \in$ task graph **do**
2:      Apply lay-based sorting;
3:      $MaxLayer =$ the number of total layers in G_t;
4:      **for** $k =$ layer 1 to $MaxLayer$ **do**
5:          **for all** task $T_i \in$ current layer **do**
6:              Find $pre(T_i)$ and $V_{one-schedule}(pre(T_i))$;
7:              Find $V_{candidate}(T_i)$;
8:          **end for**
9:          Find all possible schedule combinations of $V_{candidate}(T_i)$ for all tasks T_i in current layer;
10:          **for all** possible schedule combinations **do**
11:              Calculate $partialTP$;
12:              **if** $partialTP \geq TPConst$ **then**
13:                  Calculate $partialCost$;
14:              **else**
15:                  Continue;
16:              **end if**
17:          **end for**
18:          Select the schedule(s) with the minimum $partialCost$, if there're several schedules with the same $partialCost$, choose the one with the maximum $partialTP$;
19:      **end for**
20: **end for**
21: Calculate total $Cost$;
22: **return** TP, $Cost$;

Algorithm 4. TP-SWAP(G_t,G_n,$TPConst$)

1: **for all** $T_i \in$ task graph **do**
2:      Schedule T_i to the cheapest node, if several nodes have the same unit cost, choose the one with the maximum computing power;
3: **end for**
4: Calculate TP, $Cost$;
5: **while** $curTP < TPConst$ **do**
6:      **for all** $T_i \in$ task graph **do**
7:          $GenerateGainCandidateSetForEachTask()$;
8:          **for all** $R_j \in V_{Gain-candidate}(T_i)$ **do**
9:              Calculate $GainWeight$;
10:          **end for**
11:          Select the task with the maximum $GainWeight$ to re-assign;
12:      **end for**
13: **end while**
14: Calculate total $Cost$;
15: **return** TP, $Cost$;

$$GainWeight(j) = \frac{TP_{New}-TP_{Cur}}{Cost_{New}-Cost_{Cur}} \qquad (12)$$

where TP_{Cur} and $Cost_{Cur}$ are the throughput and cost of current schedule, respectively; TP_{New} and $Cost_{New}$ are the throughput and cost of T_i re-mapped to node R_j which is a candidate node in $V_{Gain-candidate}(T_i)$ for T_i, respectively. The algorithm keeps re-mapping by considering the greatest values of $GainWeight$ for all tasks and their candidate nodes. The complexity of this algorithm is $O(mns)$, where s is the number of swaps.

5   Performance Evaluation

We design and implement our experiments based on the GridSim [29] toolkit. The four algorithms are implemented as four separate schedulers, which can generate scheduling results for given workflows and networks. The workflow tasks are submitted to a Grid resources as advance reservations in GridSim. The cost and throughput are recorded after simulations are finished in GridSim.

5.1   Experimental Settings

Workflow and Grid Network Configurations. Given that different workflow applications and networks may have different impact on the performance of the scheduling algorithms, we develop a workflow and network generator which can randomly create varying parameters of the workflows and networks that follows a similar experimental approaches used by some previous published articles [6,20], and within a suitably selected range of values: (i) the number of tasks and the complexity of each task; (ii) the number of inter-task communications and the data transfer size between two tasks; (iii) the number of nodes and the processing power of each node; (iv) the unit execution price of each node and network link; (v) the number of network links as well as the bandwidth and the minimum link delay of each link.

In our experiments, the cost that a user needs to pay for a workflow execution (i.e. user charge) comprises of two parts, namely cost of executing tasks on nodes, and cost of transfer data of dependency edges over network links.

We represent the problem size in Table 2 for workflow scheduling as a four-tuple $(m, |E_T|, n, |E_R|)$: m tasks and $|E_T|$ dependency edges in the workflow, and n nodes with $|E_R|$ links in the network.

Performance Metrics and Experimental Scenarios. We consider the two performance metrics of throughput and execution cost, and evaluate our algorithm from the following experimental scenarios:

– Impact of budget constraint
– Impact of throughput constraint
– Impact of workflow size
– Impact of network size

Table 2. Workflow configurations

Problem index	Workflow ID	Network ID	Problem size $(m, |E_T|, n, |E_R|)$
1	1	1	10, 20, 5, 19
2	2	2	15, 25, 10, 89
3	3	4	20, 42, 15, 209
4	4	4	25, 52, 20, 379
5	5	5	30, 60, 25, 425
6	6	6	35, 72, 30, 630
7	7	7	40, 79, 35, 855
8	8	8	45, 93, 40, 1250
9	9	9	50, 96, 45, 1600
10	10	10	60, 122, 50, 2200

Incomplete network graphs are simulated due to network connectivity and facility accessibility. To conduct thorough comparison, we select different budget constraints and simulate several different sizes of workflows and networks. To set up baselines for comparison, we also developed some representative workflow scheduling algorithms for maximizing throughput (due to no existing algorithm for maximizing throughput under budget constraint) including Streamline [7] and LDP [6] (which is used to find an initial schedule in B-SWAP).

5.2 Analysis of Results

Budget Constrained Approaches. In order to compare the performance of the two algorithms for maximizing throughput under budget constraint, namely B-RATE and B-SWAP, we conduct the above-mentioned 10 sets of workflows and networks with problem sizes from small to large and give part of the results in Fig. 3. For each set, various budget constraints are considered. Generally, more budget is provided when problem size becomes larger due to more computation and communication efforts. We calculate the throughput and cost for comparison. The performance of the two proposed algorithms is further compared with Streamline [7] and LDP [6].

Figure 3 shows the throughput and cost comparison among the four algorithms, the x axis represents the budget constraints; the y axis on the left and the various bars denote the throughput value, the y axis on the right and the lines represent the actual cost of the schedule. The throughput and cost of Streamline and LDP remains constant for each budget constraint as a baseline (since they do not consider budget). We observe that in most cases, B-SWAP results in higher throughput with larger cost than that of B-RATE. This may be due to the fact that B-SWAP starts with a schedule optimized for throughput, then keep re-mapping for the largest savings in cost with the minimum throughput loss; While the B-RATE algorithm starts with a rough and un-precise distribution of budget constraint value for each layer. It is noted that under smaller budget constraints, B-RATE may fail to compute a schedule because the budget constraints for some layers might not be possible under mapping strategy.

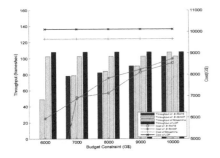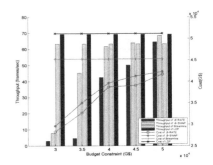

Fig. 3. Throughput and cost comparison under different budget constraints (left: problem index = 2, right: problem index = 6).

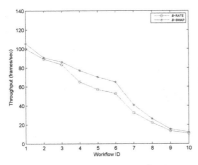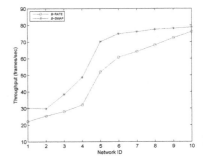

(a) Impact of workflow size (budget constraint = 80% of LDP's cost, network ID = 8)

(b) Impact of network size (budget constraint = 80% of LDP's cost, workflow ID = 5)

Fig. 4. Impact of workflow size and network size

With larger budget constraints, the two algorithms achieve more similar throughput values due to sufficient budget to play with. In comparison with Streamline and LDP algorithms, since the two algorithms aim for optimization for throughput, we observe that LDP produces the highest throughput with the highest cost though. With the increased budget, B-RATE and B-SWAP are able to achieve comparable throughputs as those from LDP. When budget constraint is set high enough, B-SWAP has the same throughput as that of LDP because no swapping procedure is needed. The costs of B-RATE and B-SWAP are much lower than that of Streamline and LDP even when their throughput values are similar. From Fig. 3, it can be seen that B-RATE's cost decreases by 8%–40% in comparison with Streamline, and decreases by 18%–45% in comparison with LDP; B-SWAP's cost decreases by 7%–35% in comparison with Streamline, and decreases by 17%–40% in comparison with LDP. The variation is due to different problem sizes and budget constraints.

The throughput measurements in Fig. 4(a) shows that B-SWAP consistently achieves higher throughput than B-RATE under the scenario of above-mentioned

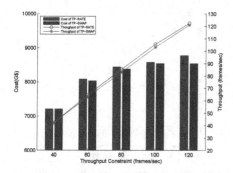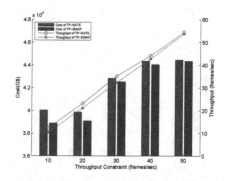

Fig. 5. Cost and throughput comparison under different throughput constraints (left: problem index = 1, right: problem index = 7).

10 workflows from small to large executed in the same network with budget constraint set to 80 % of LDP's cost. A larger workflow size obviously results in a smaller throughput, which explains the decreasing trend in each curve.

In order to evaluate the impact of network size on the performance of B-RATE and B-SWAP, we compare their throughputs under the scenario of the same workflow executed in the above-mentioned 10 networks from small to large with budget constraint set to 80 % of LDP's cost. Figure 4(b) shows that B-SWAP consistently achieves higher throughput than B-RATE. A smaller network size results in a smaller throughput due to higher resource sharing, and the curves increases quickly as network becomes larger, but the increasing trend will slow down after the network is large enough for the workflow.

Throughput Constrained Approaches. In order to compare the performance of the two algorithms for minimizing execution cost under throughput constraint, namely TP-RATE and TP-SWAP, we conduct the above-mentioned 10 sets of workflows and networks with problem sizes from small to large and give part of the results in Fig. 5. For each set, various throughput constraints are considered. We calculate the throughput and cost for comparison. To our best knowledge, since no other algorithm considers minimizing execution cost under throughput constraint, we only provide performance comparison between the two proposed approaches.

Figure 5 shows the cost and throughput comparison, the x axis represents the throughput constraints, the y axis on the left and the bars represent the actual cost, the y axis on the right and the lines represent the throughput of the schedule. We observe straightforwardly that cost gets larger when throughput constraint becomes higher. In most cases, TP-SWAP produces lower cost than TP-RATE, but its throughput is relatively smaller. This may be due to the fact that TP-SWAP starts with a greedy schedule optimized for cost, then keep re-mapping for the maximum gain in throughput for the least increase in cost whereas the TP-RATE algorithm has a partial-optimized schedule for each layer that may not be optimal for cost as an entire schedule. Therefore,

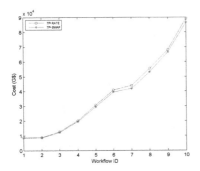
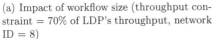
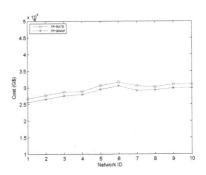

(a) Impact of workflow size (throughput constraint = 70% of LDP's throughput, network ID = 8)

(b) Impact of network size (throughput constraint = 70% of LDP's throughput, workflow ID = 5)

Fig. 6. Impact of workflow size and network size

TP-SWAP is more likely to produce throughput closer to the throughput constraint than TP-RATE. The throughput of the two algorithms gets similar when the throughput constraint becomes higher due to less available resources to produce higher throughput. With larger throughput constraints, the two algorithms achieve more similar costs because higher throughput requirement limits the selection of nodes. From Fig. 5, it can be seen that compares with TP-RATE, TP-SWAP's cost is about 0 %–3 % lower, and throughput is about 0 %–20 % smaller. The variation is due to different problem sizes and throughput constraints.

The throughput measurements in Fig. 6(a) shows that TP-SWAP consistently achieves lower cost than TP-RATE under the scenario of above-mentioned 10 workflows from small to large executed in the same network with throughput constraint set to 70 % of LDP's throughput. A larger workflow size obviously results in a larger cost, which explains the increasing trend in each curve.

In order to evaluate the impact of network size on the performance of TP-RATE and TP-SWAP, we compare their costs under the scenario of the same workflow executed in the above-mentioned 10 networks from small to large with throughput constraint set to 70 % of LDP's throughput. Figure 6(b) shows that TP-SWAP consistently achieves higher throughput than TP-RATE. A smaller network size results in a relatively smaller cost because higher resource sharing decreases the data transfer cost (since the data transfer costs of adjacent tasks scheduled on the same node are negligible).

6   Conclusions

In this paper, we considered a workflow scheduling problem for streaming applications with budget and throughput requirements for streaming applications in heterogeneous Grid environment. We proposed two algorithms, namely B-RATE and B-SWAP for budget constrained objective, and two algorithms, namely

TP-RATE and TP-SWAP for throughput constrained objective. Thorough simulation experiments under GridSim were conducted with randomly generated workflow and Grid network cases. From our simulation experiments, it could be seen that for budget constrained objective, B-SWAP algorithm outperformed the B-RATE algorithm but with a higher complexity. Compared with throughput optimized only algorithms such as Streamline and LDP, our two proposed algorithms achieved much lower execution cost with similar throughput. For throughput constrained objective, TP-SWAP outperformed TP-RATE in execution cost, but with disadvantage of a higher complexity and smaller throughput. In the future, real-life scientific workflows and real Grid networks with more dynamic scenarios for execution of the workflow will be considered.

References

1. Tannenbaum, T., Wright, D., Miller, K., Livny, M.: Condor - A Distributed Job. MIT Press, Cambridge (2002)
2. Blythe, J., Jain, S., Deelman, E., Gi, Y., Vahi, K., Mandal, A., Kennedy, K.: Task scheduling strategies for workflow-based applications in grids. In: IEEE International Symposium on Cluster Computing and the Grid (CCGrid), pp. 759–767 (2005)
3. Cao, J., Jarvis, S., Saini, S., Nudd, G.: Gridflow:workflow management for grid computing. In: 3rd International Symposium on Cluster Computing and the Grid (CCGrid), Tokyo, Japan (2003)
4. Abramson, R.B.D., Venugopal, S.: The grid economy. Proc. IEEE **93**(3), 698–714 (2005)
5. Foster, I.: Globus toolkit version 4: software for service-oriented systems. J. Comput. Sci. Technol. **21**, 513–520 (2006)
6. Gu, Y., Wu, Q.: Maximizing workflow throughput for streaming applications in distributed environments. In: 19th International Conference on Computer Communications and Networks (ICCCN) (2010)
7. Agarwalla, B., Ahmed, N., Hilley, D., Ramachandran, U.: Streamline: a scheduling heuristic for streaming application on the grid. In: The 13th Multimedia Computing and Networking Conference, pp. 69–85 (2007)
8. Condor. http://research.cs.wisc.edu/htcondor
9. DAGMan. http://research.cs.wisc.edu/htcondor/dagman/dagman.html
10. Globus. http://www.globus.org
11. Deelman, E., Singh, G., Su, M.H., Blythe, J., Gil, Y., Kesselman, C., Mehta, G., Vahi, K., Berriman, G.B., Good, J., Laity, A., Jacob, J.C., Katz, D.S.: Pegasus: a framework for mapping complex scientific workflows onto distributed systems. Sci. Program. **13**, 219–237 (2005)
12. Yu, J., Buyya, R.: A taxonomy of scientific workflow systems for grid computing. SIGMOD Rec. **34**(3), 44–49 (2005)
13. Topcuoglu, S., Wu, M.: Task scheduling algorithms for heterogeneous processors. In: 8th IEEE Heterogeneous Computing Workshop (HCW99), pp. 3–14 (1999)
14. Sonmez, O., Yigitbasi, N., Abrishami, S., Iosup, A., Epema, D.: Performance analysis of dynamic workflow scheduling in multicluster grids. In: The 19th ACM International Symposium on High Performance Distributed Computing (HPDC '10) (2010)

15. Dongarra, J., Jeannot, E., Saule, E., Shi, Z.: Bi-objective scheduling algorithms for optimizing makespan and reliability on heterogeneous systems. In: The 19th Annual ACM Symposium on Parallel Algorithms and Architectures (SPAA '07), pp. 280–288 (2007)

16. Wu, Q., Gu, Y.: Supporting distributed application workflows in heterogeneous computing environments. In: 14th International Conference on Parallel and Distributed Systems (ICPADS08), Vol. 47. pp. 8–22 (2008)

17. Wu, Q., Zhu, M., Lu, X., Brown, P., Lin, Y., Gu, Y., Cao, F., Reuter, M.: Automation and management of scientific workflows in distributed network environments. In: The 6th International Workshop of IPDPS on System Management Techniques, Processes, and Services, pp. 1–8 (2010)

18. Wu, Q., Zhu, M., Gu, Y., Brown, P., Lu, X., Lin, W., Liu, Y.: A distributed workflow management system with case study of real-life scientific applications on grids. J. Grid Comput. **10**(3), 367–393 (2012)

19. Wu, Q., Gu, Y., Lin, Y., Rao, N.: Latency modeling and minimization for large-scale scientific workflows in distributed network environments. In: The 44th Annual Simulation Symposium (ANSS 2011), pp. 205–212 (2011)

20. Gu, Y., Wu, Q., Liu, X., Yu, D.: Improving throughput and reliability of distributed scientific workflows for streaming data processing. In: The 13th IEEE International Conference on High Performance and Communications (HPCC), pp. 347–354 (2011)

21. Yu, J., Buyya, R.: A budget constrained scheduling of workflow applications on utility grids using genetic algorithms. In: Workshop on Workflows in Support of Large-Scale Science (WORKS), pp. 1–10 (2006)

22. Yuan, Y., Wang, K., Sun, X., Guo, T.: An iterative heuristic for scheduling grid workflows with budget constraints. In: International Conference on Machine Learning and Cybernetics, pp. 1700–1705 (2009)

23. Abrishami, S., Naghibzadeh, M., Epema, D.: Cost-driven scheduling of grid workflows using partial critical paths. IEEE Trans. Parallel Distrib. Sys. **23**(8), 1400–1414 (2012)

24. Yao, Y., Liu, J., Ma, L.: Efficient cost optimization for workflow scheduling on grids. In: International Conference on Management and Service Science (MASS), pp. 1–4 (2010)

25. Sakellariou, R., Zhao, H., Tsiakkouri, E., Dikaiakos, M.: Scheduling workflows with budget constraints. In: Gorlatch, S., Danelutto, M. (eds.) Integrated Research in Grid Computing, pp. 189–202. Springer, Heidelberg (2007)

26. Yu, J., Buyya, R.: Scheduling scientific workflow applications with deadline and budget constraints using genetic algorithms. Sci. Program. **14**(3–4), 217–230 (2006)

27. Yu, J., Buyya, R., Tham, C.: Cost-based scheduling of scientific workflow applications on utility grids. In: First International Conference one-Science and Grid Computing, pp. 139–147 (2005)

28. Sakellariou, R., Zhao, H.: A hybrid heuristic for dag scheduling on heterogeneous systems. In: 13th IEEE Heterogeneous Computing Workshop (HCW'04), Santa Fe, New Mexico, USA (2004)

29. Buyya, R., Murshed, M.: Gridsim: a toolkit for the modeling and simulation of distributed resource management and scheduling for grid computing. Concurr. Comput. Pract. Exp. **14**(13), 1175–1220 (2002)

Multi Resource Fairness: Problems and Challenges

Dalibor Klusáček[1,2](✉), Hana Rudová[1], and Michal Jaroš[3]

[1] Faculty of Informatics, Masaryk University,
Botanická 68a, Brno, Czech Republic
[2] CESNET z.s.p.o., Zikova 4, Prague, Czech Republic
[3] Institute of Computer Science, Masaryk University,
Botanická 68a, Brno, Czech Republic
{xklusac,hanka}@fi.muni.cz, mjaros@ics.muni.cz

Abstract. Current production resource management and scheduling systems often use some mechanism to guarantee fair sharing of computational resources among different users of the system. For example, the user who so far consumed small amount of CPU time gets higher priority and vice versa. The problem with such a solution is that it does not reflect other consumed resources like RAM, HDD storage capacity or GPU cores. Clearly, different users may have highly heterogeneous demands concerning aforementioned resources, yet they are all prioritized only with respect to consumed CPU time. In this paper we show that such a single resource-based approach is unfair and is no longer suitable for nowadays systems. We provide a survey of existing works that somehow try to deal with this situation and we closely analyze and evaluate their characteristics. Next, we propose new enhanced approaches that would allow the development of usable multi resource-aware user prioritization mechanisms. We demonstrate that different consumed resources can be weighted and combined together within a single formula which can be used to establish users' priorities. Moreover, we show that when it comes to multiple resources, it is not always possible to find a suitable solution that would fulfill all fairness-related requirements.

Keywords: Multi resource fairness · Fairshare · Penalty · Scheduling

1 Introduction

This paper is inspired by the lessons learned over the few past years when analyzing the workload of the Czech National Grid Infrastructure MetaCentrum [16]. MetaCentrum is highly heterogeneous national Grid that provides computational resources to various users and research groups. As in other systems, one of the main goal is to guarantee that computational resources are shared in a fair fashion with respect to different users and research groups [11,14]. These requirements are typically solved using the service[1] of the applied resource manager, in

---

[1] This service is commonly called a *fairshare algorithm* [2,10].

N. Desai and W. Cirne (Eds.): JSSPP 2013, LNCS 8429, pp. 81–95, 2014.
DOI: 10.1007/978-3-662-43779-7_5, © Springer-Verlag Berlin Heidelberg 2014

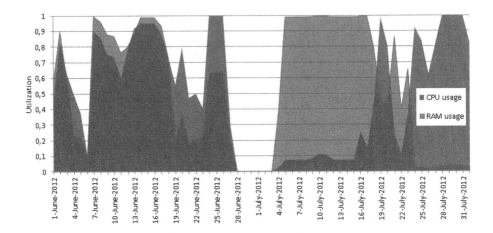

Fig. 1. An example of CPU and RAM utilization on one Zewura node.

this case the TORQUE [3]. Current fairshare algorithm measures the amount of consumed CPU time for each user and then calculates users' priorities such that the user with the smallest amount of consumed CPU time gets the highest priority and vice versa [14]. While jobs typically consume several different resources (e.g., CPU time, RAM, GPUs and HDD storage) simultaneously, the whole user prioritization scheme is based only on one parameter — consumed CPU time. Clearly, it is questionable whether such a solution can guarantee fair sharing of resources [15]. Therefore, we have performed several analysis of existing workload and quickly realized that this single resource-based fairshare algorithm is (very) unfair.

To demonstrate some of the issues found in the workload we present Fig. 1 that shows the usage of CPUs and RAM on a selected node within the Zewura cluster in MetaCentrum. This particular node has 80 CPUs and 512 GB of RAM. The figure shows that for nearly two weeks in July 2012 the jobs used at most 10 % of CPUs while consuming all available RAM memory. Clearly, the remaining 90 % of CPUs are then useless because no new job can be executed there due to the lack of available RAM. More importantly, using the standard fairshare algorithm owner(s) of these memory-demanding jobs are only accounted for using 10 % of available CPU time. However, as intuition suggests they should be accounted as if using 100 % of machine's CPU time because they effectively "disabled" the whole machine by using all of its RAM.

The solution is to extend the current single resource-based fairshare algorithm and incorporate consumption of other important job-related resources, e.g., RAM, GPUs or HDD storage. For this purpose we have studied existing works that deal with similar problems and we present their survey here. We also propose new solutions that can flexibly combine several different resources with different weights (i.e., costs) as existing works have some limitations when using several (weighted) resources together. We also define several rules that should be satisfied by considered multi resource-based fairshare formulas in order to generate fair and acceptable solutions. Based on these requirements, we analyze the suitability of considered techniques. Especially, we demonstrate weighting of different consumed resources and their combination within a single formula that is then used in the fairshare algorithm to establish priorities among users of the system. Surprisingly, we realize that — in general — it is not always possible to find a suitable solution that would fulfill all fairness-related requirements.

The structure of this paper is following. In Sect. 2 we discuss existing related works on single and multi resource-based fairness techniques. Especially, we closely describe current single resource-based fairshare algorithm as applied in MetaCentrum's TORQUE. In Sect. 3 we define several rules that should be satisfied by a prospective multi resource-based fairshare formula. Next, we present and discuss possible extensions of the fairshare algorithm that incorporate multiple resources. We also discuss whether these extensions are suitable when different resources have different weights, i.e., "cost" and/or importance. Section 4 discusses the findings of our work and suggests suitable solutions that can be applied within a multi resource-based fairshare algorithm. In Sect. 5 we conclude the paper and discuss the future work.

2   Related Work

All popular resource management systems and schedulers such as PBS [13], TORQUE [3], Moab, Maui [1], Quincy [9] or Hadoop's Fair and Capacity Schedulers [4,5] support some form of fairshare mechanism. Nice explanation of Maui's fairshare mechanism can be found in [10].

The solution currently applied in MetaCentrum's TORQUE is very similar to Maui and uses the well known *max-min* approach [8], i.e., it gives the highest priority to a user with the smallest amount of consumed CPU time and vice versa. For the purpose of this paper, we assume that a user's priority is established using a function that looks like Formula 1 [10,15].

$$F_u = \sum_{j=1}^{n} (P_j \cdot walltime_j) \qquad (1)$$

Here, the F_u is the resulting priority of a given user u that so far computed n jobs. The final value is computed as a sum of products of job penalty (P_j) and the job's walltime ($walltime_j$). Once the priorities are computed for all users, the user with the smallest value of F_u then gets the highest priority in a job queue. Such a formula is a general form of a function that can be used to establish ordering of users. It represents the simplest version, that does not use a so called decay algorithm [10]. Decay algorithm is typically applied to determine the value of F_u with respect to aging, i.e., it specifies how the effective fairshare usage is decreased over the time[2]. For example, Maui's fairshare algorithm utilizes

---

[2] In Maui's terminology, *fairshare usage* represents the metric of utilization measurement [10]. Typically, fairshare usage expresses the amount of consumed CPU time of a given user.

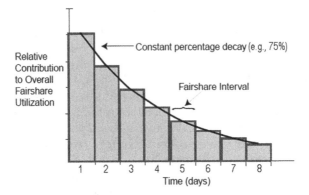

Fig. 2. Effective fairshare usage based on the decay algorithm that reflects aging. This image is adopted from [10].

the concept of fairshare windows each covering a particular period of time. An administrator may then specify how long each window should last, how fairshare usage in each window should be weighted, and how many windows should be evaluated in obtaining the final effective fairshare usage [10]. For example, an administrator may wish to make fairshare adjustments based on the usage of resources during the previous 8 days. To do this, he or she may choose to evaluate 8 fairshare windows each consisting of 24 h periods, with a decay, i.e., aging factor of 0.75 as seen in Fig. 2. For simplicity, we will not consider the decay algorithm in the formulas as its inclusion is straightforward.

When computing F_u, a proper computation of the job's penalty P_j is the key problem. In the rest of the paper we assume that the value of P_j is a real number from the interval $[0, 1]$, and we discuss several variants of P_j computation. Commonly, fairshare algorithms only consider a single resource, typically CPU time. In such a case, the penalty function P_j for a given job j can be described by Formula 2, where $req_{CPU,j}$ is the number of CPUs allocated to a given job j and $avail_{CPU}$ is the total amount of CPUs available in the system.

$$P_j = \frac{req_{CPU,j}}{avail_{CPU}} \tag{2}$$

Clearly, the penalty of a given user's job j is proportional to the number of CPUs it requires as P_j expresses the ratio of consumed to available CPUs, i.e., the relative CPU usage[3]. The resulting distribution of such penalties is linear, and the highest penalty (1.0) is obtained when a user's job consumes all available CPUs in the system.

As we already mentioned in Sect. 1, the analysis of existing MetaCentrum's workloads has quickly identified that such an approach is clearly unfair.

---

[3] In MetaCentrum, resources allocated (i.e., reserved) to a given job cannot be used by other jobs even if those resources are not fully used. Therefore, in the whole paper we measure CPU, RAM, etc., requirements as the amount of a given resource that has been allocated for a job, even if actual job's requirements are smaller.

There were jobs that required few CPUs and (almost) all RAM memory (see Fig. 1). Therefore, those remaining CPUs could not be utilized by remaining users since there was no free RAM left. The classical — single resource-based — fairshare mechanism computed according to consumed CPU time is then absolutely unacceptable as the users with high RAM requirements are not adequately penalized in comparison with those users who only need (a lot of) CPUs. Of course, similar findings can be done concerning other resources such as GPUs or HDD storage.

Although the single resource-based fairshare algorithm is inadequate, many systems are still using it today [5,8,9,12]. Surprisingly, the so called multi resource fairness seems to be a rather new area of researchers' interest as there are only few works that address this problem specifically [7,8,12,15]. For example, the recent *Dominant Resource Factor (DRF)* [8] suggests to perform max-min fairshare algorithm over so called dominant user's share. Dominant share is the maximum share that a user has been allocated of any resource. Such a resource is then called a *dominant resource*. Sadly, some parts of the paper are not very clear. For example, the pseudo-code of DRF algorithm does not correspond with the algorithm's textual description. Moreover, the resulting DRF allocation is formulated using a linear programming notation. However, the paper does not explain how non-integer results should be handled. As discussed in [12] which builds upon the results of [8], if a given user is allowed to execute, e.g., 0.76 jobs we cannot use such a solution unless user's jobs are continuously divisible [6]. For common grid and cluster environment, this is rarely the case. Similar situation applies for [7], which proposes new definition for the simultaneous fair allocation of multiple continuously divisible resources called *bottleneck-based fairness (BBF)*. In BBF, an allocation of resources is considered fair if every user either gets all the resources she wishes for, or else gets at least her entitlement on some bottleneck resource, and therefore cannot complain about not receiving more. Beside that, the tradeoffs of using multi resource-based fairness algorithms like DRF are discussed in [12]. Especially, the overall efficiency is of interest, e.g., the amount of unused resources is studied. Apart from DRF, the paper proposes the use of other approaches such as so called *Generalized Fairness on Jobs (GFJ)*. Unlike DRF, GJF measures fairness only in terms of the number of jobs allocated to each user. Users requiring more resources are thus treated equally [12]. From our point of view, such a notion of fairness is impractical as it allows to cheat easily by "packing" several small jobs as a one large job. Last but not least, all approaches proposed in [12] or in [7] make the assumption that all jobs and resources are continuously divisible which is rather unrealistic for our purposes. In our previous work [15], we have proposed multi resource-based penalty function that uses a product of relative resources' requirements. In Sect. 3.2 we show that this function is less suitable than other approaches. Also, Moab or Maui schedulers allow the system administrator to combine CPU and, e.g., RAM consumptions within the fairshare function [2,10] using so called *processor equivalent (PE)* mechanism [10]. It is based on the application of *max* function that determines a job's most constraining resource consumption and translates it into an equivalent processor count [10]. In fact, this solution uses similar idea as the DRF. Although PE mechanism is available in several production schedulers, we did not find any work that would specifically discuss its suitability. Also Moab's and Maui's documentation did not bring much insight into this solution [1,2].

In the following section, we define several major principles that should be followed by a multi resource-based fairshare algorithm and we closely analyze selected promising multi resource-based fairshare metrics that are either based on existing works or are our own contribution.

3   Multi Resource-Based Fairshare Algorithm

As discussed in previous section, the core part of the fairshare algorithm is the *penalty function*. Therefore, using the results from the literature, we now present and analyze several variants of multi resource-based job penalty functions that — beside the common CPU consumption — also consider additional consumed resources. Before we start, we first formulate several basic rules that are to be followed by an ideal multi resource-based penalty function. These rules are a result of several discussions that were held within the MetaCentrum team and reflect the specific requirements of MetaCentrum. We believe that these rules are general enough, still we are aware that for different institutions they may be either too restrictive or incomplete.

(1) **Multiple resources:** When calculating the value of penalty, the function should not consider only one type of consumed resource, e.g., CPUs.

(2) **Nondominant resources:** Penalty function should consider the consumption of nondominant resources as well. In another words, if two different jobs have the same consumption of a given dominant resource then the one having smaller consumption of nondominant resources should receive smaller penalty.

(3) **Max-min penalty:** Maximum penalty (i.e., 1) should be applied whenever a job completely utilizes at least one resource since the corresponding machine is then practically unusable for other jobs. Similarly, a job obtains minimum penalty (i.e., 0) only when it does not consume any resource at all[4].

(4) **Linearity:** Penalty function should be linear with respect to a given consumed resource. The linearity is important factor that guarantees that a user cannot cheat by dividing his or her (large) job into several smaller jobs that would — due to the nonlinear character of the penalty — together receive smaller penalty than the original (large) job.

(5) **Weights:** For a given resource, penalty function should allow to use weights that express the importance or the "cost" of that resource.

---

[4] Max-min penalty rule defines when P_j reaches its minimum and maximum. Apparently, no "real" job should ever receive minimum penalty since it always consumes some resources.

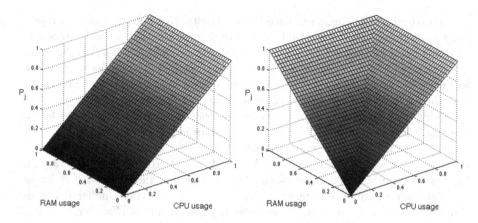

Fig. 3. Single resource CPU-based penalty (left) and *max*-based penalty function (right).

In the following text, we consider general formulas that allow inclusion of r different resources. The x-th resource is denoted as x where $x \in (1,..,r)$. For better readability, all figures that illustrate these formulas will however only contain the two most important resources — CPUs and RAM.

We start with an illustration of the penalties that are obtained when using classical CPU-based single resource penalty that has been shown in Formula 2. The resulting distribution of such penalties can be illustrated by the graph shown in Fig. 3 (left). Clearly, the penalty of a given user's job j has no relation to RAM consumption and is only proportional to the number of required CPUs as P_j expresses the ratio of consumed to available CPUs. This function is therefore impractical as it breaks all rules except for the "linearity" rule 4.

In order to resolve the unfairness of the single resource-based fairshare metric we analyze/propose several candidate penalty formulas that somehow incorporate additional resource requirements.

3.1 Dominant Resource-Based Penalty

Existing works [1,2,8,10] suggest to measure and apply *dominant resource*-based penalty. It means that a user is penalized according to the maximum relative share he or she has been allocated of any resource [8]. In another words, instead of combining all resource requests together, only the maximum (most restricting) relative request is considered and penalized accordingly. The penalty is then computed using Formula 3 and the corresponding distribution of penalties is depicted in Fig. 3 (right).

$$P_j = \max \left(\frac{req_{1,j}}{avail_1}, .., \frac{req_{r,j}}{avail_r} \right) \tag{3}$$

Compared to the single resource-based penalty, this penalty function represents several benefits. First of all, it is very simple function so both users and system administrators will find it easy to understand. Second, it solves the problem described in Sect. 1, i.e., it adequately penalizes highly asymmetric requests, following the rule 3. Last but not least, unlike some of the functions that will be discussed in next section, this penalty is linear, fulfilling the rule 4.

Sadly, this penalty also represents several drawbacks. Although it does follow the rule 1, it does not fulfill the rule 2, i.e., it does not consider the nondominant resources at all. Therefore, users are not forced to better estimate their requests concerning nondominant resources. As a side effect, this penalty is not fair. Consider two users with equal dominant resource demands but with different nondominant resource requirements. Clearly, the one having smaller demands should be less penalized as he or she consumes less resources. However, they will both receive the same penalty, disregarding their real resource consumptions, which breaks the rule 2. We believe that this is an unfair behavior. The second problem is that we cannot apply resource weights in a reasonable manner. In reality, different resources are rarely considered as equally important. In fact, some resources are more important than others. For example, in MetaCentrum, the common sense is that CPUs are more "expensive" than, e.g., RAM. When necessary, it is often possible to increase the amount of RAM on a given machine while it is not possible to increase the number of CPUs. Therefore, the requirement is to apply resource-specific weights when computing the penalty function. As we show now, in case of Formula 3 this process is somehow tricky. There are two basic extensions of Formula 3 that involve weights and we show them in Formula 4 and 5. Both of them guarantee that the values of P_j will remain within the interval $[0, 1]$.

$$P_j = \min\left(1, \max\left(w_1 \frac{req_{1,j}}{avail_1}, .., w_r \frac{req_{r,j}}{avail_r}\right)\right) \tag{4}$$

$$P_j = \frac{\max\left(w_1 \frac{req_{1,j}}{avail_1}, .., w_r \frac{req_{r,j}}{avail_r}\right)}{\max\left(w_1, .., w_r\right)} \tag{5}$$

Here, the weight of a given resource x is denoted as w_x and we assume that for every resource x the weight $w_x > 0$. There are two major problems with the weighted max-based functions. The first problem (A) is that in some situations we often cannot distinguish between full and partial consumption of the most "expensive" resource. The second problem (B) is that sometimes we cannot properly penalize total consumption of "cheap" resources. As stated by the rule 3, if a job fully consumes some resource on a given machine, we require full penalty for such a job as it "disabled" the whole machine that cannot be used to process other jobs. Let us consider Formula 4 first. Problem (A) appears whenever the most expensive resource has its weight $w_{most} > 1$. For example, let $w_{most} = 2$. Then every job requiring at least $1/2$ of that resource will always receive maximum penalty. Clearly, this behavior is not fair. Problem (B) can appear when $w_{most} \leq 1$. Then it can easily happen, that we cannot properly penalize full consumption of some "cheap" resource. For example, let the fully consumed "cheap" resource has weight $w_{least} = 0.1$ while the weight of the most expensive resource is, e.g., $w_{most} = 1$ and its utilization is only 50 %. Then Formula 4 resolves as $P_j = \min(1, \max(0.5, 0.1)) = 0.5$. Clearly, instead of $P_j = 1$ we only get 0.5, failing to meet the requirements described by the rule 3. In case of Formula 5, the problem (A) is eliminated, however the second problem (B) can still appear. For example, let the fully consumed "cheap" resource has $w_{least} = 1$. Let the "expensive" resource be only occupied by, e.g., 10 % with $w_{most} = 2.0$. Then Formula 5 resolves as $P_j = \max(0.2, 1.0)/2 = 0.5$. Clearly, instead of $P_j = 1$ we only get 0.5, failing to meet the requirements described by the rule 3. Therefore, max-based penalty also breaks the "weights" rule 5. Based on these findings we have decided to analyze whether there is a chance to find a new penalty function that would overcome aforementioned problems.

3.2 Penalties Based on Combination of All Resources

Following text summarizes our attempts to develop a new penalty function that would also reflect nondominant resources as required by the rule 2. Three types of penalty functions are considered and their strengths and weaknesses are discussed in the following text.

$$W = \sum_{x=1}^{r} w_x \tag{6}$$

$$P_j = \prod_{x=1}^{r} \frac{req_{x,j}}{avail_x} \tag{7}$$

$$P_j = \left(\prod_{x=1}^{r} \left(\frac{req_{x,j}}{avail_x} \right)^{w_x} \right)^{\frac{1}{W}} \tag{8}$$

The first candidate depicted by Formula 7 uses a *product* of each resource's relative requirement. Originally, this function has been used only on two resources [15] where relative CPU and RAM requirements have been multiplied. The idea behind this approach is that consumed CPUs and RAM can be represented as 2D objects, where the multiplication represents de facto a "rectangle area" of consumed resources [15], thus reflecting consumption of both CPUs and RAM. The resulting distribution of penalties is illustrated by Fig. 4 (left).

Sadly, this penalty function is not very suitable. As can be seen in the graph, the function assigns low penalties for highly asymmetric requests, breaking the rule 3. For example, if a user consumes all CPUs and little RAM the resulting penalty is very low compared to a scenario where "symmetric" user's job consumes all available CPUs and RAM. This appears to be unacceptable and very unfair behavior. Our analysis quickly revealed that this penalty also breaks the "linearity" rule 4. The problem lies in the adopted idea of "rectangle area", i.e., in the multiplication of CPU and RAM requests. Consider following simple scenario with two users in a system consisting of 10 CPUs and 10 GB of RAM.

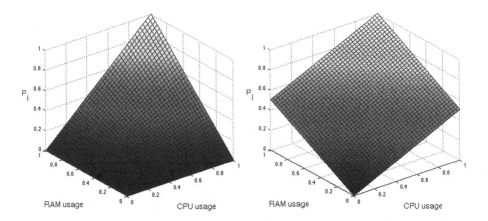

Fig. 4. Product-based penalty (left) and sum-based penalty function (right).

The first user requests 9 CPUs and 9 GB of RAM and thus gets the penalty $P_j = 0.9 \cdot 0.9 = 0.81$. The second user wants to run 9 jobs, each requiring 1 CPU and 1 GB of RAM. The total penalty for the second user is therefore $P_1 + .. + P_9 = 9 \cdot (0.1 \cdot 0.1) = 0.09$. However, both users consumed the same amount of resources. Apparently, the multiplication is a bad idea which leads to nonlinear behavior that may produce different penalties for the same amount of consumed resources. Due to the associative property of multiplication, we cannot apply weights by multiplying each resource's usage by its weight. Instead, we have to apply slightly more complicated function as is presented in Formula 8[5].

In the next attempt we have removed the multiplication and applied a *sum*-based function instead, to guarantee linear behavior. The resulting penalty function is shown in Formula 9 that summarizes all relative resource requests. Corresponding distribution of penalties is shown in Fig. 4 (right).

$$P_j = \frac{1}{r} \sum_{x=1}^{r} \frac{req_{x,j}}{avail_x} \tag{9}$$

$$P_j = \frac{1}{W} \sum_{x=1}^{r} w_x \frac{req_{x,j}}{avail_x} \tag{10}$$

This formula is linear (rule 4) and considers all resources (rules 1, 2) and can be extended to support weights as shows Formula 10. Still, it has one major drawback since it does not assign maximum penalty when a given resource is fully consumed, i.e., it breaks the important "max-min penalty" rule 3.

As a result, we propose a *root*-based penalty function that removes most of the problems mentioned for Formulas 2–10. This penalty function is shown in Formula 11 (symmetric version) and Formula 12 (weighted version), respectively. Corresponding distributions of penalties are depicted in Fig. 5.

---

[5] The W parameter used in Formula 8 and lately in Formula 10 and Formula 12 is computed using Formula 6.

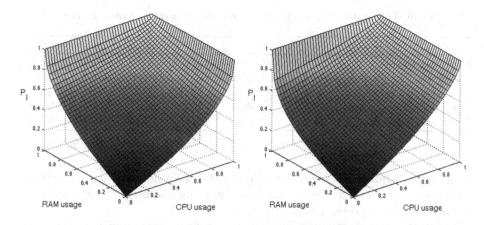

Fig. 5. Root-based penalty function (left) and its weighted version (right).

$$P_j = 1 - \sqrt[r]{\prod_{x=1}^{r} \left(1 - \frac{req_{x,j}}{avail_x}\right)} \tag{11}$$

$$P_j = 1 - \left(\prod_{x=1}^{r} \left(1 - \frac{req_{x,j}}{avail_x}\right)^{w_x}\right)^{\frac{1}{W}} \tag{12}$$

As can be seen in Fig. 5 (left) the function represents good compromise between the pure dominant resource-based *max* function and the aforementioned functions that combine all resources. More precisely, this *root*-based penalty follows the rules 1, 2, 3 and 5 as we show in the following discussion. The function combines all consumed resources, thus it fulfills the rules 1 and 2. Notably, unlike the *max*-based function, it also reflects all nondominant resources, i.e., it motivates users to better estimate all resource-related parameters. It also follows the rule 3 as it assigns reasonably high penalties for jobs with asymmetric requests, especially total consumption of selected resource results in a full penalty. Last but not least, it can be easily extended to follow the "weights" rule 5 as depicts Formula 12. Using weights, the corresponding distribution of penalties is then adjusted as shown in Fig. 5 (right). In this case we have chosen $w_{CPU} = 2.0$ and $w_{RAM} = 1.0$ which results in a steeper shape of CPU-related curve. Also, RAM-related curve has changed, having lower initial elevation that only increases when RAM usage approaches its upper limit. Still, one problem remains—the root-based penalty function breaks the "linearity" rule 4.

4   Summary and Discussion

In this paper we have presented several problems that arise when seeking for truly fair and flexible multi resource-based penalty function. The overall results are

Table 1. Suitability of penalty functions with respect to required rules.

	rule 1	rule 2	rule 3	rule 4	rule 5
CPU-based penalty (Formula 2)	NO	NO	NO	**YES**	NO
Max-based penalty (Formula 3)	**YES**	NO	**YES**	**YES**	NO
$Product$-based penalty (Formula 8)	**YES**	**YES**	NO	NO	**YES**
Sum-based penalty (Formula 10)	**YES**	**YES**	NO	**YES**	**YES**
$Root$-based penalty (Formula 12)	**YES**	**YES**	**YES**	NO	**YES**

presented in Table 1 that summarizes capabilities of considered penalty functions with respect to those five rules that were established in order to represent our requirements on a proper penalty function.

None of the presented functions fulfills all requirements at once. In fact, it is impossible to find a function that would fulfill all five rules, especially the rule 2, the rule 3 and the rule 4 cannot be fulfilled at the same time by one function. For example, as soon as the desired function follows the "max-min penalty" rule 3 it cannot fulfill the rules 2 and 4 at the same time. For simplicity, let us assume a scenario with two resources. If the rule 3 is to be followed, then the desired function must create a surface that comprises the "zero point" (no resource is consumed at all) and the two "maximum lines" (at least one resource is consumed completely) which are highlighted in black color in Fig. 6. Since the "zero point" and the "maximum lines" do not lie in a plane, full linearity of such a function is unattainable. Only partial linearity (linearity with respect to only one resource) as prescribed by the rule 4 is attainable by the function depicted in Fig. 6 (left). However, such a function clearly fails to follow the rule 2. On the other hand, the rule 2 can be fulfilled if we allow the surface to be curved and smooth as seen for the function in Fig. 6 (right), but then the linearity is broken even in terms of the rule 4.

Thus, if we are decided to follow the rules 2 and 3, we therefore must break the rule 4, i.e., the linearity. Fortunately, it is possible to minimize the adverse effects of non-linearity by requiring that the desired function will assign linear penalties at least when the corresponding jobs have symmetric requirements concerning the relative amount of used resources. This requirement means that the desired function's surface is to comprise also the line connecting the "zero point" and the interconnection point of the two "maximum lines" (all resources consumed completely). As can be check-verified, the *root*-based function, including its weighted version, fulfills this requirement.

Still, some of the functions mentioned above are more suitable than the others. The final decision on what penalty function should be applied is however highly individual as different people and/or organizations may have different notion of "what is fair" when it comes to multiple resources [8,12]. From our point of view, CPU-based penalty as well as *product* and *sum*-based penalties are not very good candidates. Clearly, single resource CPU-based penalty function fails to meet all rules except for the "linearity" rule 4. As we have already shown

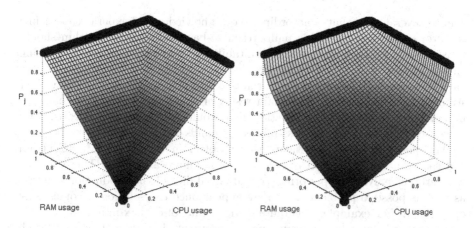

Fig. 6. Non-smooth, *max*-based penalty function vs. smooth, *root*-based penalty function (right).

in Sect. 3.2, *product*-based penalty is a very bad candidate while *sum*-based penalty function breaks the important "max-min penalty" rule 3 very heavily (see Fig. 4 (right)).

From our perspective, only two suitable candidates remain: *max*-based penalty and *root*-based penalty. *Max*-based penalty function (Formula 3) fails to fulfill the rule 2. Moreover, once weights are applied they can cause breaking of the rule 3 (see discussion in Sect. 3.1). Therefore, in Table 1 we claim that *max*-based penalty function cannot fulfill the "weights" rule 5. *Root*-based penalty fulfills all rules except for the "linearity" rule 4, which is not desirable as it allows users to cheat in some situations. For example, instead of one large job a user can submit two smaller jobs. As a result, he or she will receive smaller penalty. This particular problem can be considered as serious. However, in real life users are often motivated to minimize their requirements concerning available resources. For example, in Ohio Supercomputer Center (OSC) long jobs are only allowed if a user is able to reasonably explain why he or she needs to run such a long experiment [18]. Moreover, parallel jobs have smaller maximal runtime limit compared to serial jobs in OSC. The reason is that long and/or massively parallel jobs can cause fragmentation of system resources [19,20]. On the other hand, short jobs that are either serial or require only a small amount of CPUs are very suitable for common schedulers as they can be used for backfilling [17].

5   Conclusion and Future Work

This paper addressed an urgent real life job scheduling problem. The goal was to maintain the fairness among different users of the system. The novelty of our work is related to the fact that we consider *multiple* consumed resources when establishing users' priorities. In the area of parallel job scheduling, this problem is very urgent and seems to be rather unexplored. Therefore, we have defined several rules that — according to our knowledge and experience — define the properties that a suitable multi resource-based fairshare algorithm should satisfy. Next, we have discussed the suitability of existing approaches, focusing on the crucial penalty functions. Beside the existing *max*-based functions we have also proposed several other variants of penalty functions and show their strengths and weaknesses. The main result of this paper is the fact that it is impossible to find a penalty function that would satisfy all five rules that we have used to express the fairness-related demands.

We plan to further investigate this problem in the future. MetaCentrum will soon start to use multi resource-based fairshare algorithm. Therefore, we will further analyze the performance and suitability of the production solution as well as possible problems that may appear once the solution becomes fully operational. For example, it is quite obvious that our "max-min penalty" rule 3 is too severe for jobs requiring special resources that are not needed by all jobs, e.g., GPUs. If a given job consumes all GPUs on a machine, it does not mean that such a machine cannot execute other jobs. Therefore, in such special situations this rule is probably too severe and shall be relaxed in the future.

Acknowledgments. We highly appreciate the support of the Grant Agency of the Czech Republic under the grant No. P202/12/0306. The access to the MetaCentrum computing facilities provided under the programme LM2010005 funded by the Ministry of Education, Youth, and Sports of the Czech Republic is highly appreciated. The Zewura workload log was kindly provided by the Czech NGI MetaCentrum. The access to the CERIT-SC computing and storage facilities provided under the programme Center CERIT Scientific Cloud, part of the Operational Program Research and Development for Innovations, reg. no. CZ. 1.05/3.2.00/08.0144 is appreciated.

References

1. Adaptive Computing Enterprises, Inc. Maui Scheduler Administrator's Guide, version 3.2, February 2013. http://docs.adaptivecomputing.com
2. Adaptive Computing Enterprises, Inc. Moab workload manager administrator's guide, version 7.2.1, February 2013. http://docs.adaptivecomputing.com
3. Adaptive Computing Enterprises, Inc. TORQUE Admininstrator Guide, version 4.2.0, February 2013. http://docs.adaptivecomputing.com
4. Apache.org. Hadoop Capacity Scheduler, February 2013. http://hadoop.apache.org/docs/r1.1.1/capacity_scheduler.html
5. Apache.org. Hadoop Fair Scheduler, February 2013. http://hadoop.apache.org/docs/r1.1.1/fair_scheduler.html
6. Blazewicz, J., Drozdowski, M., Markiewicz, M.: Divisible task scheduling - concept and verification. Parallel Comput. 25(1), 87–98 (1999)
7. Dolev, D., Feitelson, D.G., Halpern, J.Y., Kupferman, R., Linial, N.: No justified complaints: on fair sharing of multiple resources. In: Proceedings of the 3rd Innovations in Theoretical Computer Science Conference, ITCS '12, pp. 68–75. ACM, New York (2012)
8. Ghodsi, A., Zaharia, M., Hindman, B., Konwinski, A., Shenker, S., Stoica, I.: Dominant resource fairness: fair allocation of multiple resource types. In: 8th USENIX Symposium on Networked Systems Design and Implementation (2011)

9. Isard, M., Prabhakaran, V., Currey, J., Wieder, U., Talwar, K., Goldberg, A.: Quincy: fair scheduling for distributed computing clusters. In: SOSP'09 (2009)
10. Jackson, D.B., Snell, Q.O., Clement, M.J.: Core algorithms of the Maui scheduler. In: Feitelson, D.G., Rudolph, L. (eds.) JSSPP 2001. LNCS, vol. 2221, pp. 87–102. Springer, Heidelberg (2001)
11. Jain, R., Chiu, D.-M., Hawe, W.: A quantitative measure of fairness and discrimination for resource allocation in shared computer systems. Technical report TR-301, Digital Equipment Corporation (1984)
12. Joe-Wong, C., Sen, S., Lan, T., Chiang, M.: Multi-resource allocation: fairness-efficiency tradeoffs in a unifying framework. In: INFOCOM (2012)
13. Jones, J.P.: PBS Professional 7, administrator guide. Altair, April 2005
14. Kleban, S.D., Clearwater, S.H.: Fair share on high performance computing systems: what does fair really mean? In: Third IEEE International Symposium on Cluster Computing and the Grid (CCGrid'03), pp. 146–153. IEEE Computer Society (2003)
15. Klusáček, D., Ruda, M., Rudová, H.: New fairness and performance metrics for current grids. In: Cracow Grid Workshop, pp. 73–74. ACC Cyfronet AGH (2012)
16. MetaCentrum, February 2013. http://www.metacentrum.cz/
17. Mu'alem, A.W., Feitelson, D.G.: Utilization, predictability, workloads, and user runtime estimates in scheduling the IBM SP2 with backfilling. IEEE Trans. Parallel Distrib. Syst. 12(6), 529–543 (2001)
18. Ohio Supercomputer Center. Batch Processing at OSC, February 2013. https://www.osc.edu/supercomputing/batch-processing-at-osc
19. Shmueli, E., Feitelson, D.G.: Backfilling with lookahead to optimize the performance of parallel job scheduling. In: Feitelson, D.G., Rudolph, L., Schwiegelshohn, U. (eds.) JSSPP 2003. LNCS, vol. 2862, pp. 228–251. Springer, Heidelberg (2003)
20. Tsafrir, D., Etsion, Y., Feitelson, D.G.: Backfilling using system-generated predictions rather than user runtime estimates. IEEE Trans. Parallel Distrib. Syst. 18(6), 789–803 (2007)

Reducing Energy Costs for IBM Blue Gene/P via Power-Aware Job Scheduling

Zhou Zhou[1][✉], Zhiling Lan[1], Wei Tang[2], and Narayan Desai[2]

[1] Department of Computer Science,
Illinois Institute of Technology, Chicago, IL, USA
{zzhou1,lan}@iit.edu
[2] Mathematics and Computer Science Division,
Argonne National Laboratory, Argonne, IL, USA
{wtang,desai}@mcs.anl.gov

Abstract. Energy expense is becoming increasingly dominant in the operating costs of high-performance computing (HPC) systems. At the same time, electricity prices vary significantly at different times of the day. Furthermore, job power profiles also differ greatly, especially on HPC systems. In this paper, we propose a smart, power-aware job scheduling approach for HPC systems based on variable energy prices and job power profiles. In particular, we propose a 0-1 knapsack model and demonstrate its flexibility and effectiveness for scheduling jobs, with the goal of reducing energy cost and not degrading system utilization. We design scheduling strategies for Blue Gene/P, a typical partition-based system. Experiments with both synthetic data and real job traces from production systems show that our power-aware job scheduling approach can reduce the energy cost significantly, up to 25 %, with only slight impact on system utilization.

Keywords: Energy · Power-aware job scheduling · Resource management · Blue Gene · HPC system

1 Introduction

With the vast improvement in technology, we are now moving toward exascale computing. Many experts predict that exascale computers will have millions of nodes, billions of threads of execution, hundreds of petabytes of inner memory, and exabytes of persistent storage [1]. Exascale computers will have unprecedented scale and architectural complexity different from the petascale systems we have now. Hence, many challenges are expected to emerge during the transition to exascale computing. Four major challenges—power, storage, concurrency, and reliability—are identified where current trends in technology are insufficient and disruptive technical breakthroughs will be needed to make exascale computing a reality [2]. In particular, the energy and power challenge is pervasive, affecting every part of a system. Today's leading-edge petascale systems consume

N. Desai and W. Cirne (Eds.): JSSPP 2013, LNCS 8429, pp. 96–115, 2014.
DOI: 10.1007/978-3-662-43779-7_6, © Springer-Verlag Berlin Heidelberg 2014

between 2 and 3 MW per petaflop [2]. It is generally accepted that an exaflop system should consume no more than 20 MW; otherwise their operating costs would be prohibitively expensive.

High-performance computing generally requires a large amount of electricity to operate computer resources and to cool the machine room. For example, a high-performance computing (HPC) center with 1,000 racks and about 25,000 square feet requires 10 MW of energy for the computing infrastructure and an additional 5 MW to remove the dissipated heat [3]. At the Argonne Leadership Computing Facility (ALCF), our systems consume approximately $1 million worth of electricity annually. As of 2006, the data centers in the United States were consuming 61.4 billion kWh per year [4], an amount of energy equivalent to that consumed by the entire transportation manufacturing industry (the industry that makes airplanes, ships, cars, trucks, and other means of transportation) [5]. Since the cost of powering HPC systems has been steadily rising with growing performance, while the cost of hardware has remained relatively stable, it is argued that if these trends were to continue, the energy cost of a large-scale system during its lifetime could surpass the equipment itself [6].

Several conventional approaches to reducing energy cost have been adopted by organizations operating HPC systems. For instance, a popular and intuitive strategy is to manipulate the nodes within an HPC system through techniques such as dynamic voltage and frequency scaling, power state transitions, and the use of separation in hot and cold aisles. Meanwhile, new cooling technologies, load-balancing algorithms, and location-aware computing have been proposed as new ways to reduce the energy demand of HPC centers [7].

In this paper we develop and analyze a new method to reduce the energy cost of operating large-scale HPC systems. Our method relies on three key observations.

1. *Electricity prices vary.* In many districts in the United States with wholesale electricity markets, the price varies on an hourly basis. Sometimes the variation can be significant as much as a factor of 10 from one hour to the next [7]. HPC centers often make a contract with the power companies to pay variable electricity prices. A common arrangement is that HPC centers pay less for electricity consumed during an off-peak period (nighttime) than during an on-peak period (daytime) [4].

2. *Job power consumption differs.* Studies have shown that most HPC jobs have distinct power consumption profiles. For example, in [8] the authors analyzed the energy characteristics of the production workload at the Research Center Juelich (FZJ) and found that their jobs have a power consumption ranging from 20 kW to 33 kW per rack on their Blue Gene/P system. Usually, an application has relatively high power consumption during its computational phases, and its power consumption drops during the communication or I/O phase [8]. For example, I/O-intensive jobs and computation-intensive jobs have totally different energy-consuming behaviors leading to variation in their power consumption.

3. *System utilization cannot be impacted in HPC.* Most conventional power saving approaches focus on manipulating nodes by turning off some nodes or
   putting the system into an idle phase during the peak price time. An imme-
   diate consequence of these approaches is that they lower system utilization
   [4]. Lowering system utilization for energy saving is not tolerable for HPC
   centers, however. HPC systems require a significant capital investment; and
   hence making efficient use of expensive resources is of paramount importance
   to HPC centers. Unlike Internet data centers that typically run at about 10–
   15 % utilization, systems at HPC centers have a typical utilization of 50–80 %
   [9], and job queues are rarely empty because of the insatiable demand in science and engineering. Therefore, an approach is needed that can save energy
   cost while maintaining relatively high system utilization.

We argue that HPC systems can save a considerable amount of electric costs
by adopting an intelligent scheduling policy that utilizes variable electricity
prices and distinct job power profiles—without reducing system utilization. More
specifically, we develop a power-aware scheduling mechanism that smartly selects
and allocates jobs based on their power profiles by preferentially allocating the
jobs with high power consumption demands during the off-peak electricity price
period. Our design is built on three key techniques: a scheduling window, a 0-1
knapsack model, and an on-line scheduling algorithm. The scheduling window
is used to balance different scheduling goals such as performance and fairness;
rather than allocating jobs one by one from the wait queue, our scheduler makes
decisions on a group of jobs selected from the waiting queue. We formalize our
scheduling problem into a standard 0-1 knapsack model, based on which we
apply dynamic programming to efficiently solve the scheduling problem. The
derived 0-1 knapsack model enables us to reduce energy cost during high electricity pricing period with no or limited impact to system utilization. We use
our on-line scheduling algorithm together with the scheduling window and 0-1
knapsack model to schedule jobs on Blue Gene/P.

By means of trace-based simulations using real job traces of the 40-rack Blue
Gene/P system at Argonne, we target how much cost saving can be achieved
with this smart power-aware scheduling. One major advantage of using real job
traces from production systems of different architectures is to ensure that experimental results can reflect the actual system performance to the greatest extent.
Experimental results show that our scheduling approach can reduce energy bills
by 25 % with no or slight loss of system utilization and scheduling fairness. We
also perform a detailed analysis to provide insight into the correlation between
power and system utilization rate, comparing our power-aware scheduling with
the default no-power-aware scheduling. We also conduct a sensitivity study to
explore how energy cost savings and utilization can be affected by applying different combinations of power ranges and pricing ratio.

The remainder of the paper is organized as follows. Section 2 discusses related
studies on HPC energy issues. Section 3 describes our methodology, including
the scheduling window, 0-1 knapsack model, and on-line scheduling algorithm.
Section 4 describes our experiments and results. Section 5 draws conclusion and
presents future work.

2   Related Work

Research on power- or energy-aware HPC systems has been active in recent years. Broadly speaking, existing work has mainly focused on the following topics: hardware design, processor adjustment, computing nodes controlling and power capping.

Energy-efficient hardware is being developed so that the components consume energy more efficiently than do standard components [10]. Several researchers [11,12] argue that the power consumption of a machine should be proportional to its workload. According to [12] a machine should consume no power in idle state, almost no power when the workload is very light, and eventually more power when the workload is increased. However, power consumption does not strictly follow this because of the various job behaviors during runtime. In [8], the authors discuss these phenomena by presenting core power and memory power for a job on Blue Gene/P.

Dynamic voltage and frequency scaling (DVFS) is another widely used technique for controlling CPU power since the power consumption of processors occupies a substantial portion of the total system power (roughly 50 % under load) [10]. DVFS enables a process to run at a lower frequency or voltage, increasing the job execution time in order to gain energy savings. Some research efforts on applying DVFS can be found in [13–15]. Nevertheless, DVFS is not appropriate for some HPC systems. For example, DVFS is both less feasible and less important for the Blue Gene series because it does not include comparable infrastructure and already operates at highly optimized voltage and frequency ranges [8]. Green Destiny [16] are build based on low frequency process to achieve the goal of energy efficiency which leaves little space for DVFS which performs better on systems equipped with high frequency processors.

In a typical HPC system, nodes often consume considerable energy in idle state without any running application. For example, an idle Blue Gene/P rack still has a DC power consumption of about 13 kW. Some nodes are shut down or switched to a low-power state during the time of low system utilization [10,17]. In [13] the authors designed an approach that can dynamically turn nodes on and off during running time. Jobs are concentrated onto fewer nodes, so that other idle nodes can be shut down to save energy consumption. Experiments on an 8-node cluster show about 19 % energy savings. In their testbed, the time used to power on the server is 100 s, while the time to shut down is 45 s, causing approximately 20 % degradation in performance.

Many large data centers use power capping to reduce the total power consumption. The data center administrator can set a threshold of power consumption to limit the actual power of the data center [6]. The total power consumption is kept under a predefined power budget so that an unexpected rise in power can be prevented. The approach also allows administrators to plan data centers more efficiently to avoid the risk of overloading existing power supplies. The idea of our scheduling borrows the idea of using power capping as a way to limit the power consumption of the system. However, our work is different from the conventional power capping approach in several aspects. First, we do not control the total power consumption through adjusting the frequency of CPU or power consumption of other components. Second, our goal is not to reduce the overall power consumption; instead, we aim at reducing energy cost by considering various job power ranges and dynamic electricity prices.

3 Methodology

In this section, we present the detailed scheduling methodology. As mentioned earlier, our scheduling design is built on three key techniques: scheduling window, 0-1 knapsack problem formulation, and on-line scheduling.

3.1 Problem Statement

User jobs are submitted to the system through a batch job scheduler. The job scheduler is responsible for allocating jobs in the wait queue to compute nodes. Before performing job scheduling, we have made two essential assumptions: (1) electricity prices keep changing during the day, with significant variation between low and high prices; (2) HPC jobs have different power profiles caused by different characteristics, which are available to the job scheduler at job submission. Also, our expected scheduling method should be based on the following design principles: (1) the scheduling method should save considerable energy cost by taking advantage of variable electricity prices and job power profiling, (2) there should be no or only minor impact to system utilization, and (3) job fairness should be preserved as much as possible. When electricity price is high (i.e., during the on-peak period), in order to save energy costs, we reduce the total amount of power consumed by the jobs allocated on the system. To limit the total power consumption, we set an upper bound denoted as the power budget that the system cannot exceed. Thus, our scheduling problem is as follows: How can we schedule jobs with different power profiles, without exceeding a predefined power budget and at the same time not affecting system utilization and not breaking the fairness of scheduling as much as possible?

Figure 1 illustrates a typical job-scheduling scenario on a 9-node cluster. Assume we have 5 jobs to be scheduled, which come in the order J1, J2, J3, J4, and J5. Job 1 stays at the head of the waiting queue and Job 5 at the tail. A 9-node atom cluster (one core per node) is ready to run these jobs. Each job is labeled with its requested number of nodes and total power consumption inside the rectangle. A job scheduler is responsible for dispatching jobs to its allocated nodes. Other unnecessary components are ignored because we focus only on the scheduling issue in terms of job size and power. We assume at this time that the electricity price is staying in the on-peak period and the power budget is 150 W for the whole system. The two rectangles in the right part of Fig. 1 represent two potential scheduling solutions. The upper one stands for the typical behavior of the backfilling scheduler where the jobs' power is not a concern. Once the scheduling decision for this time slot is made, there will be no changes unless some jobs cannot acquire needed resources. As shown in this

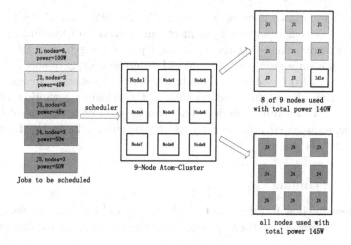

Fig. 1. Scheduling 5 jobs using traditional (top right) and power-aware scheduling (bottom right) separately.

figure, two jobs (J1 and J5) occupy eight nodes, leaving one node idle because J3, J4, and J5 all require more than one node. So at this time 8 out of 9 nodes are running jobs, with a total power of 140 kW. In contrast, the rectangle in the lower right corner shows another possible combination of jobs. Its aim is to choose jobs whose aggregated power consumption will not exceed the power budget and to try to utilize nodes as much possible. Instead of choosing jobs in a first com, first served (FCFS) manner, it searches the waiting queue for an optimal combination of jobs that can achieve the maximum system utilization and do not break the power budget constraint. As a consequence, we can see J3, J4, and J5 are picked up and put on the cluster. With their total size exactly equivalent to the cluster size, their total power is 145 W, which does not exceed the power budget.

3.2 Scheduling Window

Balancing fairness and system performance is a critical concern when developing schedulers. The simplest way to schedule jobs is to use a strict FCFS policy plus backfilling [18,19]. It ensures that jobs are started in the order of their arrivals. FCFS plus EASY backfilling is widely used by many batch schedulers; indeed, it has been estimated that 90 % to 95 % of batch schedulers use this default configuration [20,21]. Under FCFS/EASY, jobs are served in FCFS order, and subsequent jobs continuously jump over the first queued job as long as they do not violate the reservation of the first queued job.

In our design, we use a window-based scheduling mechanism to avoid breaking the fairness of job scheduling as much as possible. Rather than allocating jobs one by one from the front of the queue as adopted by existing schedulers, our method allocates a window of jobs at a time. The selection of jobs into the window is to guarantee certain fairness, while the allocation of the jobs in the window onto system resources is to meet our objective of maximizing system utilization without exceeding the predefined power budget. The job scheduler makes decisions on a group of jobs selected from the waiting queue. Jobs within the group are called to be in a scheduling window. To ensure fairness as much as possible, the job scheduler selects jobs in the scheduling window based the system's original scheduling policy. This can be seen as a variant of FCFS in that this window-based approach treats the group of jobs in the front of the wait queue with the same priority.

3.3   Job Scheduling

We now describe how to formalize the scheduling problem listed in Sect. 3.1 into a 0-1 knapsack model. We then present dynamic programming to efficiently solve the model.

0-1 Knapsack Model. Suppose there are S available nodes in the system, J jobs as $\{j_i | 1 \leq i \leq J\}$ to be scheduled, and a power budget denoted as PB. Hence we can formalize the problem into a classical 0-1 knapsack model as follows:

Problem 1. *To select a subset of $\{j_i | 1 \leq i \leq J\}$ such that their aggregated power consumption is no more than the power budget, with the objective of maximizing the number of nodes allocated to these jobs.*

For each job j_i, we associate it with a gain value v_i and weight w_i. Here v_i represents the number of nodes allocated to the job, which will be elaborated in the next subsection, and w_i denotes its power consumption, which is usually measured in kilowatts per node or kilowatts per rack.

Problem 2. *To determine a binary vector $X = \{x_i | 1 \leq i \leq J\}$ such that*

$$maximize \sum_{1 \leq i \leq J} x_i \cdot v_i, \ x_i = 0 \ or \ 1$$

$$subject \ to \ \sum_{1 \leq i \leq j} x_i \cdot w_i \leq PB. \tag{1}$$

Job Power Profiling. To make an intelligent job allocation, we must precisely model the job power consumption. The IBM Blue Gene series is representative of contiguous systems, which means that only logically contiguous subsets of nodes can be grouped to serve a single job. For instance, in Blue Gene/P systems, the basic unit of job allocation is called midplane, which includes 512 nodes connected via a 3D torus network [22]. Two midplanes are grouped together to form a 1024-node rack. Hence a job can be allocated more nodes than it actually requests.

Calculating job power consumption of a job on a contiguous system is a bit complicated. Because of the existence of the basic allocation unit, some nodes in the group serving a job may stay idle. Therefore, we derive the job power consumption as follows.

$$w_i = P_{work\_nodes} + P_{idle\_nodes} \qquad (2)$$

As shown in this equation, the total power consumption of job j_i is the sum of two parts: that of the working nodes P_{work_nodes} and that of the idle nodes P_{idle_nodes}.

To calculate P_{work_nodes} and P_{idle_nodes}, we take the Blue Gene/P system as a simple example. We get the following formulas.

$$\begin{cases} P_{work\_nodes} = \frac{N_i}{N_i^{alloc}} \cdot \frac{P_i}{1024} \\ P_{idle\_nodes} = \frac{N_i^{alloc} - N_i}{N_i^{alloc}} \cdot \frac{P_{idle}}{1024} \end{cases} \qquad (3)$$

In Eq. 3, P_i is the power consumption of job j_i, which is measured in kW per rack; N_i is the number of nodes j_i requests; and N_i^{alloc} is the number of nodes j_i actually get allocated. Sometimes $N_i \neq N_i^{alloc}$ because there exists a basic allocation unit (512-node midplane). $\frac{P_i}{1024}$ and $\frac{P_{idle}}{1024}$ denote the power consumption in kW/node transformed from kW/rack with a rack consisting of 1,024 computing nodes. P_i and P_{idle} can be obtained by querying the historical data of a job recorded by a power monitor. Many HPC systems have been equipped with particular hardware and software to detect the running information (e.g., LLView for Blue Gene/P; see [8]).

Dynamic Programming. After setting up the gain value and weight, the 0-1 knapsack model can be solved in pseudo-polynomial time by using a dynamic programming method [23]. To avoid redundant computation, when implementing this algorithm we use the tabular approach by defining a 2D table G, where $G[k, w]$ denotes the maximum gain value that can be achieved by scheduling jobs $\{j_i | 1 \leq i \leq k\}$ with no more than the power budget as w, where $1 \leq k \leq J$. $G[k, w]$ has the following recursive feature.

$$G[k, w] = \begin{cases} 0 & k = 0 \ or \ w = 0 \\ G[k-1, w] & w_i \geq w \\ max(G[k-1, w], v_i + G[k-1, w - w_i]) & w_i \leq w \end{cases} \qquad (4)$$

The solution $G[J, PB]$ and its corresponding binary vector X determine the selection of jobs scheduled to run. The computation complexity of Eq. 4 is $O(J \cdot PB)$.

3.4   On-Line Scheduling on Blue Gene/P

We apply the 0-1 knapsack model after the scheduling decision has been made. The detailed scheduling steps are as follows.

Table 1. Experiment configuration

Workload	Intrepid (BG/P) at Argonne National Lab.
No. of nodes	40,960 (40 racks)
No. of jobs	March, 2009: 9709; April, 2009: 10503
	May, 2009: 7925; June, 2009: 8317
	July, 2009: 8241; Aug, 2009: 7592
Price period	On-peak (9am–11pm)
	Off-peak (11pm–9am)
Pricing ratio	On-peak:Off-peak = 1:3, 1:4, 1:5
Job power profile	20 to 33 kW per rack
	30 to 90 kW per rack
	30 to 120 kW per rack
Power budget	50 %, 60 %, 70 %, 80 %, 90 %

Step 1: Use a traditional scheduling method to select a set of jobs denoted as J.

Step 2: Decide whether it is an on-peak period. If so, go to Step 3. If not, set J as the optimal solution, and go to Step 5.

Step 3: Apply the 0-1 knapsack model to the job set J using weight and value functions, and get the optimal combination of jobs.

Step 4: Release allocated nodes of jobs that are not in the optimal set.

Step 5: Start jobs in the optimal set.

4   Evaluation

We evaluate our power-aware scheduling algorithm by using trace-based simulations. In particular, we use the event-driven simulator called Qsim [24], which supports simulation of the BG/P system and its partition-based job scheduling. We extend Qsim to include our power-aware scheduling method. In this section, we describe the experiment configuration and our evaluation metrics. We then present our experimental results by comparing our power-aware scheduling with the default power-agnostic scheduling. Table 1 shows the overall configuration of our experiment that will be described in the next subsection.

4.1   Experiment Configuration

Job Trace. Our experimental study is based on real job traces from workloads collected from two different systems: one workload is from the 40-rack Blue Gene/P system called Intrepid at Argonne. Intrepid is a partitioned torus system, so nodes can be allocated in order to connect them into a job-specific torus network [25]. One major advantage of using real job traces is that experimental results from simulation are more convincing and can reflect the system performance to the greatest extent. For Intrepid, we use a six-month job trace from the machine (40,960 computing nodes) collected by Cobalt, a resource manager developed at Argonne [26]. It contains 52,287 jobs recorded from March 2009 to August 2009. We apply our power-aware scheduling algorithm on a monthly base to see the results for months. By doing so, we are able to examine our algorithm under diverse characteristics of jobs such as different numbers of jobs and various job arriving rate.

Dynamic Electricity Price. In our experiments, we assume the most common type of variable electricity price, namely, on-peak/off-peak pricing. Under this pricing system, electricity costs less during off-peak periods (from 11pm to 9pm) and more when used during on-peak periods (from 9am until 11pm) [4]. Here we are not concerned about the absolute value of electricity price. Instead we care only about the ratio of on-peak pricing to off-peak pricing because one of our goals is to explore how much energy cost can be saved under our smart power-aware scheduling as compared with a default job scheduler without considering power or energy. According to the study listed in [7], the most common ratio of on-peak and off-peak pricing varies from 2.0 to 5.0. Hence we use three different ratios, 1:3, 1:4, and 1:5, in our experiments. In the figures in the following sections, we use "PR" to denote "pricing ratio" for short.

Job Power Profile. Because we lack the power information directly related to the testing workloads, we use the field data listed in [8] to estimate the approximate power consumption of jobs for our workloads. For the Intrepid workload, job power ranges between 20 and 33 kW per rack. We assign each job a random power value within this range using normal distribution, which fits the observation in [8] that most jobs fall into the 22 to 24 kW per rack range. For definiteness and without loss of generality, we apply another two sets of ranges as 30 to 90 kW and 30 to 120 kW per rack. These numbers should not be taken too literally since they are used to represent a higher ratio between high-power and low-power jobs for the newest supercomputers. In the following sections, we use "power" to denote the meaning "power per rack" for short.

Power Budget. We evaluate five power budgets in our experiments as follows. We first run the simulation using the default scheduling policy and monitor the runtime power of the system; we then calculate the average power and set it as the baseline value. Respectively, we set the power budget to 50 %, 60 %, 70 %, 80 %, and 90 % of the baseline value.

4.2 Evaluation Metrics

Our power-aware scheduling has three targets: saving energy cost, impacting system utilization only slightly, and preserving a certain degree of fairness.

Energy Cost Saving. This metric represents the amount of the energy bill that we can reduce by using our power-aware scheduling, as compared with the default scheduling approach without considering power or energy. In detail, the energy cost is calculated by accumulation during runtime. Because the price changes at different time periods, a monitor is responsible for calculating the current energy cost as an extension to Qsim.

System Utilization Rate. This metric represents the ratio of the utilized node-hour compared with the total available node-hours. Usually it is calculated as an average value over a specified period of time.

Fairness. Currently, there is no standard way to measure job fairness. Previous work on fairness of scheduling includes using "fair start time" [27] and measuring resource quality [28,29]. To study the fairness of our power-aware scheduling, we propose a new metric by investigating the temporal relationship between the start times of jobs. Because we adopt a scheduling window when apply the 0-1 knapsack algorithm, Any job within this window can be selected for scheduling. Such scheduling may disrupt the execution order between jobs included in that window. Here we introduce a new metric called "inverse pair." This idea is borrowed from the concept of permutation inverse in discrete mathematics. In combinatorial and discrete mathematics, a pair of element of (p_i, p_j) is called an inversion in a permutation p if $i \geq j$ and $p_i \leq p_j$ [30]. Similarly, we build a sequence of jobs, S, based on their start time using a traditional job scheduling method. S_i denotes the start time of job J_i. Also we build another sequence of jobs, called P, using our power-aware job scheduling method. In the same way P_i denotes the start time of job J_i. In sequence S and P, for a pair of jobs J_i and J_j, if $S_i \leq S_j$ and $P_i \geq P_j$, we call jobs J_i and J_j an "inverse pair." We count the total number of inverse pairs to assess the overall fairness. This metric reflects the extent of disruption to job execution caused by using budget controlling.

4.3   Results

Our experimental results are presented in four different groups. First, we evaluate energy cost saving gained by using our power-aware scheduling policy. Second, we study the impact to system utilization after using our scheduling policy. Third, we study the extent to which scheduling fairness is impacted by our power-aware scheduling policy. We also conduct detailed analysis of how the average power and system utilization change within a day. In the three groups above, we use the power range 20 to 33 kW of real systems and a pricing ratio 1:3 to present detailed analysis. We then conduct a complementary sensitivity study on energy cost savings and system utilization using different combinations of power ranges and pricing ratios.

Energy Cost Savings. Figure 2 presents the energy cost saving of six months on BG/P. In this figure, each group of bars represents one month in our job log. In each group, one single bar represents a power budget value (i.e., "PB-50 %" means power budget is set to 50 % of the baseline value). Obviously, our power-aware scheduling approach can help reduce energy cost significantly for BG/P systems. We notice that a lower power budget can save more energy cost than can a higher power budget. Intuitively, a higher power budget limits the power usage during the on-peak period more than a lower power budget does. The bars within each group appear to have a decreasing trend with higher power budget, with only two exceptions: in June a power budget of 90 % can save a little more than one of 80 %, and similarly in May. The largest energy cost savings happen

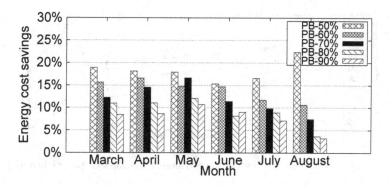

Fig. 2. Energy cost savings with power 20 to 33 kW per rack and pricing ratio 1:3.

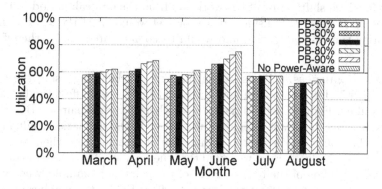

Fig. 3. Utilization with power 20 to 33 kW per rack and pricing ratio 1:3.

in August, as much as 23 % with a power budget of 50 %. For the other five months, using a power budget of 50 % can achieve more than 15 % cost savings. Even when using the highest power budget (PB-90 %), most months can achieve more than 5 % energy cost savings.

Impact on Utilization. Figure 3 shows the system utilization of six months on BG/P. The bars are similar to those in Fig. 2, and in each group there is an additional bar for the default scheduling method without power-aware scheduling. The figure shows that the system utilization is roughly 50 % to 70 %, which is comparable to many real scientific computing data centers and grids [12,31]. Two features are prominent. First we observe that our power-aware scheduling approach only slightly affects the system utilization rate. Unlike energy cost savings, the disparity between high and low power budget is not large, compared with the base value. For example, the most utilization drop is in June when the original utilization rate using default scheduling policy is around 75 %, while using a power budget of 50 % results in a utilization rate of 62 %. Second, whereas five power budgets are used in July, the utilization rates are almost the same, around 55 %. This phenomenon is caused by our power-aware scheduling

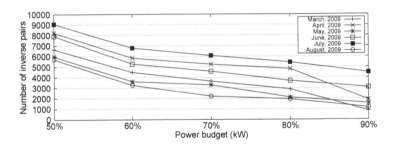

Fig. 4. Fairness of scheduling under power range 20 to 33 kW per rack and pricing ratio 1:3.

approach, which shifts some of the workload from the on-peak period to the off-peak period. We note that using a power budget would affect the utilization rate only during the on-peak period and would be compensated during the off-peak period.

Impact on Fairness. We assess the fairness of scheduling using the metric "inverse pair." Her we evaluate how the power budget will affect the fairness of job scheduling. Figure 4 depicts the total number of inverse pairs on BG/P. The x-axis represents the power budget as introduced in the simulation configuration section. The y-axis denotes the total number of inverse pairs when we impose different power budgets. First we found that the number of inverse pairs occupies only a small portion of the total number of job pairs. For example, when we use a 50 % power budget job log from March 2009 on BG/P, the number of inverse pairs is nearly 7,000, and the total number of job pairs in the job sequence is about 10^7 (9,709 jobs and $C^2_{9709} \approx 10^8$). From Fig. 4 we can clearly see that the number of inverse pairs decreases as the power budget goes up; generally, the trend shows a linear decline as the power budget grows up. Even under the lowest power budget (50 %) the total order of job executions is not affected too much, with the number of inverse pairs up to 8,000. Moreover, for all months, the number of inverse pairs dropped by nearly 50 % when the power budget rose from 50 % to 60 %. We found that the number of inverse pairs is also related to the number of jobs in the job trace. Intuitively, a larger power budget is beneficial to scheduling more jobs and not disrupting their relatively temporal relationship.

Correlation Between Power and Utilization. So far, we have studied the energy cost savings and system utilization rate under our power-aware scheduling approach. Here we present detailed results of the power and instant utilization within a day and how power-aware scheduling affects them. Figure 5(a) shows the average power in a day during March 2009 of a BG/P job trace. The x-axis represents the time in one day measured in minute. The y-axis represents the instant system power consumption recorded at each time point. The black line above minute = 540 splits the time of a day into two periods of which the left part represents the off-peak period, whereas the right parts represents on-peak

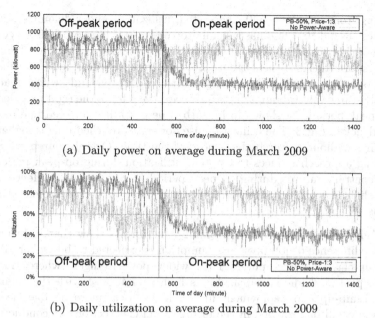

(a) Daily power on average during March 2009

(b) Daily utilization on average during March 2009

Fig. 5. Average power and utilization of BG/P using default no power-aware job scheduling (green line) power 20 to 33 kW per rack and pricing ratio 1:3 (red line).

period. The green line represents a traditional system power pattern using the default scheduling policy. This reflects a common behavior of system power with relatively low power consumption early in the morning and higher during the rest of the day. Remember that in our simulation configuration, we set the on-peak period to be 9am–11pm. Hence, we find that the system power with power-aware scheduling (red line) starts to go down around the time where minute = 540. We can see that the red line is always below around 50 % of the baseline value as half of the power of the green line. And we can also see that during the off-peak period where minute goes from 0 to 540, the system is running at a higher power rate indicated by the red line. The reason is that along with power-aware scheduling during on-peak period some jobs are delayed and get a chance to be run after on-peak period. These jobs can be seen as being "pushed" to off-peak period. This situation leads to more jobs in the waiting queue, causing more power consumption than the original scheduling method does. This fits what we expect, namely, that during the on-peak period less energy should be consumed and during the off-peak period more energy should be consumed.

Figure 5(b) shows the average utilization within a day for job log March 2009. The black dashed line where minute = 540 still acts as the splitting point between off-peak period and on-peak period. Obviously, we can see the curve of the utilization line conforms very closely to that in Fig. 5. This fits the conclusion of multiple studies [6, 12] which have indicated that CPU utilization is a good estimator for power usage. First we examine the left part of the dashed line.

Beginning from minute = 540, the system utilization under default scheduling fluctuates around 80 % and has a small drop off to 70 % later on. This is typical in the real world because systems are always highly utilized in daytime where more jobs are submitted into the system. Also from minute = 540, system utilization under power-aware scheduling policy starts to drop off and swiftly reaches a relatively stable value about 40 % to 50 %. Now we refer to the right part denoting the off-peak period. As shown in Fig. 5(b), the green line and red line resemble the tendency in Fig. 3. The utilization use power-aware scheduling is higher than scheduling without power budget most of the time. Overall, our power-aware scheduling approach reduces the system utilization during on-peak period and on the contrary raise it during off-peak period as compensation. Hence, it has only a slight impact on the whole system utilization, as we presented in the previous section.

Sensitivity Study. Our initial profiling experiments show that in future systems the difference of job power consumption is expected to be higher. Today's leadership-class supercomputers have wider power ranges, where the ratio between peak and idle state can be as high as 1:4. Also with the smart grid project ramp-up and deployment in North America, more flexible electricity price policy will be provided in the future. So in this section, we conduct a sensitivity study to explore the potentiality of how different combinations of power and pricing ratio will affect our evaluation metrics. We use three power ranges, 20 to 30 kW, 30 to 90 kW, and 30 to 120 kW, along with three pricing ratios, 1:3, 1:4, and 1:5, in our experiments.

Figure 6 presents the energy cost savings under different combinations of power ranges and pricing ratios. First we can see that our power-aware scheduling approach also works under these scenarios. For all months, a power budget of 50 % can lead to more than 10 % energy cost savings. The largest energy cost savings can achieve more than 25 %, as shown in Fig. 6(e). We interpret these figures as follows.

First, we compare energy cost savings under variable power ranges and fixed pricing ratios. We observe that a narrower power range is likely to save more energy cost savings than is a wider power range. For example, when the pricing ratio is fixed to 1:4, the effect of a power range of 20 to 33 kW is greater than that of power range 30 to 90 kW and 30 to 120 kW in all months. Also under the same pricing ratio 1:4, a power range 30 to 90 kW results in greater energy cost savings than in almost all the months with a power range of 30 to 120 kW. The reason is that the majority of jobs in the BG/P log are small and thus require nodes less than 2 racks, which can have many more idle nodes. With many small jobs running in the systems, the system power tends to be lower than on systems where job sizes are more uniformly distributed. As a result, imposing a power budget cannot constrain the power of the whole system as much as that under a narrower power range.

Second, we focus on savings under a fixed power range and variable pricing ratio. Obviously, higher pricing ratios produce more energy cost savings in every month. Since some portion of the system power usage is shifted from the on-peak

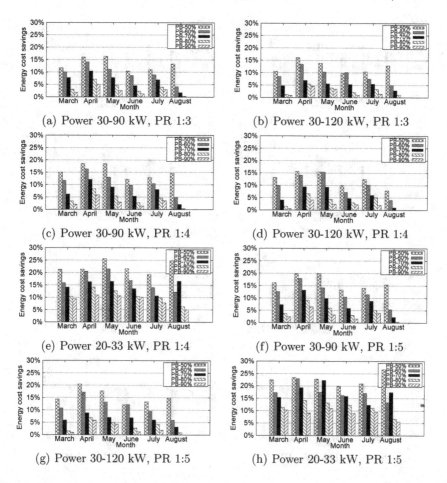

Fig. 6. Energy cost savings under various combinations; "Power" is the power range per rack, and "PR" is the pricing ratio.

period to the off-peak period, higher pricing ratios lead to more difference in the cost of the amount of power transferred. Hence we believe one can saving save energy costs with a personalized electricity pricing policy in the future.

Figure 7 shows the system utilization rates under different combinations of power ranges and pricing ratios. Since the pricing ratio does not influence the utilization, we focus only on variable power ranges. First, similar to Fig. 3, our power-aware job scheduling brings minor impact to system utilization rate. The largest utilization drop is in June in Fig. 7(e), a drop of about 15 %. Second, we observe that system utilization rates under wider power ranger are higher in some months. For example, in Fig. 7(g) when the price is fixed at 1:5, using a power range of 30 to 120 kW gives rise to higher utilization in June than does a power range of 20 to 33 kW. This result reflects the role of our 0-1 knapsack algorithm. Under the same power budget, a wider power range can generate a

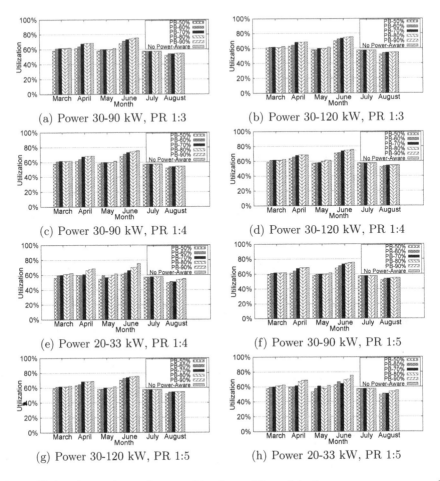

Fig. 7. Utilization under various combinations; "Power" is the power range per rack and "PR" is the pricing ratio.

more optimal solution because of the larger choosing space. But we notice that the effect is not that obvious because in BG/P the system resources released by jobs each time are relatively small compared with the whole system size, thus leaving little space for optimizing the system utilization rate.

4.4   Results Summary

In summary, our trace-based experiments have shown the following.

- Our power-aware scheduling approach can effectively reduce the energy cost by up to 25 %. For HPC centers such as the ALCF, this energy cost savings is translated into over $250,000 saving per year.
- This energy cost savings comes at the expense of a slight impact on system utilization during the on-peak price period. We also observe a modest increase

in system utilization during the off-peak price period. In other words, the overall system utilization does not change much on a daily base.

- While our scheduling window preserves some degree of scheduling fairness, some jobs, especially those having high power consumption, will be delayed; but the delay is limited to a day.
- Based on our sensitivity study, we find that our power-aware job scheduling has a high potential to save energy costs and maintain system utilization.

5 Conclusion and Future Work

In this paper, we have presented a smart power-aware scheduling method to reduce electric bills for HPC systems under the condition of limiting the impact on system utilization and scheduling fairness. The design explores variable electricity prices and distinct job power profiles. Our approach contains three key techniques: a scheduling window, 0-1 knapsack, and on-line scheduling algorithm. Using real workloads from BG/P, we have demonstrated that our power-aware scheduling can effectively save energy costs with acceptable loss to system metrics such as utilization.

This is our first step in investigating power-aware job scheduling to address the energy challenge for HPC. We plan to extend our work in several ways. First, we will explore data analysis technology on historical data in order to examine power profiles for HPC jobs at various production systems; our aim is to enable us to predict job power profiles at their submission. Additionally, we are enhancing our power-aware scheduling with an adaptive self-tuning mechanism; the resulting job scheduler will be able to adjust its decision to external conditions such as electricity price automatically during operation. We also plan to integrate this work with our prior studies on fault-aware scheduling [21,24,32].

Government License

Acknowledgment. This work was supported in part by the U.S. National Science Foundation grants CNS-0834514 and CNS-0720549 and in part by the U.S. Department of Energy, Office of Science, Advanced Scientific Computing Research under contract DE-AC02-06CH1135. We thank Dr. Ioan Raicu for generously providing high-performance servers for our experiments.

References

1. Zhou, Z., Tang, W., Zheng, Z., Lan, Z., Desai, N.: Evaluating performance impacts of delayed failure repairing on large-scale systems. In: 2011 IEEE International Conference on Cluster Computing (CLUSTER), pp. 532–536 (2011)
2. Bergman, K., Borkar, S., Campbell, D., Carlson, W., Dally, W., Denneau, M., Franzon, P., Harrod, W., Hiller, J., Karp, S., Keckler, S., Klein, D., Lucas, R., Richards, M., Scarpelli, A., Scott, S., Snavely, A., Sterling, T., Williams, R.S., Yelick, K., Bergman, K., Borkar, S., Campbell, D., Carlson, W., Dally, W., Denneau, M., Franzon, P., Harrod, W., Hiller, J., Keckler, S., Klein, D., Kogge, P., Williams, R.S., Yelick, K.: Exascale computing study: technology challenges in achieving exascale systems (2008)
3. Patel, C., Sharma, R., Bash, C., Graupner, S.: Energy aware grid: global workload placement based on energy efficiency. In: Proceedings of IMECE (2003)
4. Goiri, I., Le, K., Haque, M., Beauchea, R., Nguyen, T., Guitart, J., Torres, J., Bianchini, R.: Greenslot: scheduling energy consumption in green datacenters. In: 2011 International Conference on High Performance Computing, Networking, Storage and Analysis (SC), pp. 1–11 (2011)
5. Jossen, A., Garche, J., Sauer, D.U.: Operation conditions of batteries in PV applications. Sol. Energy **76**, 759–769 (2004)
6. Fan, X., Weber, W.-D., Barroso, L.A.: Power provisioning for a warehouse-sized computer. In: Proceedings of the 34th annual International Symposium on Computer Architecture, ISCA '07, pp. 13–23. ACM, New York (2007)
7. Qureshi, A., Weber, R., Balakrishnan, H., Guttag, J., Maggs, B.: Cutting the electric bill for internet-scale systems. In: Proceedings of the ACM SIGCOMM 2009 conference on data communication, SIGCOMM '09, pp. 123–134. ACM, New York (2009)
8. Hennecke, M., Frings, W., Homberg, W., Zitz, A., Knobloch, M., Böttiger, H.: Measuring power consumption on IBM Blue Gene/P. Comput. Sci. Res. Dev. **27**(4), 329–336 (2012)
9. Parallel workload archive. http://www.cs.huji.ac.il/labs/parallel/workload/
10. Mämmelä, O., Majanen, M., Basmadjian, R., Meer, H., Giesler, A., Homberg, W.: Energy-aware job scheduler for high-performance computing. Comput. Sci. Res. Dev. **27**(4), 265–275 (2012)
11. Meisner, D., Sadler, C., Barroso, L., Weber, W., Wenisch, T.: Power management of online data-intensive services. In: 2011 38th Annual International Symposium on Computer Architecture (ISCA), pp. 319–330 (2011)
12. Barroso, L., Holzle, U.: The case for energy-proportional computing. Computer **40**(12), 33–37 (2007)
13. Pinheiro, E., Bianchini, R., Carrera, E.V., Heath, T.: Load balancing and unbalancing for power and performance in cluster-based systems. In: Proceedings of the Workshop on Compilers and Operating Systems for Low, Power (COLP'01) (2001)
14. Liu, Y., Zhu, H.: A survey of the research on power management techniques for high-performance systems. Softw. Pract. Exper. **40**, 943–964 (2010)
15. Lee, E., Kulkarni, I., Pompili, D., Parashar, M.: Proactive thermal management in green datacenters. J. Supercomput. **60**(2), 165–195 (2012)
16. Feng, W., Warren, M., Weigle, E.: The bladed beowulf: a cost-effective alternative to traditional beowulfs. In: Proceedings 2002 IEEE International Conference on Cluster Computing, 2002, pp. 245–254 (2002)

17. Hikita, J., Hirano, A., Nakashima, H.: Saving 200 kw and $200 k/year by power-aware job/machine scheduling. In: IEEE International Symposium on Parallel and Distributed Processing, 2008, IPDPS 2008, pp. 1–8 (2008)
18. Etsion, Y., Tsafrir, D.: A short survey of commercial cluster batch schedulers, Technical report. The Hebrew University of Jerusalem, Jerusalem (2005)
19. Feitelson, D., Weil, A.: Utilization and predictability in scheduling the IBM SP2 with backfilling. In: Parallel Processing Symposium, 1998, IPPS/SPDP 1998. In: Proceedings of the 1st Merged International Parallel Processing Symposium and Symposium on Parallel and Distributed Processing 1998, pp. 542–546 (1998)
20. Tsafrir, D., Etsion, Y., Feitelson, D.: Backfilling using system-generated predictions rather than user runtime estimates. IEEE Trans. Parallel Distrib. Syst. **18**(6), 789–803 (2007)
21. Li, Y., Lan, Z., Gujrati, P., Sun, X.-H.: Fault-aware runtime strategies for high-performance computing. IEEE Trans. Parallel Distrib. Syst. **20**(4), 460–473 (2009)
22. IBM Blue Gene team: Overview of the IBM Blue Gene/P project. IBM J. Res. Dev. **52**(1.2), pp. 199–220 (2008)
23. Cormen, T.H., Stein, C., Rivest, R.L., Leiserson, C.E.: Introduction to Algorithms, 2nd edn. McGraw-Hill Higher Education, New York (2001)
24. Tang, W., Lan, Z., Desai, N., Buettner, D.: Fault-aware, utility-based job scheduling on Blue Gene/P systems. In: IEEE International Conference on Cluster Computing and Workshops, 2009, CLUSTER '09, pp. 1–10 (2009)
25. Tang, W., Lan, Z., Desai, N., Buettner, D., Yu, Y.: Reducing fragmentation on torus-connected supercomputers. In: 2011 IEEE International Parallel Distributed Processing Symposium (IPDPS), pp. 828–839 (2011)
26. Cobalt resource manager. http://trac.mcs.anl.gov/projects/cobalt
27. Sabin, G., Kochhar, G., Sadayappan, P.: Job fairness in non-preemptive job scheduling. In: International Conference on Parallel Processing, 2004, ICPP 2004, vol. 1, pp. 186–194 (2004)
28. Sabin, G., Sadayappan, P.: Unfairness metrics for space-sharing parallel job schedulers. In: Feitelson, D.G., Frachtenberg, E., Rudolph, L., Schwiegelshohn, U. (eds.) JSSPP 2005. LNCS, vol. 3834, pp. 238–256. Springer, Heidelberg (2005)
29. Tang, W., Ren, D., Lan, Z., Desai, N.: Adaptive metric-aware job scheduling for production supercomputers. In: 2012 41st International Conference on Parallel Processing Workshops (ICPPW), pp. 107–115 (2012)
30. Pemmaraju, S., Skiena, S.: Computational Discrete Mathematics: Combinatorics and Graph Theory with Mathematica. Cambridge University Press, New York (2003)
31. Rodero, I., Guim, F., Corbalan, J.: Evaluation of coordinated grid scheduling strategies. In: 11th IEEE International Conference on High Performance Computing and Communications, 2009, HPCC '09, pp. 1–10 (2009)
32. Tang, W., Desai, N., Buettner, D., Lan, Z.: Analyzing and adjusting user runtime estimates to improve job scheduling on the Blue Gene/P. In: IEEE International Symposium on Parallel Distributed Processing (IPDPS) 2010, pp. 1–11 (2010)

Heuristics for Resource Matching in Intel's Compute Farm

Ohad Shai[1,2], Edi Shmueli[1], and Dror G. Feitelson[3]($\boxtimes$)

[1] Intel Corporation, MATAM Industrial Park, Haifa, Israel
{ohad.shai,edi.shmueli}@intel.com
[2] Blavatnik School of Computer Science, Tel-Aviv University,
Ramat Aviv, Tel-Aviv, Israel
[3]* School of Computer Science and Engineering,
The Hebrew University, Jerusalem, Israel
feit@cs.huji.ac.il

Abstract. In this paper we investigate the issue of resource matching between jobs and machines in Intel's compute farm. We show that common heuristics such as Best-Fit and Worse-Fit may fail to properly utilize the available resources when applied to either cores or memory in isolation. In an attempt to overcome the problem we propose Mix-Fit, a heuristic which attempts to balance usage between resources. While this indeed usually improves upon the single-resource heuristics, it too fails to be optimal in all cases. As a solution we default to Max-Jobs, a meta-heuristic that employs all the other heuristics as sub-routines, and selects the one which matches the highest number of jobs. Extensive simulations that are based on real workload traces from four different Intel sites demonstrate that Max-Jobs is indeed the most robust heuristic for diverse workloads and system configurations, and provides up to 22 % reduction in the average wait time of jobs.

Keywords: NetBatch · Job scheduling · Resource matching · Simulation · Best-Fit · Worse-Fit · First-Fit

1 Introduction

Intel owns an Internet-scale distributed compute farm that is used for running its massive chip-simulation workloads [3,5, p. 78]. The farm is composed of tens of thousands of servers that are located in multiple data centers that are geographically spread around the globe. It is capable of running hundreds of thousands of simulation jobs and tests simultaneously, and handles a rate of thousands of newly incoming jobs every second.

This huge compute capacity is managed by an in-house developed highly-scalable two-tier resource management and scheduling system called NetBatch. At the lower level NetBatch groups the servers into autonomous clusters that are referred to in NetBatch terminology as Physical Pools. Each such pool contains

N. Desai and W. Cirne (Eds.): JSSPP 2013, LNCS 8429, pp. 116–135, 2014.
DOI: 10.1007/978-3-662-43779-7_7, © Springer-Verlag Berlin Heidelberg 2014

up to thousands of servers and is managed by a single NetBatch entity that is called the Physical Pool Manager or PPM. The role of the PPM is to accept jobs from the upper level, and to schedule them on underlying servers efficiently and with minimal waste.

At the upper level NetBatch deploys a second set of pools that are called Virtual Pools. Just like in the lower level, each virtual pool is managed by a single NetBatch component that is called the Virtual Pool Manager or VPM. The role of the VPMs is to cooperatively accept jobs from the users and distribute them to the different PPMs in order to spread the load across the farm. Together, these two layers, VPMs at the top and PPMs at the bottom, strive to utilize every compute resource across the farm. This paper focuses on the work done at the PPM level.

A basic requirement in NetBatch is the enforcement of fair-share scheduling among the various projects and business units within Intel that share the farm. Fair-share begins at the planning phase where different projects purchase different amounts of servers to be used for their jobs. These purchases eventually reflect their share of the combined resources. Once the shares are calculated, they are propagated to the PPMs where they are physically enforced. (The calculation and propagation mechanisms are beyond the scope of this paper.)

To enforce fair-share the PPM constantly monitors which jobs from which projects are currently running and the amount of resources they use. The PPM then selects from its wait queue the first job from the most eligible project (the project whose ratio of currently used resources to its share of the resources is the smallest) and tries to match a machine to that job. If the matching succeeds, the job is scheduled for execution on that machine. Otherwise, a reservation is made for the job, and the process is repeated while making sure not to violate previously made reservations. Such reservations enable jobs from projects that are lagging behind to obtain the required resources as soon as possible.

Matching machines to jobs is done using any of a set of heuristics. For example, one may sort the list of candidate machines according to some pre-defined criteria — e.g. increasing number of free cores or decreasing amount of free memory — and then traverse the sorted list and select the first machine on which the job fits. This leads to variants of Best-Fit and Worse-Fit schemes. Good sorting criteria reduce fragmentation thus allowing more jobs to be executed, and are critical for the overall utilization of the pool. Alternatively one may opt to reduce overhead and use a First-Fit heuristic.

The sorting criteria are programmable configuration parameters in NetBatch. This allows one to implement various matching heuristics and apply them on different resources to best suit the workload characteristics and needs. NetBatch also allows individual jobs to specify different heuristics, while the pool administrator can set a default policy to be used for all jobs.

In this paper we argue that no heuristic applied to a single resource in isolation can yield optimal performance under all scenarios and cases. To demonstrate our point we use both simple test cases and workload traces that were collected at four large Intel sites. Using the traces, we simulate the PPM behavior when applying the different heuristics to schedule the jobs. We show that depending on the workload different heuristics may be capable of scheduling a higher number of jobs.

In an attempt to overcome the problem we develop "Mix-Fit" — a combined heuristic that tries to balance the use of cores and memory. Intuitively this should reduce fragmentation at the pool. However, while generally better than the previous heuristics, Mix-Fit too fails to yield optimal assignments in some cases.

As an alternative, we propose a meta-heuristic we call "Max-Jobs". Max-Jobs is not tailored towards specific workloads or configurations. Instead, it uses the aforementioned heuristics as sub-routines and chooses, in every scheduling cycle, the one that yields the highest number of matched jobs. This overcomes corner cases that hinder specific heuristics from being optimal in all cases, and conforms well to the NetBatch philosophy of maximizing resource utilization in every step. We demonstrate, through simulation, that Max-Jobs yields lower wait times by up to 22 % for all jobs in average under high loads.

The rest of this paper is organized as follows. Section 2 provides more details on the problem of matching machines to jobs, and explores the performance of commonly used heuristics. Section 3 then describes the Mix-Fit heuristic, followed by the Max-Jobs meta-heuristic in Sect. 4, and simulation results in Sect. 5. Section 6 briefly presents related work, and Sect. 7 concludes the paper.

2   Matching Machines to Jobs

As described above, matching machines to jobs at the PPM is done by choosing the most eligible job from the wait queue, sorting the list of candidate machines according to some pre-defined criterion, traversing the sorted list, and selecting the first machine on which the job fits[1]. This is repeated again and again until either the wait queue or the list of machines are exhausted. At this point the PPM launches the chosen job(s) on the selected machine(s) and waits for the next scheduling cycle.

A job may be multithreaded, but we assume that each job can fit on a single (multicore) machine. In principle NetBatch also supports parallel jobs (called "MPI jobs") that span multiple machines, but in practice their numbers at the present time are small. The only added difficulty in supporting such jobs is the need to allocate multiple machines at once instead of one at a time.

There are many criteria by which the machines can be sorted. In this paper we focus on the number of free cores and amount of free memory, as this suits well the workload in Intel which is characterized by compute-intensive memory-demanding jobs. Though I/O is definitely a factor, and some jobs do perform large file operations, there are some in-house solutions that are beyond the scope of this paper that greatly reduce the I/O burden on the machines.

---

[1] This is done for practical reasons since trying all combinations is time consuming.

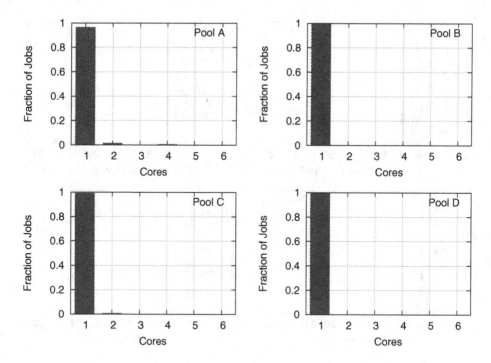

Fig. 1. Jobs' cores requirements: the vast majority of the jobs are serial and require a single CPU core in order to execute.

Figures 1 and 2 show the distribution of the jobs' cores and memory require-ments in four large pools at different locations across the Intel farm[2]. The data comes from traces [1] that were collected at the PPM level during a one-month period, and which contain up to 13 million jobs each. As can be seen in the figures, the vast majority of the jobs are serial (single-thread jobs, requiring a single CPU core in order to execute). Memory requirements are mostly 8 GB and below, but there are jobs that require 16 GB, 32 GB, or even more memory (not shown) in order to execute. These observations are consistent across the pools.

The two ways to sort the machines by available cores or memory are in increasing or decreasing order. Sorting them by *increasing* amount of free cores or memory and selecting the first machine on which the job fits effectively imple-ments the Best-Fit heuristic. Best-Fit is known to result in a better packing of jobs, while maintaining unbalanced cores (or memory) usage across the machines in anticipation for future jobs with high resource requirements. Sorting the machines by *decreasing* amount of free cores or memory implements the Worse-Fit heuristic. Worse-Fit's advantage is in keeping resource usage balanced across machines, which is particularly useful for mostly-homogeneous workloads. For completeness we also mention First-Fit. First-Fit's advantage is in its simplicity,

---

[2] The requirements are specified as part of the job profile at submit time.

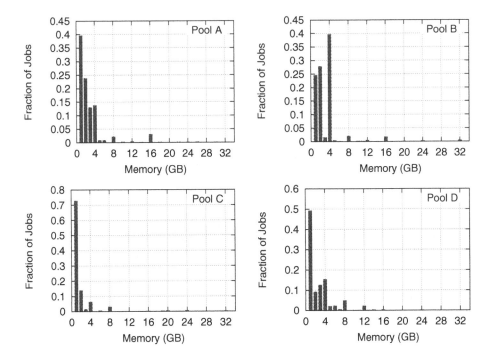

Fig. 2. Jobs' memory requirements: demands are mostly 8 GB and below, but there are jobs that require 16 GB, 32 GB or even more memory in order to execute.

as it does not require the sorting of the machines. Our tests, however, revealed that it performs poorly in our environment, so we do not refer to it further in this paper.

We argue that no single heuristic, when applied to a single resource in isolation, can yield optimal performance under all workload scenarios. To demonstrate our point we begin by providing simple synthetic examples showing how different heuristics match different number of jobs under different workload conditions. We then put theory to the test by running simulations on the aforementioned traces, demonstrating the effectiveness of the different heuristics under different workloads.

2.1 Synthetic Examples of Heuristics Failures

In our examples we consider two machines, A and B, each having four cores and 32 GB of memory. Assume that 8 jobs are queued at the PPM in the following priority order: two jobs of one core and 16 GB of memory, and then 6 jobs of one core and 4 GB of memory. As can be seen in Fig. 3(a), Best-Fit matches the first two jobs with machine A, totally exhausting its memory, and the next four jobs with machine B, thereby exhausting its cores. The end result is two unutilized

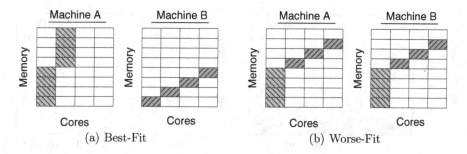

Fig. 3. Scenario for which Worse-Fit (right) is better than Best-Fit (left). Memory is depicted in 4 GB blocks. Shading indicates mapping of a job to a certain core and certain blocks of memory. Note that both cores and memory are mapped exclusively to distinct jobs.

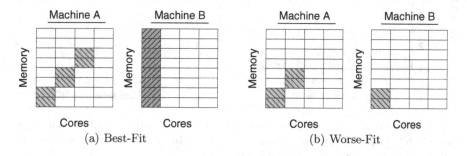

Fig. 4. Scenario for which Best-Fit (left) is better than Worse-Fit (right).

cores on machine A, half the memory unutilized on machine B, and two jobs that remain pending at the PPM. Worse-Fit on the other hand matches the first two jobs on different machines, which leaves enough free space (cores and memory) for all the remaining 6 jobs to be matched. This is illustrated in Fig. 3(b).

Another example is illustrated in Fig. 4. The priority order here is 3 jobs of one core and 8 GB, followed by one job of one core and 32 GB of memory. As can be seen, Worse-Fit spreads the first three jobs on different machines, which doesn't leaves enough memory for the 32 GB job to be matched. Best-Fit on the other hand matches the first three jobs on machines A, which allows the 32 GB to be matched with machine B.

2.2 Observations from the Workloads

Machines currently available on the market typically have multi-core CPUs and large amounts of memory. Therefore, we may expect to see situations similar to the ones described above. In addition, jobs comes with core and memory requirement, and in most cases jobs are allocated one per core. This may waste cycles due to wait states and I/O, but makes things much more predictable.

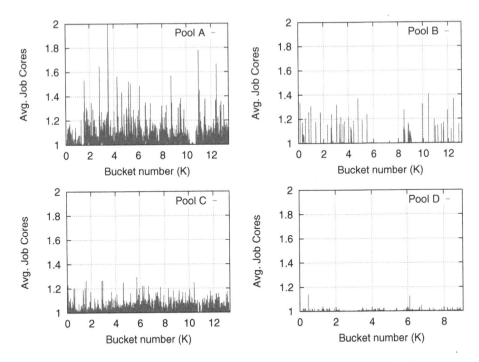

Fig. 5. Bursts in jobs cores requirements: pool A is the burstiest. Pool B's bursts are sparse, while pool C's have only a small amplitude. In pool D there are virtually no bursts of jobs requiring more than one core.

To characterize the use of cores and memory in each of the pools, we used the traces mentioned above, and partitioned them into buckets of 1000 jobs each. This resulted in 13 K buckets for pools A, B, and C, and 10 K buckets for pool D. Such small buckets allow us to observe bursts of activity that deviate from the average.

Figures 5 and 6 show the jobs' average cores and memory requirements in each of the buckets, for each of the four pools, respectively. As can be seen, different pools exhibit different magnitudes of bursts of jobs with high core or memory demands. Pool A is the most bursty in both dimensions; it is the only pool that had a bucket in which the average job core requirement is higher than 2, and multiple buckets in which the average memory requirement is larger than 20 GB.

Pool B exhibits sparse bursts of jobs with high core demands, but intense bursts of high memory requirements. Pool C exhibits continuous moderate core demands, and also relatively steady memory bursts. Finally, pool D has virtually no bursts of jobs requiring more than one core, but it does exhibit bursts of high memory demands, along with periods of particularly low memory requirements.

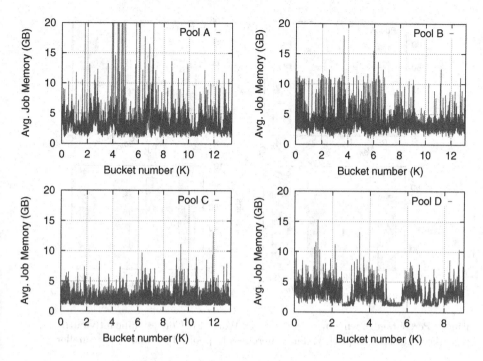

Fig. 6. Bursts in jobs memory requirements: pools A and B are the most bursty; A in particular has bursts that exceed 20 GB on average. Pool C is somewhat steadier, while pool D exhibits periods of particularly low memory demands between the bursts.

2.3   Comparing Heuristics

To demonstrate the effectiveness of the different heuristics under different work-loads we performed the following experiment. We used the buckets described above, assigned all jobs in each bucket a submit time of 0, and gave each heuristic an opportunity to try and match, in simulation, as many jobs as possible from each bucket on a small synthetic pool of empty machines (total of 512 cores); jobs that could not be matched were simply skipped. For each bucket we then counted the number of jobs matched by each heuristic, and gave the winning heuristic(s) (the one(s) who matched the highest number of jobs) a point.

The results are shown in Fig. 7. As can be seen, Worse-Fit-Cores significantly outperforms all other heuristics (collecting the highest percentage of wins) in pool A. It is also the best heuristic in pools B, C, and D, but the differences there are smaller. There is little difference among Best-Fit-Memory, Worse-Fit-Memory, and Best-Fit-Cores, although Worse-Fit-Memory is consistently slightly better than the other two. Notably, for pool D where there is virtually no core fragmentation as indicated in Fig. 5 there seems to be little difference between the performance of the different heuristics.

An important observation is that though Worse-Fit-Cores appears to be the preferred heuristic, it did *not* win in all cases. This is shown by the gap between

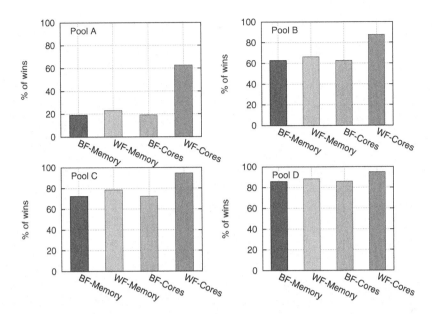

Fig. 7. Percentage of wins by each heuristic: Worse-Fit-Cores significantly outperforms the other heuristics in pool A. The differences in pools B, C, and D are smaller.

the Worse-Fit-Cores bars and the 100 % mark, indicating that in 6–37 % of the experiments other heuristics performed better. These gaps are the motivation for the Mix-Fit heuristic proposed next.

3   Mix-Fit

As demonstrated in the previous section, none of the one-dimensional heuristics is capable of maximizing the number of matched jobs under all workload scenarios. In this section we propose a new heuristic, Mix-Fit, that takes into account both cores and memory in an attempt to overcome the problem.

3.1   Balanced Resource Usage

The basic idea behind Mix-Fit is to try and reach balanced resource utilization across both cores and memory. This is achieved by considering the *configured* ratio of cores to memory on each machine, and matching the job with the machine on which the ratio of *used* cores to memory, together with this job, is closest to the configured ratio.

To see how this is done, envision a grid representing possible resource combinations (as was done in Figs. 3 and 4). Each column represents a CPU core, and each row a block of memory (the sizes of such blocks are not really important as long as they are used consistently; they should correspond to the smallest unit being allocated). Assuming that cores and memory blocks are assigned exclusively to jobs, an allocation may be portrayed as a sequence of shaded squares on this grid, where each job is represented by a sequence of memory-squares in a specific core-column.

The configured ratio is represented by the diagonal of this grid, and the used ratio by the line connecting the top-right point of the grid with the top-right point of the last job. Mix-Fit defines a parameter, α, that denotes the angle between these two lines. Note that the used ratio is calculated after allocating the job being considered, so machines on which this job does not fit are excluded from the discussion. Mix-Fit then matches the job with the machine with the minimal α value. In case of a tie, the first machine with the minimal value is used.

Two important notes. First, The grid is drawn such that memory and cores are normalized to the same scale in each machine separately, thereby creating a square. This prevents the scale from affecting the angle. Second, the angle is based on lines emanating from the top right corner. It is also possible to have a similar definition based on the origin (i.e. the bottom-left corner). Choosing the top-right corner leads to higher sensitivity when the machine is loaded, which facilitates better precision in balancing the resources in such cases.

Let's see an example. Three machines are available, each with 4 cores and 32 GB of memory. Machine A already has one job with 24 GB, Machine B has 2 jobs with 8 GB each, and Machine C has one job with 2 cores and 4 GB memory and another job with 1 core and 4 GB memory. The next job that arrives requires one core and 8 GB of memory. The various α values of all three machines including the newly arrived job are demonstrated in Fig. 8. The machine selected by Mix-Fit in this case is B where $\alpha = 0$.

To demonstrate why this may be expected to improve over the previous heuristics we will use the same examples we used above. Consider Fig. 3, where Worse-Fit yielded the best match. After matching the first 16 GB job with machine A, Mix-Fit will match the second 16 GB job with machine B, as this will lead to a smaller α value as can be seen in Fig. 9(a). It will then match the remaining 4 GB jobs with both machines until all cores get utilized. As can be seen in Fig. 9(b) the end result is identical to Worse-Fit.

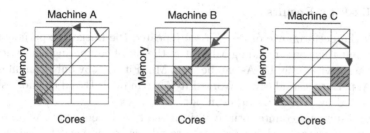

Fig. 8. Example of various α angles calculated by Mix-Fit. The selected machine in this case is B where $\alpha = 0$.

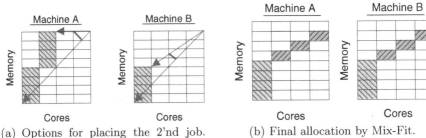

(a) Options for placing the 2'nd job.   (b) Final allocation by Mix-Fit.
The angle on machine B is smaller.

Fig. 9. Mix-Fit behavior for the example in Fig. 4. The end result is identical to Worse-Fit.

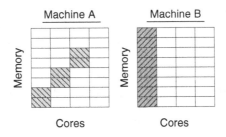

Fig. 10. Jobs allocated by Mix-Fit for the example in Fig. 4. The result is identical to Best-Fit.

Next, lets re-examine Fig. 4 where Best-Fit yielded the best results. In this scenario Mix-Fit will match the first three 8 GB jobs with machine A, and then the 32 GB job with machine B, replicating the behavior of Best-Fit. Note that α would have been the same for the second 8 GB, whether it would have been matched on machine A or B. But as noted above, in such cases the First-Fit heuristics is used as a tie breaker and hence the job is matched with machine A. As can be seen in Fig. 10 the end result is identical to Best-Fit.

3.2 Mix-Fit's Results

To check the performance of Mix-Fit we repeated the buckets experiment from Sect. 2.3, but this time including Mix-Fit in the set of competing heuristics. The results are shown in Fig. 11. As can be seen, Mix-Fit wins by only a small margin in pool A, performs similarly to Worse-Fit-Cores in pools B and D, and is slightly outperformed by Worse-Fit-Cores in pool C.

These results are counterintuitive, since in a two-dimensional environment of cores and memory, where both resources are subject to sudden deflation by bursts of jobs with high demands, a reasonable strategy would be to try and balance the usage between the resources, in order to secure a safety margin against bursts of

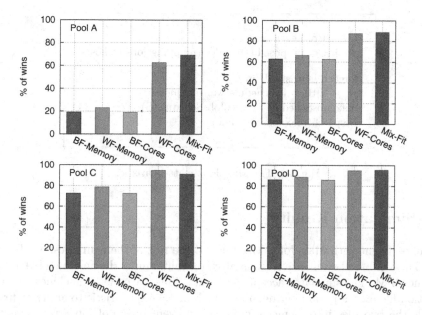

Fig. 11. Percentage of wins by each heuristic: Mix-Fit wins by only a small margin in pool A, performs similarly to Worse-Fit-Cores in pools B and D, and is slightly outperformed by Worse-Fit-Cores in pool C.

any kind. This strategy, however, which Mix-Fit employs, seems to yield some improvement only under the most bursty situations (pool A). This leads us to default to a meta-heuristic, Max-Jobs, which is described next.

4   The Max-Jobs Meta-heuristic

The experiment described above indicates that counterintuitively, Mix-Fit does not yield the best performance in all pools. As an alternative, we therefore suggest the use of the Max-Jobs meta-heuristic.

A meta-heuristic is an algorithm that employs other heuristics as subroutines. In our case, Max-Jobs uses all of the heuristics described before: Best-Fit-Cores, Best-Fit-Memory, Worse-Fit-Cores, Worse-Fit-Memory, and Mix-Fit. At each scheduling cycle, Max-Jobs picks the best schedule produced by any of these heuristics for this cycle. In other words, the meta-algorithm runs all the available heuristics as black-boxes and selects the one with the best result for the currently queued jobs. The target function defining "best" is maximizing the number of jobs assigned to machines in this cycle. Importantly, additional heuristics can be added later and the system will take advantage of them in those cases that they perform the best.

Pseudo-code for the Max-Jobs meta-heuristic is given in Fig. 12.

```
L – list of heuristics
S – list of proposed schedules (mapping jobs to hosts)

foreach heuristic H in L
     S[H] = H.Schedule(waitingQueue)
maxJobsSchedule = MaxJobsSchedule(S)
Dispatch(maxJobsSchedule)
```

Fig. 12. The Max-Jobs meta-heuristic.

5   Simulation Results

To experiment with Max-Jobs, Mix-Fit and the rest of the heuristics, we developed a Java-based event-driven simulator [10] that mimics the matching behavior at the PPM. The simulator accepts as input a jobs trace file, a machines configuration file, and a parameter defining which matching heuristic to apply. It first loads the two files into memory, building an event queue of job arrival events sorted according to the timestamps from the trace (hence preserving the original arrival order and inter-arrival times of the jobs), and a list of machine objects according to the configuration.

The scheduling function is invoked by the scheduler at regular intervals, as is commonly done in many large-scale systems. In our simulations we used an interval of 30 seconds. This allows the scheduling overhead to be amortized over multiple jobs that are handled at once, and may also facilitate better assignments of jobs to machines, because the scheduler can optimize across a large number of jobs rather than treating them individually.

In each scheduling cycle, the scheduler begins by picking the first arrival event from the queue and trying to match a machine to the arriving job using the selected heuristic[3]. If the matching succeeds the job is marked as "running" on the selected machine, and a completion event is scheduled in the event queue at a timestamp corresponding to the current time plus the job's duration from the trace. Otherwise a reservation is made for the job. Specifically the machine with the highest available memory is reserved for the job for its future execution, thus preventing other jobs from being scheduled to that machine during the rest of the scheduling cycle.

For the workload we used the traces that were described in Sect. 2, and which contains 9–13 million jobs each. The parameters we used from the traces are the jobs' arrival times, runtime duration, and the number of cores and amount of memory each job requires in order to execute (see Figs. 1 and 2 for the distributions). For the machines we used a special NetBatch command to query the present machine configurations from each of the pools on which the traces were collected.

---

[3] For simplicity we skipped the fair-share calculation.

Our initial simulations revealed that the original load in the traces is too low for the wait queue in the simulated PPM to accumulate a meaningful number of jobs. This may stem from fact that the load in the month in which the traces were collected was particularly low, or that the configuration has changed by the time we ran the machines query (a few months later). In any case the results were that all heuristics performed the same.

To overcome this problem we increased the load by multiplying the jobs arrival time by a factor, β, that is less than or equal to one. The smaller the value of β, the smaller the inter-arrival times become between the jobs, which increases the rate of incoming jobs and the load on the simulated pool. We ran high-load simulations with β values ranging between 0.58–0.95. In the figures below, we translate the β values into an actual load percentage for each pool.

Metrics that were measured are the average wait time of jobs, the average slowdown, and the average length of the waiting queue during the simulation. The results are shown in Figs. 13, 14, 15, for each metric, respectively. Since the metrics are dependent and the results are similar between the metrics, we will only discuss the differences between the heuristics and pools.

In correlation with the buckets experiment in Fig. 11, Mix-Fit showed marked improvement over the other heuristics in pool A, and was able to reduce the waiting time by 22 %, slowdown by 23 %, and queue length by 22 % under the highest loads simulated.

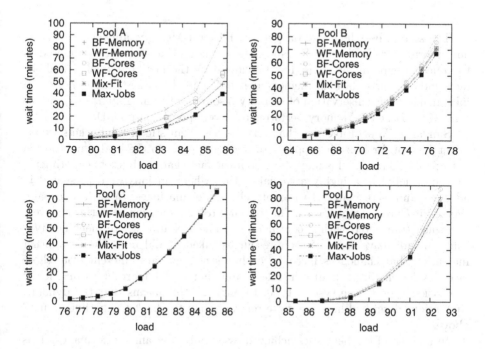

Fig. 13. Average wait time of jobs. System load is expressed as percent of capacity.

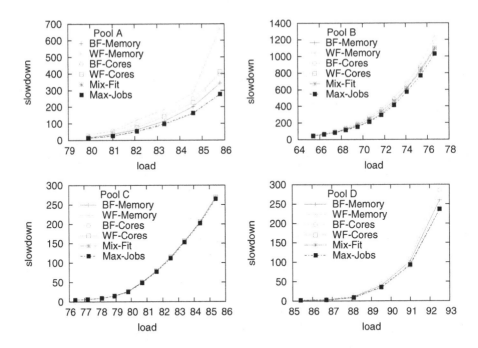

Fig. 14. Average slowdown of jobs.

The second-best heuristic on pool A, Best-Fit-Memory, appears to slightly outperform Mix-Fit in pool B, especially in the mid-range load, as opposed to the buckets experiment. This may be caused by the fact that pool B had the most intense bursts of high memory demands and the largest fraction of 4 GB jobs, making the conservation of memory resources of prime importance. At the same time, Best-Fit-Memory performs relatively poorly on pool D.

Similarly, Worse-Fit-Cores that was the best heuristic in the buckets experiment (except for Mix-Fit) appears to perform poorly in the load simulation in both pools A and B. This may stem from the fact that the buckets experiments were conducted in a highly artificial setting where all jobs were presented in advance, and were matched to empty clusters of machines. In such a scenario Worse-Fit-Cores — which is similar to round-robin allocation — performed well, but when confronted with a continuous on-line scenario, where machines typically already have some of their resources taken, it did not. This is another indication that challenges faced by on-line schedulers are different from those faced by batch (or off-line) schedulers, and that it is important to match the simulation type to the system type. In our case this means that the dynamic simulations described here are more relevant than the bucket experiments used above.

In pool C all the heuristics achieved essentially the same performance. This reflects an unchallenging workload that can be handled by any heuristic.

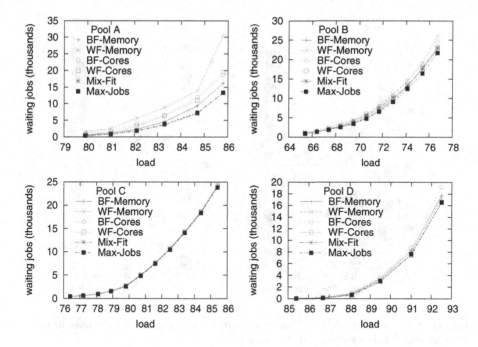

Fig. 15. Average wait-queue length.

Finally, in pool D Mix-Fit had similar results to the second best heuristic, Worse-Fit-Cores. It looks like the non-bursty nature of that pool gives an advantage to balancing heuristics such as Worse-Fit-Cores.

Figure 16 shows the fraction of times each heuristic was selected by Max-Jobs. As can be seen, Mix-Fit is dominant, even more than in the above buckets experiment, but still getting as low as 73 % in pool A. Best-Fit-Memory is markedly better than Worse-Fit-Cores especially in pools A and D.

As expected, the Max-Jobs meta-heuristic is the best scheme all around, and seems to be largely robust against workload and configuration variations. This is due to the fact that it uses the best heuristic at each scheduling cycle. However, its final result (in terms of average performance across all the jobs in the trace) is not necessarily identical to that of the best heuristic that it employs. On one hand, Max-Jobs can be better than each individual heuristic, as happens for example in pool B. This is probably because it can mix them as needed, and use a different heuristic for different situations as they occur. On the other hand, Max-Jobs is sometimes slightly inferior to the best individual heuristic, as seen for example in pool A. This is probably due to situations in which packing jobs very densely leads to reduced performance in a successive scheduling round.

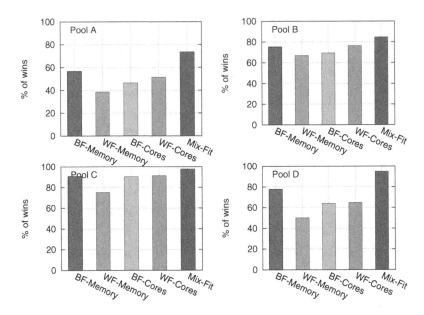

Fig. 16. Selected heuristics by Max-Jobs. Sum is more than 100 % because in many cases several heuristics produced the same result.

6   Related Work

There are very few externally available publications that relate to NetBatch. Zhang et al. investigated the use of dynamic rescheduling of NetBatch jobs between pools which improves utilization at the farm level [17]. Our work in effect complements theirs by focusing on utilization improvements within the individual pools.

The question of assigning machines to jobs has received some attention in the literature. Xiao et al. studied a problem similar to ours and also concluded that one-dimensional strategies yields sub-optimal performance [16]. In their work, however, cores are considered shared resources, and thus the investigation focused on the interference between the jobs. Amir et al. proposed a load balancing scheme where the targets for process migration are selected so as to avoid saturation of any single resource [2]. This is similar to avoiding high α values in our terminology.

The idea of symbiotic scheduling is also related to our work. Symbiotic scheduling attempts to find sets of jobs that complement each other and together use the system resources effectively. This was initiated in the context of hyper-threading (or simultaneous multithreading) processors [6,13], and extended also to the domain of clusters [15].

Meta-schedulers like the Max-Jobs approach have also been used before. For example, Talby used such a meta-scheduler to select among different versions of backfilling in scheduling large-scale parallel machines [14]. However, this was done by simulating recent work in the background and then switching to the version that looks best. Such an approach depends on an assumption of locality, meaning that the future workload will also benefit from this version. In our work we actually run all the contending variants on the jobs in the queue, and select the one that indeed achieves more assignments.

Another meta-scheduler example is the portfolio scheduler [4] that was developed in parallel to our work. The portfolio scheduler is a general-purpose mechanism that applies to scientific computing with various target functions for scheduling. Max-Jobs on the contrary, applies to batch systems and its target function is specified as maximizing the total number of running jobs.

It should be noted that due to the assumption that cores and memory are allocated exclusively to jobs, our problem is not directly related to the well-known 2D bin-packing problem. In particular, it is not allowed to pack multiple jobs with limited memory requirements onto the same core [8]. It does, however, correspond the problem of allocating virtual machines to physical servers which has gained much attention in resent years. This has been called the *vector bin-packing problem*, since the allocation can be depicted as the vector-sum of vectors representing the resource requirements of individual virtual machines [9]. This directly corresponds to our depiction of rectangles that connect at their corners in Figs. 3, 4, etc.

The ideas suggested for vector bin-packing are all very similar to our Mix-Fit algorithm. For example, they are also based on normalizing the resources and creating a square (or multi-dimensional cube, if there are more resources than 2). The available resources are then represented by a diagonal vector, the consumption by other vectors, and the basic idea is to try to make these vectors close to each other. However, the details may differ.

Mishra and Sahoo [8] describe the SandPiper algorithms used in Xen, and the VectorDot algorithm [12]. They show that both suffer from failures similar to the ones we demonstrated in Sect. 2. For example, the VectorDot algorithm uses the dot product of the consumed resources vector and the request vector to identify requests that are orthogonal to the current usage, and thus may be expected to complement it. However, this is subject to artifacts because the lengths of the vectors also affect the result. They then suggest a rather complex approach for identifying complementary vectors based on a discretization of the space called the "planar resource hexagon". They did not, however, evaluate its performance compared to existing heuristics.

Panigrahy et al. study a wide range of First-Fit-Decreasing-based algorithms [9]. The idea is to combine the requirements for different resources in some way into a single number, and then pack in a decreasing order. However, this approach loses the important geometrical structure of the problem. They therefore also consider heuristics based on the dot product or the maximal required resource. The evaluations are based on presumed synthetic distributions. Compared with these previous works, our approach of using just the angle between two vectors is among the simplest. Basing the comparison at the top-right corner for improved discrimination seems to be novel. It would be interesting to evaluate the effect of these details, but our results so far indicate that they may not have much impact for real workloads.

Lee et al. investigated the problem of virtual machines allocation taking into consideration the consolidation of virtual machines onto the same physical platform, and the possible resulting resource contention [7]. In principle such considerations are also applicable to our work. However, we note that the configuration of NetBatch pools is such that I/O and bandwidth are seldom a bottleneck.

Finally, it is important to remember that since the PPM considers the jobs one at a time there is a limit on the optimizations that can be applied. Looking further into the queue and considering more than one job may yield significant improvements [11].

7   Conclusions

Matching jobs with resources is an NP-hard problem. The common practice is therefore to rely on heuristics to do the matching. In this paper we investigated the problem of resource matching in Intel's compute farm, and showed that none of the well-known heuristics such as Best-Fit or Worse-Fit yield optimal performance in all workload scenarios and cases. This stems from two reasons. First, these heuristics focus on a single resource, either cores or memory, whereas in reality the contention may apply to the other resource. To address this problem we implemented a specialized heuristic, Mix-Fit, that takes both resources into account and tries to create an assignment that leads to a balanced use of the resources. In principle this can be extended to more than two resources. While this too failed to be optimal in all cases, it did show some improvement under certain conditions.

Second, the nature of dynamically changing demands prevent a specific use-case-tailored algorithm to be optimal for all cases. For that, we proposed a meta-heuristic called Max-Jobs, that is not tailored to a specific workload or scenario. Rather, it uses the other heuristics as black-boxes, and chooses, in every scheduling cycle, the one that yields the maximal number of matched jobs. We have demonstrated through simulations that max-jobs is highly competitive with all the individual heuristics, and as such is robust against changes in workload or configuration.

References

1. The parallel workloads archive (2013). http://www.cs.huji.ac.il/labs/parallel/workload
2. Amir, Y., Awerbuch, B., Barak, A., Borgstrom, R.S., Keren, A.: An opportunity cost approach for job assignment in a scalable computing cluster. IEEE Trans. Parallel Distrib. Syst. 11(7), 760–768 (2000)
3. Bentley, B.: Validating the Intel® Pentium® 4 microprocessor. In: Proceedings of the 38th Design Automation Conference, pp. 244–248, June 2001

4. Deng, K., Verboon, R., Ren, K., Iosup, A.: A periodic portfolio scheduler for scientic computing in the data center. In: 17th Workshop on Job Scheduling Strategies for Parallel Processing (JSSPP 2013), Boston, USA, May 2013
5. Evans, N.D.: Business Innovation and Disruptive Technology: Harnessing the Power of Breakthrough Technology for Competitive Advantage. Financial Times Prentice Hall, Upper Saddle River (2003)
6. Eyerman, S., Eeckhout, L.: Probabilistic job symbiosis modeling for SMT processor scheduling. In: 15th Intel Conference Architecture Support for Programming Language & Operating Systems, pp. 91–102, March 2010
7. Lee, S., Panigrahy, R., Prabhakaran, V., Ramasubramanian, V., Talwar, K., Uyeda, L., Wieder, U.: Validating heuristics for virtual machines consolidation. Technical report MSR-TR-2011-9, Microsoft Research, January 2011
8. Mishra, M., Sahoo, A.: On theory of VM placement: anomalies in existing methodologies and their mitigation using a novel vector based approach. In: IEEE Intel Conference Cloud, Computing, pp. 275–282 (2011)
9. Panigrahy, R., Talwar, K., Uyeda, L., Wieder, U.: Heuristics for vector bin packing. Technical report, Microsoft Research (2011)
10. Shai, O.: Batch simulator (simba). Open source project hosted (2012). http://code.google.com/p/batch-simulator
11. Shmueli, E., Feitelson, D.G.: Backfilling with lookahead to optimize the packing of parallel jobs. J. Parallel Distrib. Comput. 65, 1090–1107 (2005)
12. Singh, A., Korupolu, M., Mohapatra, D., Server-storage virtualization: integration and load balancing in data centers. In: SC 2008: High Performance Computing, Networking, Storage and Analysis, pp. 1–12 (2008)
13. Snavely, A., Tullsen, D.M.: Symbiotic jobscheduling for a simultaneous multithreading processor. In: 9th Intel Conference Architecture Support for Programming Language & Operating Systems, pp. 234–244, November 2000
14. Talby, D., Feitelson, D.G.: Improving and stabilizing parallel computer performance using adaptive backfilling. In: 19th Intel Parallel & Distributed Processing Symposium, April 2005
15. Weinberg, J., Snavely, A.: Symbiotic space-sharing on SDSC's dataStar system. In: Frachtenberg, E., Schwiegelshohn, U. (eds.) JSSPP 2006. LNCS, vol. 4376, pp. 192–209. Springer, Heidelberg (2007)
16. Xiao, L., Chen, S., Zhang, X.: Dynamic cluster resource allocations for jobs with known and unknown memory demands. IEEE Trans. Parallel Distrib. Syst. 13(3), 223–240 (2002)
17. Zhang, Z., Phan, L.T.X., Tan, G., Jain, S., Duong, H., Loo, B.T., Lee, I.: On the feasibility of dynamic rescheduling on the intel distributed computing platform. In: Proceedings 11th Intel Middleware Conference Industrial track, pp. 4–10. ACM, New York (2010)

On Task Assignment in Data Intensive Scalable Computing

Giovanni Agosta, Gerardo Pelosi[✉], and Ettore Speziale

Dipartimento di Elettronica, Informazione e Bioingegneria – DEIB,
Politecnico di Milano, Piazza Leonardo da Vinci, 32, 20133 Milan, Italy
agosta@acm.org, {gerardo.pelosi,ettore.speziale}@polimi.it

Abstract. MapReduce and other Data-Intensive Scalable Computing paradigms have emerged as the most popular solution for processing massive data sets, a crucial task in surviving the "Data Deluge". Recent works have shown that maintaining data locality is paramount to achieve high performance in such paradigms. To this end, suitable task assignment algorithms are needed. Current solutions use round-robin task assignment policies, which was shown to yield suboptimal results. In this paper, we propose and evaluate new algorithms for task assignment on a model of the Hadoop framework, comparing them with state-of-the-art solutions proposed in theoretical works as well as with the current Hadoop polices.

1   Introduction

The data-intensive computing paradigm has recently received significant attention in both research and industrial ICT communities due to the exponential increase of data available for analytical processing–the so-called "Data Deluge" [8]. The cloud computing scenario represents the most important arena where the potential impact and the effectiveness of data-intensive computing are most visible. The Cloud is an abstraction for the complex infrastructure underlying the Internet and refers to both the applications delivered as services over the network and the hardware and software resources that provide those services. As a key concept, the cloud computing paradigm shifts data storage and computing power away from the user endpoints, across the network, and into large clusters of machines hosted by cloud providers (e.g., Amazon, Google). The research challenges aimed at exploiting the full potential of data-intensive computing lie in designing clusters and software frameworks to improve performance of massive simultaneous computations, energy efficiency, and reliability of the provided services. In this regard, *MapReduce* is the leading software framework, composed of both a programming model and an associated run-time system, introduced by Google in 2004 to support distributed computing on large data sets, through splitting the workload over large clusters of commodity PCs [5,6]. A critical issue to achieve good performance on large scale *MapReduce* systems lies in ensuring that as many data accesses as possible are executed locally. To this

N. Desai and W. Cirne (Eds.): JSSPP 2013, LNCS 8429, pp. 136–155, 2014.
DOI: 10.1007/978-3-662-43779-7_8, © Springer-Verlag Berlin Heidelberg 2014

end, a data processing job is parallelized in a set of tasks, which are assigned to servers which will execute them. However, purely locality-based scheduling may lead to long latencies, since a specific computation may access data stored on busy servers. Thus, locality-aware, latency minimizing scheduling algorithms have been designed [7] to reduce latency while still exploiting locality.

We present an algorithm for task assignment on a cluster of servers that balances latency and resource usage, while also taking into account the workload running on the target cluster. The proposed algorithm is able to achieve an efficient tradeoff between latency and resource usage through employing a novel heuristic technique. A simulation-based analysis of the performance of the proposed algorithm against the state-of-the-art solutions is presented, showing that it is able to obtain lower latencies than the standard locality aware round-robin strategy [1], as well as lower resource consumption than the flow-based algorithm reported in [7] together with a better computational complexity. Moreover, we show that our algorithm and the flow-based one are Pareto-optimal with respect to latency and resource consumption, while the round-robin is not. On the other hand, the present work does not deal with fault tolerance in MapReduce systems. While this is also a critical issue in achieving performances, it is a different issue from load balancing, which is best covered with specialized approaches that act during the task execution rather than at task assignment. We also do not deal with job scheduling, and therefore with fair-share scheduling among users, as this goal is better achieved at the level of job scheduling.

The remainder of the paper is organized as follows. Section 2 reports a brief summary of MapReduce systems. Section 3 describes the proposed task assignment algorithm and its properties. Section 4 presents the evaluation of the algorithm, in comparison with existing practices and theoretical works. Section 5 provides an overview of closely related works, and Sect. 6 draws some conclusions and highlights future directions.

2   Background

A *MapReduce* system is a framework for distributed computation over large data sets that implements both the MapReduce programming model and an associated run-time system. It mimics the functional programming constructs *map* and *reduce* and enables the programmer to abstract from common distributed programming issues such as: load balancing, network performances and fault-tolerance. In spite of its simplicity, the MapReduce programming model turns out to effectively fit many problems encountered in the practice of processing large data sets although a preliminary decomposition of the problem into multiple MapReduce jobs is often needed [3,9]. Typical applications are Web indexing, report generation, click-log file analysis, financial analysis, data mining, machine learning, bioinformatics and scientific simulations [5,6]. The programming model is based on the iteration over data-independent inputs where the required operations are: (i) computation of key/value pairs from each piece of input (*map* phase); (ii) grouping of all intermediate values by the key value; (iii) reduction of each data group to a few computed values (*reduce* phase). Word counting is a toy example that considers a set of text documents as input and a list of the occurrences of each word as output, where the key/value pair is given by "word"/"counting" instances. Actual implementations of both proprietary [5,6] and open-source [1] instances of a *MapReduce* system employ dedicated clusters of commodity machines. Each cluster is managed by a *master* server that is in charge of keeping track of all jobs while they are queued and processed in the distributed system. A *job-tracker* running on the master server schedules the received jobs and assigns their tasks on target *slave* servers. Each slave server runs a *task-tracker* that schedules the corresponding tasks, on a first-come/first-served strategy, consistently with the local computational resources and operating system policies. Due to the simplicity of the MapReduce programming model, a user will seldom submit a single job, since, the composition of more jobs in complex workloads (or applications) allows to take better advantage of the system. A MapReduce application is, in general, a Directed Acyclic Graph (DAG) where the nodes represent jobs and the arcs represent data dependences [3]. Therefore a job can only be executed after all of its predecessors have been completed.

Canonical solutions to the scheduling of a DAG solve a constrained optimization problem where the figure of merit is the expected latency of every job and the constraints are represented by the available resources. A variant of this setting is to employ the minimization of resources as a figure of merit, and the maximum latency allowed for each job as a constraint. However, these strategies cannot be applied in the job-tracker, because they need a precise knowledge of the foreseen latency of each job as well as the available resources. The latency of a MapReduce job is not trivial to predict. This is due to both the heterogeneity of applications submitted by different users, and to the presence of straggled tasks and execution failures, which can change unpredictably the actual latency of the executed job [10]. In addition, the submission rate of the jobs in a Data Intensive Scalable Computing (DISC) cluster is quite low — on average, one job per 2–3 min [4,10] — and thus the time to fill a queue of jobs to schedule is high. Given the aforementioned considerations, the scheduling strategy for the job-tracker of a MapReduce system should take into account the cluster workload variation over time. Therefore, *online* scheduling algorithms represent the prime choice. Indeed, proprietary and open-source MapReduce systems adopt online scheduling strategies. Apache Hadoop [2] is an open-source Java implementation of *MapReduce*, originally designed to implement parallel processing in local networks, whose job-tracker employs a round-robin strategy (over the available resources) to assign the tasks in each job over the slave servers. A more accurate task assignment algorithm is proposed in [7], where the authors describe a flow-based algorithm aimed at minimizing the completion time of the considered job and show how such solution is near-optimal within an additive constant from the optimum solution obtained through the fully combinatorial exploration of task assignments. We extend the abstract system model presented in [7], to effectively obtain a trade-off between job latency and throughput. Moreover, through taking into account a pre-existing workload, we better represent the challenges of an on-line task assignment.

3   A Locality Aware and Bounded Latency Approach

In this section, we introduce the main contribution of this work, a *Locality Aware Bounded Latency* (LABL) task assignment algorithm. We will now provide some preliminary concepts and definitions, followed by a description of the algorithm. We describe the formal properties of the LABL task assignment algorithm, and show that its running time complexity is linear w.r.t. the size of the input job.

3.1   Preliminaries

Definition 1. *A* job *is a set of* tasks, $T = \{t_1, \ldots, t_m\}$. *The tasks are mutually independent and do not have any control or data dependencies among them. Thus, the job can be fully parallelized.*

In a *MapReduce* implementation, the tasks are partitioned between *map* and *reduce* operations. The *reduce* tasks must be scheduled after the *map* tasks have completed [1]. Without loss of generality, it is safe to model jobs as composed only of *reduce* tasks or only of *map* tasks. A job composed of both types of tasks is split in two homogeneous jobs for the purpose of the model, with the provision that the *reduce* job is scheduled only after the corresponding *map* job has completed. Note also that, in practice, the distribution of latencies of *reduce* tasks is remarkably similar to that of *map* tasks [10], so it is not necessary to keep track of *map* and *reduce* jobs separately.

Definition 2. *A* cluster *is a set of homogeneous* servers, $S = \{s_1, \ldots, s_n\}$, *each of which is assumed to be able to execute a given task with the same execution time, provided that a copy of the corresponding data is locally accessible.*

The locality of the data processed as the input of each task is crucial for the performance of the whole system. Indeed, the overall performance in terms of both job latency and total system workload largely depends on the initial data placement on the cluster.

Definition 3. *Given a job T and a cluster S, a* data placement function ρ *specifies the subset of servers where the execution of a task t can be completed through accessing a local copy of the necessary data.*

$$\rho : T \mapsto 2^S \text{ and } \forall t \in T, \rho(t) \subseteq S$$

The number of data copies available for a given task $t \in T$ is denoted as $|\rho(t)|$. A task t is denoted as local *to a server s if $s \in \rho(t)$, and as* remote *otherwise.*

As previously mentioned, the considered abstract model assumes a set of homogeneous tasks and a set of homogeneous servers, in such a way that all the tasks which data is locally available run in the same amount of time (w_{loc}) and all tasks running on servers where remote data accesses must be employed also exhibit the same execution time (w_{rem}). The execution time experienced by the latter type of tasks depends on the total number of remote data accesses observed in the system. However, the additional overhead (with respect to the execution time of a task accessing data in place) does not incur in large variations when the network traffic of the system is in a steady state [7]. Therefore, the usual conservative assumption about the execution time experienced by tasks accessing remote data (fitting most of the practical environments) considers these execution times constant (over the entire set of tasks). In particular, the execution times are three times higher than the ones of tasks accessing data in place [7,11].

Definition 4. *Given a job T and a cluster S, an* assignment *corresponds to the execution of a number of tasks $\{t_1, \ldots, \} \subseteq T$ on a single server $s \in S$, and is denoted as a pair $(s, \{t_1, \ldots, \})$. A Task Assignment, $\mathcal{A}$, is a collection of pairs (s', T') with $s' \in S$, $T' \subseteq T$, such that every task in T and every server in S is present in one and only one assignment.*

$$\mathcal{A} = \begin{cases} (s', T') : s' \in S, T' \subseteq T \\ \forall s'' \in S, T'' \subseteq T \; \nexists (s'', T'') : s'' = s' \vee T'' = T' \end{cases}$$

The assignment of tasks to servers dynamically influences the subsequent assignment choices, due to the potential change of both network traffic and workload level of the cluster. The *job-tracker*, running on the *master* server, is the system actor in charge of orchestrating the workload distribution thus, it can dynamically evaluate the *load* of each server. Assuming w_{loc} and w_{rem} as the unitary task execution times for processing local and remote data, respectively, the evaluation of any server load is abstracted through the definition of the following function. We call the time w_{loc} a *unit of work*.

Definition 5. *Let T be a job, S be a cluster, and $\mathcal{A}$ a given task assignment. The* load *of any server $s \in S$ is evaluated through a function, ϕ, which maps s to the numerical value of its current workload (measured in units of work). The workload of s in assignment $\mathcal{A}$ includes the set of tasks $\widehat{T} \subseteq T$, such that $(s, \widehat{T}) \in \mathcal{A}$. Then,*

$$\phi(s) = \phi_s + w_{loc}|\widehat{T}_{loc}| + w_{rem}|\widehat{T}_{rem}|$$

where $\widehat{T}_{loc} = \{t \in \widehat{T} : s \in \rho(t)\}$ and $\widehat{T}_{rem} = \{t \in \widehat{T} : s \notin \rho(t)\}$ denote the sets of task that access data to be processed locally or remotely, respectively, while ϕ_s is a constant factor that takes into account the load due to the tasks that are already running on s before the assignment $(s, \widehat{T})$ is put into effect.

Note that, without loss of generality, we consider that at least one server s_0 has an initial workload $\phi_{s_0} = 0$, i.e., there is at least one free server. To understand the rationale of this choice, consider a load ϕ for a given cluster S, leading to an assignment $\mathcal{A}$. Now, consider a second load ϕ' such that $\forall s \in S, \phi'_s = \phi_s + 1$. The same assignment is generated under this second workload, except that the starting time of each task is increased by one unit of time. Thus, to provide a uniform scale for latency measurements, we normalize ϕ so that the condition $\exists s_0 \in S \mid \phi_{s_0} = 0$ holds.

3.2 Optimization Goals

Given a job T and a cluster S, the proposed task assignment strategy aims at achieving a tradeoff between the *job latency* and the total *resource accounting* of the target cluster. The figures of merit used to evaluate the effectiveness of a task assignment algorithm `alg` and the resulting Task Assignment $\mathcal{A}$ are:

(i) The *resource accounting* is defined as the total number $C_{\mathtt{alg}}(T)$ of units of work consumed to execute the job:

$$C_{\mathtt{alg}}(T) = \sum_{s \in S} (\phi(s) - \phi_s)$$

(ii) The *latency* $l_{\mathtt{alg}}(T)$ is defined as the maximum completion time for a task of the job, normalized to the minimum starting time for a task:

$$l_{\mathtt{alg}}(T) = \max_{s \in S} \phi(s)$$

(iii) The *throughput* is defined as the ratio $R_{\mathtt{alg}}(T)$ between the number of tasks in the job and its resource accounting:

$$R_{\mathtt{alg}}(T) = \frac{|T|}{C_{\mathtt{alg}}(T)}$$

3.3 Lower Bounds for the Expected Job Latency

We start from the insight that it is possible to drive the online task assignment procedure taking as a reference a lower bound on the job latency. Such a reference allows the assignment procedure to start with a predetermined minimum job latency limit, discarding unfeasible scenarios a-priori and taking into account remote assignments that would not be considered under lower latency limits. Given a job T and a idle cluster S (i.e., $\forall s \in S, \phi_s = 0$), if each task can access the data to be processed on every server locally (i.e., $\forall t \in T, \rho(t) = S$), then a trivial lower bound for the job latency is given by $\lceil w_{\mathrm{loc}}|T|/|S| \rceil$. Weakening these assumptions through removing either the hypothesis that each server is initially idle or the hypothesis of a uniform placement of data for each task, leads to solve two simpler problems prior to apply any task assignment operation. These problems are more formally stated as follows.

Problem 1. Let S be a cluster with initial workload defined as $\phi(s) = \phi_s, \forall s \in S$, and T be a set of tasks that can locally access the data to be processed on any server S: $\forall t \in T \; \rho(t) = S$.

Considering the execution cost of each task as w_{loc} (i.e., ignoring the impact of the data placement), a lower bound for the job latency is computed a-priori as:

$$l^* = \left\lceil \frac{w_{\mathrm{loc}}|T|}{|S|} + \frac{1}{|S|} \sum_{s \in S} \phi(s) \right\rceil$$

The straightforward solution of Problem 1 follows from considering each task as a local one since the data is assumed to be uniformly replicated on each server.

Problem 2. Let S be a cluster with initial workload defined as $\phi(s) = \phi_s$, $\forall s \in S$, and T be a set of tasks whose data is replicated on servers according to a data placement function $\rho : T \mapsto 2^S$. Assuming a limit l for the expected job latency, the set S can be partitioned as $S = S_{\mathrm{inf}}[l] \cup S_{\mathrm{sup}}[l] \cup S_{\mathrm{busy}}[l]$, where $S_{\mathrm{sup}}[l] = \{s \in S | l - \phi_s \geq w_{\mathrm{rem}}\}$ is the set of servers that can only execute local tasks within the latency limit l, $S_{\mathrm{busy}}[l] = \{s \in S | l - \phi_s \leq 0\}$ is the set of servers that are busy with workload from previous jobs. Finally, the set of servers that cannot execute remote tasks within the latency limit l is $S_{\mathrm{inf}}[l] = S \backslash (S_{\mathrm{inf}}[l] \cup S_{\mathrm{busy}}[l])$. The set of tasks T can also be partitioned as $T = T_{\mathrm{loc}}[l] \cup T_{\mathrm{rem}}[l]$, where $T_{\mathrm{rem}}[l] = \{t \in T | \rho(t) \subseteq S_{\mathrm{busy}}[l]\}$ is the set of tasks that can only be executed remotely within l and $T_{\mathrm{loc}}[l] = T \backslash T_{\mathrm{rem}}[l]$ is the set of tasks that can be run within l on servers with local access to data.

Considering the execution time of any task in T_{loc} as w_{loc} and the execution time of any task in T_{rem} as w_{rem} ($> w_{\mathrm{loc}}$), a lower bound for the expected job latency is derived as:

$$l^{**} = \min_{l \geq 0} \left\{ \begin{array}{l} \displaystyle\sum_{s \in S_{\mathrm{sup}}} \left\lfloor \frac{l - \phi_s}{w_{\mathrm{rem}}} \right\rfloor \geq |T_{\mathrm{rem}}[l]| \\[2ex] \displaystyle\sum_{s \in S_{\mathrm{sup}} \cup S_{\mathrm{inf}}} (l - \phi_s) \geq a[l] \end{array} \right.$$

where $a[l]$ is the cost of the execution of the given job following an "ideal" assignment of both local and remote tasks within the latency limit l (in this way, the data placement function is employed only for partitioning the job in the local $T_{\mathrm{loc}}[l]$ and remote $T_{\mathrm{rem}}[l]$ task sets but not to solve assignment conflicts, if any):

$$a[l] = w_{\mathrm{rem}}|T_{\mathrm{rem}}[l]| + w_{\mathrm{loc}}|T_{\mathrm{loc}}[l]|$$

The first inequality states that the servers in S_{sup} can provide, as a whole, enough units of work to manage the execution of all remote tasks within the latency limit of l, while the second inequality constraints the available number of units of work on the entire cluster to be greater than the resource allocation needed to schedule each local task locally and each remote task remotely assuming no resource conflict. Therefore, the minimum among the aforementioned latency limits gives a lower bound l^{**} which guarantee a more accurate estimate with respect to the previous bound l^*, thus allowing to initialize our on-line assignment algorithm with a threshold that guarantee a faster convergence.

3.4   Task Assignment Algorithm

The LABL Task Assignment algorithm, reported in Fig. 1, takes as input a job T, a cluster S and a lower bound l for the expected job latency that will be employed to drive the assignments computed as output. The initial value of the job latency limit l is equal to the lower bound l^{**}, computed as shown in

Algorithm: TASKASSIGNMENT

Input: $S = \{s_1, \ldots, s_m\}$, set of servers
$T = \{t_1, \ldots, t_n\}$, set of tasks
l, initial server load limit;

Output: $A = \{(s, \widehat{T}) : s \in S, \widehat{T} \in \wp(T);$
$\forall (s', \widehat{T}'), (s'', \widehat{T}''), s' \neq s'' \wedge \widehat{T}' \cap \widehat{T}'' = \emptyset\}$,
set of assignments;

// Place tasks on servers through trading off the job latency and data movement

```
1   A ← ∅;
2   while T ≠ ∅ do
3       S_inf ← {s ∈ S, l − w_rem < φ(s) < l};
4       S_sup ← {s ∈ S, 0 ≤ φ(s) ≤ l − w_rem};
5       T_loc ← {t ∈ T, ρ(t) ∩ {S_inf ∪ S_sup} ≠ ∅};
6       T_rem ← {t ∈ T, ρ(t) ∩ (S \ {S_inf ∪ S_sup}) = ∅};
```

// **Phase I: Place most constrained tasks in T_{loc} on most loaded servers unable to execute a remote task while limiting their load under l (i.e., servers in S_{inf}). $T_{loc} \cup T_{rem} = T$**

```
7       while S_inf ≠ ∅ do
8           s ← EXTRACTMOSTLOADEDSRV (S_inf) // Get s∈S s.t. φ(s)>φ(s_i), ∀s_i∈S, s_i≠s
9           T̃ ← ρ⁻¹(s) // Set containing tasks working on s local data
10          T̂ ← ∅ // Set of tasks foreseen to be assigned to s
11          while T̃ ≠ ∅ and φ(s) ≤ l do
12              t ← EXTRACTMOSTCONSTRAINEDTASK (T̃) // Get t∈T̃ s.t. |ρ(t)|<|ρ(t_i)|, ∀t_i∈T̃, t_i≠t
13              T̂ ← T̂ ∪ {t};
14          A ← A ∪ {(s, T̂)};
15          T_loc ← T_loc \ T̂;
```

// **Phase II: Place remote tasks on servers s having a load s.t. $l - \phi(s) \geq w_{rem}$**

```
16      if CONSIDERREMOTEASSIGNMENTS (l) = true then
17          S'_sup ← ∅;
18          Â ← ∅;
19          while T_rem ≠ ∅ ∧ S_sup ≠ ∅ do
20              t ← EXTRACTTASK (T_rem);
21              s ← EXTRACTSRV (S_sup);
22              T̂ ← EXTRACTASSIGNMENT (Â, s);
23              T̂ ← T̂ ∪ {t};
24              Â ← Â ∪ {(s, T̂)};
25              if φ(s) ≤ l − (w_rem) then
26                  S'_sup ← S'_sup ∪ {s};
27              if S_sup = ∅ then
28                  S_sup ← S'_sup; S'_sup ← ∅;
29          A ← A ∪ Â;
```

// **Phase III: Place tasks on less loaded servers, storing the corresponding data**

```
30      T ← T_loc ∪ T_rem;
31      T̃ ← ∅;
32      while T ≠ ∅ do
33          t ← EXTRACTTASK (T);
34          s ← EXTRACTLEASTLOADEDSRV (ρ(t));
35          if φ(s) + w_loc ≤ l then
36              T̂ ← EXTRACTASSIGNMENT (A, s);
37              T̂ ← T̂ ∪ {t}; A ← A ∪ {(s, T̂)};
38          else
39              T̃ ← T̃ ∪ {t};
40      T ← T̃;
41      l ← l + 1;
42  return A
```

Fig. 1. Locality Aware and Bounded Latency (LABL) Task Assignment algorithm

the previous section. The main loop of the algorithm iterates until all tasks are assigned to a server and is structured in three phases each of which acts on a different partition of the set of slave servers. At the beginning, the following subsets of servers and tasks are considered. S_{inf} includes all servers that can execute at least one local task within the limit l but not a remote one, while S_{sup} includes those servers that can execute at least one remote task within the limit l (lines **3–4**). Servers in the complementary set $S_{\text{busy}} = S \backslash (S_{\text{inf}} \cup S_{\text{sup}})$ will not be considered until the limit l for the job latency is increased, thus leading to consider them in S_{inf} or S_{sup} in subsequent iterations of the main loop. The job T is partitioned in two subsets: T_{loc} and T_{rem}, where T_{loc} includes any task that can be executed on at least one server in $S_{\text{inf}} \cup S_{\text{sup}}$ and T_{rem} includes any task that can only be executed remotely before the limit l (lines **5–6**).

The body of the main loop is divided in three phases. In the first phase (lines **7–15**), we assign as many tasks as possible from T_{loc} to servers in S_{inf}, without exceeding the limit l. The tasks from T_{loc} are selected in ascending order of $|\rho(t)|$ (i.e., ranked by the number of servers where they can access data locally), so as to assign first those tasks that can only be executed on few servers, and are therefore more likely to cause violations of the target latency l. This is due to the fact that the initial value of l is l^{**}, which has been computed without taking into account the effect of many tasks having data on a small group of servers. In the second phase (lines **16–30**), we assign tasks from T_{rem} to servers in S_{sup}, without exceeding the limit l. During the first iteration of the main loop, all tasks from T_{rem} might be assigned, because the limit l is initially set to l^{**}, which guarantees that all tasks that need to be executed remotely can be completed within l^{**}. In the third phase (lines **31–41**), we assign as many tasks as possible from T_{loc} to servers in S_{sup}, without exceeding the limit l. Finally, if some tasks are still unassigned, the algorithm increases the limit l by one unit, recomputes the four subsets (T_{loc}, T_{rem}, S_{inf}, S_{sup}) and iterates the three phases. Note that the second phase forces the assignment of as many remote tasks as possible, employing time that could be usefully exploited by other jobs in return for a potentially very low latency gain. Thus, the algorithm triggers the execution of the second phase through a *threshold function* (CONSIDERREMOTEASSIGNMENTS at line **16**) that is *true* until a given latency limit is reached, and *false* thereafter.

3.5   Example

To understand the behavior of the LABL algorithm, we compare it to the locality-aware round-robin [1] and flow-based algorithms [7], using a limited number of servers, $|S| = 10$, and tasks, $|T| = 20$. The task execution times are set at $w_{\text{loc}} = 1$, $w_{\text{rem}} = 3$. Figure 2 reports the considered data placement, with a maximum data replication factor of 2. Figure 3 reports assignments generated by the round-robin algorithm [1] and the flow-based algorithm [7], while Fig. 4 shows assignments generated by the LABL algorithm, when the execution of the second phase is stopped after the first iteration. The round-robin algorithm cycles through the list of servers in a pre-determined arbitrary order until all tasks have been assigned (in the example, starting from s_1, then s_2, s_3, etc.).

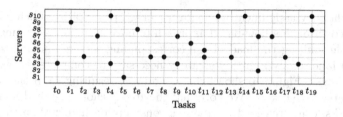

Fig. 2. Data placement

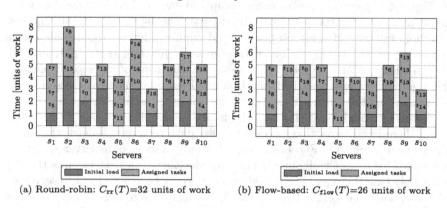

(a) Round-robin: $C_{rr}(T)$=32 units of work

(b) Flow-based: $C_{flow}(T)$=26 units of work

Fig. 3. Round-robin (a) and Flow-based (b) Assignments

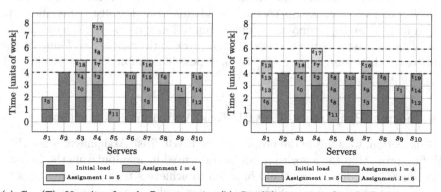

(a) $C_{LABL}(T)$=20 units of work. Remote assignment performed with load threshold l=4

(b) $C_{LABL}(T)$=24 units of work. Remote assignments performed with load threshold $l \in \{4,5\}$

Fig. 4. Locality Aware and Bounded Latency Task Assignments

At each step, a task is assigned to a server. The algorithm tries to exploit the data placement by assigning a local task to the current server. If this is not possible, a remote task is assigned. The greedy choices of the round-robin algorithm results in a final assignment (see Fig. 3a) with high job latency and high resource consumption ($l_{rr} = 8$, $C_{rr}(T) = 32$). The approach reported in [7] improves the round- robin strategy and describes an algorithm that allows to choose the minimum latency assignment among a list of $|T|$ possibilities. Each assignment is computed through a flow-based approach to maximize the assignment of local tasks (while limiting the load of the corresponding servers under a temporary threshold) followed by a greedy strategy necessary to complete the assignment of remote tasks. Figure 3b shows the assignment resulting from the aforementioned strategy ($l_{\text{flow}} = 6$). We note that the greedy choice, applied to assign the remote tasks, can often lead to resource consumption higher than the minimal one: $C_{\text{flow}}(T) = 26 > 20$.

Figure 4 depicts the assignments computed by the LABL algorithm when taking as input an initial job latency limit $l = 4$. The algorithm exhibits different behaviors in terms of total job latency and minimization of resource allocation depending on the configuration of the *threshold function* (see Fig. 1, line **16**: CONSIDERREMOTEASSIGNMENTS) that stops the execution of the second phase of the algorithm from a specified iteration on. Figure 4a, shows the assignments obtained when the second phase is executed only at the first iteration.

Note that this has no effect on the final assignment since, at the first iteration, there is no tasks that needs to access data remotely. Indeed, the initial servers load specified in Fig. 4a suggests that only tasks local to server s_2 may be considered for remote assignment. The data placement function specifies that t_{15} is the only task that can be assigned on s_2, however t_{15} is also local to server s_7. Thus, t_{15} has to be assigned on s_7. The final assignment in Fig. 4a uses resources sparingly ($C_{\text{LABL}}(T) = 20$, equal to the minimum), at the cost of an increased latency ($l_{\text{LABL}} = 8$). To decrease latencies, it is necessary to consider the explicit handling of remote tasks up to the second iteration (Fig. 4b). This allows to assign tasks t_8 and t_{13} remotely, contributing to lower the overall latency, at the cost of an increased resource usage. With respect to the assignment found by the flow-based algorithm, we achieve the best possible combination of job latency $l_{\text{LABL}} = 6$ and resource usage $C_{\text{LABL}}(T) = 24$.

3.6   Formal Properties of LABL Task Assignment Algorithm

In this section, we analyze the properties the LABL Task Assignment algorithm. We first prove that the algorithm can be configured by manipulating the CONSID-ERREMOTEASSIGNMENTS threshold function to achieve strong properties on load balance and resource usage. Subsequently, we analyze the computational complexity of the LABL algorithm.

Theorem 1. *Under the condition that* CONSIDERREMOTEASSIGNMENTS *is true for all iterations of the main loop, the LABL Task Assignment algorithm produces an assignment* $\mathcal{A}_{LABL}$ *with*

$$\max_{s \in S} \phi(s) \leq \min_{s \in S} \phi(s) + w_{\text{rem}}$$

Proof. Let $s_{\max}$ be one of the servers such that the latency of the computed assignment is $l_{\text{LALB}} = \phi(s_{\max})$ and $s_{\min}$ be another server such that the execution of the tasks on it makes its final completion time $\phi(s_{\min})$ equal to the minimum latency among the servers in S. The proof will be developed through a *reductio ad absurdum*. Assume that $\phi(s_{\max}) > \phi(s_{\min}) + w_{\mathrm{rem}}$ holds at the end of the LABL algorithm execution, and that the latency of the computed assignment is $l_{\mathrm{LABL}} = l_{\mathrm{out}}$. Such an hypothesis implies that in the last-but-one iteration of the outer loop of the LABL algorithm, there was a number n of tasks that could not be assigned within the latency limit $l = l_{\mathrm{out}} - 1$. In the case $n = 1$, this task would have been assigned to the server $s_{\min}$ in the phase II of the algorithm, as the hypothesis guarantees enough resources for the remote execution of it. This contradicts the initial assumption as the aforementioned last iteration would not have occurred, and therefore the latency of the computed assignment would have been $l_{\mathrm{LABL}} = l_{\mathrm{out}} - 1$.

In case $n > 1$, each task can be sequentially assigned for remote execution to a server, starting from the one having workload equal to $\phi(s_{\min})$, as long as the number of tasks and the number of servers satisfying the condition $\phi(s) + w_{\mathrm{rem}} \leq l_{\mathrm{out}} - 1$ allows the assignments. If all tasks are assigned, then the last iteration would not have occurred, thus having the same conditions of the former case. Otherwise, the remaining tasks must be assigned at the next iteration when $l = l_{\mathrm{out}}$ as the servers in the last-but-one iteration could have included only tasks requesting an execution time in $[w_{\mathrm{loc}}, w_{\mathrm{rem}} - 1]$ which is not obviously the case. In the last iteration there would have been only servers that could satisfy assignments of tasks with an execution time ranging from w_{loc} to w_{rem}. Therefore the difference between the maximum and the minimum workload would be $\phi(s_{\max}) - \phi(s_{\min}) \leq w_{\mathrm{rem}}$, that contradicts the hypothesis.

Corollary 1. *If Theorem 1 holds and the server $s_{\min} \in S$ with minimum workload satisfies the condition $\phi(s_{\min}) \leq l^{**}$, then the optimal latency l^{opt} for the given assignment problem is bounded as:* $l_{\mathrm{LABL}} - w_{\mathrm{rem}} \leq l^{\mathrm{opt}} \leq l_{\mathrm{LABL}}$.

Proof. The lower bound given by l^{**} is lesser than or equal to l^{opt} by definition, while l^{opt} is, in turn, lesser than or equal to the latency limit computed by the LABL algorithm: $l^{**} \leq l^{\mathrm{opt}} \leq l_{\mathrm{LABL}}$. Now, if Theorem 1 holds, then $l_{LABL} = \phi(s_{\max})$ and $\phi(s_{\min}) \geq l_{\mathrm{LABL}} - w_{\mathrm{rem}}$. Therefore, noting that l^{**} must be greater than or equal to $\phi(s_{\min})$, leads to the thesis.

Theorem 2. *The LABL Task Assignment algorithm, under the condition that* CONSIDERREMOTEASSIGNMENTS *is false for all values of $l > l^{**}$, produces an assignment $\mathcal{A}_{\mathrm{LABL}}$ with a total resource usage*

$$C_{\mathrm{LABL}}(T) \leq l^{**} \times |S| - \sum_{s \in S} \phi_s$$

Proof. If CONSIDERREMOTEASSIGNMENTS is false for all l except l^{**}, the second phase of the LABL algorithm is executed only once, that is the assignment of remote tasks is performed only in the first iteration (i.e., when $l = l^{**}$).

If all the tasks are assigned in the first iteration (that is, the algorithm computes a final latency $l_{\mathrm{out}} = l^{**}$) then the resource allocation in terms of units of work is due to the servers in $S_{\mathrm{sup}} \cup S_{\mathrm{inf}} = S \backslash S_{\mathrm{busy}}$, as in S_{busy} there are only servers with a workload that doesn't allow to cope with either local or remote tasks. Therefore the following relation holds:

$$\sum_{s \in S_{\text{sup}} \cup S_{\text{inf}}} (l^{**} - \phi_s) \geq \sum_{s \in S} (l^{**} - \phi_s)$$

The term in the right side of the previous inequality ($C_{\text{LABL}} \leq \sum_{s \in S} (l^{**} - \phi_s) = l^{**} \times |S| - \sum_{s \in S} \phi_s$) is always smaller than the left one, as the workload of servers in S_{busy} is by definition greater than or equal l^{**}.

If the LABL assignment algorithm terminates with $l_{\text{out}} > l^{**}$, then through remembering that the latency limit given by l^{**} guarantees (by definition) that the whole cluster S can allocate all the remote tasks (see the first condition in the definition of l^{**} in Sect. 3.3), and following the theorem hypothesis the assignment of tasks in the first and third phase of the algorithm will proceed through allocating the tasks locally, it is easy to infer that the whole number of units of work actually spent by the cluster (C_{LABL}), at the end of the computation, will not be greater than $l^{**} \times |S| - \sum_{s \in S} \phi_s$.

Theorem 3. *The LABL Task Assignment algorithm operates in time*

$$\mathcal{O}\left(\log |T| \times |T| \times \max_{t \in T} |\rho(t)|\right)$$

where $|T|$ is the number of tasks and $\max_{t \in T}(|\rho(t)|)$ is the maximum number of data copies available for a task.

Proof. We represent $\rho(t)$ as adjacency lists sorted by server load and $\rho^{-1}(s)$ as adjacency lists sorted by $|\rho(t)|$. The sorting of subsets of T can be performed employing a counting sort algorithm, and has therefore $\mathcal{O}(|T| + \max_{t \in T} |\rho(t)|)$ complexity, since there are at most $\max_{t \in T} (|\rho(t)|)$ keys. The sorting of subsets of S can also be performed employing a counting sort algorithm, and has therefore $\mathcal{O}(|S| + \max_{s \in S} \phi(s))$ complexity, since there are at most $\max_{s \in S} \phi(s)$ keys. Note that the maximum values of $|\rho(t)|$ and $\phi(s)$ are two orders of magnitude smaller than $|T|$ and $|S|$ in real world cases, so using counting sort or other distribution sort algorithms is a reasonable choice. In particular, $\phi(s) \leq \max\{\phi_s, l^{**}\}$ initially, and $\phi(s) \leq \max\{\phi_s, l\}$ in successive iterations.

Computing the four sets S_{inf}, S_{sup}, T_{loc} and T_{rem} amounts to a single scan of S and T. Since in general $|S| < |T|$, the construction is overall $O(|T|)$. The first phase scans the entire S_{inf}. At most w_{rem} tasks are assigned for each $s \in S_{\text{inf}}$, since doing otherwise would lead to violating the latency bound. The complexity of this phase is therefore $\mathcal{O}(|S|)$. The second phase scans the entire T_{rem}, and assigns all tasks to the least loaded servers in a round robin way. The complexity of this phase is straightforward, as it performs $\mathcal{O}(|T_{\text{rem}}|)$ operations, which is also $\mathcal{O}(|T|)$. While the complexity of the third phase, as explained in Fig. 1 is $\mathcal{O}(|T|)$, it is possible to implement it by iterating on the servers in S_{sup} and assigning as many task to each server as it can handle within the latency bound. This leads to a complexity of $\mathcal{O}(|S|)$.

Overall, we have a complexity that is bounded by $\mathcal{O}\left(|T| + \max_{t \in T} |\rho(t)|\right) + \mathcal{O}\left(|S| + \max_{s \in S} \phi(s)\right)$ for each iteration of the main loop. Since we increase l by one at each iteration, the number of iterations of the main loop is given by $l_{\text{LABL}} - l^{**}$, where l_{LABL} is the latency of the assignment. Note that, even if we allocated every task remotely, l_{LABL} would be limited by

$$l_{\text{LABL}} \leq \left(w_{\text{rem}}|T| + \sum_{s \in S} \phi_s\right)/|S|$$

Considering that $l^{**} \leq (w_{\text{loc}}|T| + \sum_{s \in S} \phi_s)/|S|$, it follows that $l_{\text{LABL}} - l^{**} \leq (w_{\text{rem}} - w_{\text{loc}})|T|/|S|$. In general, it can be assumed that $|T| \simeq c|S|$, where c is a small factor typically ranging in $\{2 \ldots 10\}$, therefore the outer loop is executed only a fixed number of times [5,10]. However, we ensure this by means of the threshold limit of l imposed by CONSIDERREMOTEASSIGNMENTS. Thereafter, we perform a reduced loop including only the first and third phases. This reduced loop, per se, has a complexity $\mathcal{O}\left(|T|^2\right)$, but it can be usefully restructured w.r.t. the general presentation to reduce the complexity. Specifically, since we are now only assigning tasks t to servers in $\rho(t)$, we can simply work as follows: for each $s \in S$, compute a set $R_s = \{t \in \rho^{-1}(s) \text{ift} \in T\}$, and sort each set by $|\rho(t)|$.

We now iterate over the servers $s \in S$ in a round-robin way, removing one element of R_s at each iteration and assigning it to s if it has not been already assigned. This guarantees completion in:

$$\mathcal{O}\left(\log|T| \times \sum_{s \in S} |R_s|\right) = \mathcal{O}\left(\log|T| \times |T| \times \max_{t \in T} |\rho(t)|\right)$$

4   Simulation Results

We conducted an experimental campaign to compare the behavior of the LABL Task Assignment with the round-robin and flow-based algorithms. We employed as a starting point a real-world configuration from [5], which provides statistical data on the execution of MapReduce jobs at Google during an entire month.

The experiments are conducted in a simulation environment, scheduling one job on a set of servers having an existing workload. This is done to simulate the online scheduling process: given the mean inter-arrival time of 2–3 min reported in [4,10], the job tracker will have completed the scheduling process of the job before a second one arrives. On the other hand, due to the long computation times, previously scheduled jobs will still be active while the new one is being scheduled. The simulation assumes tasks to require the same time w_{loc} to be executed on any server storing the necessary data. Since the time w_{loc} also represents a *unit of work*, we will consider $w_{\text{loc}} = 1$ in all experiments. Whenever a task is assigned to a server that does not have the required data, the data must be fetched, leading the execution time to increase to w_{rem}. We set $w_{\text{rem}} = 3$ in all experiments, following the same approach as [7]. We explore a configuration space considering a number of servers $|S| = \{1600, \ldots, 2000\}$ and a number of tasks $|T| = \{3200, \ldots, 3500\}$, though we will only show subsets of the overall

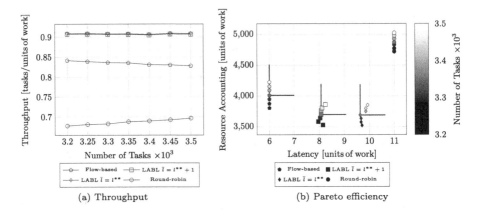

(a) Throughput   (b) Pareto efficiency

Fig. 5. Performance of analyzed algorithms

configuration space in some experiments for the sake of clarity. The data placement is randomly determined such that $|\rho(t)|$ is in the range $[1, \rho_{max}]$ for all tasks, where ρ_{max} is a parameter fixed at 4 in all experiments, except when evaluating the sensitivity of the algorithms to the replication factor. In all the experiments, the initial load is randomly assigned, within the range $[0, 5]$. In all cases, the reported data has been obtained as the average of the results gathered from 30 runs of the same experiment.

4.1   Performance Overview

The experiment reported in Fig. 5 compares the effectiveness of the LABL Task Assignment with both the round-robin and flow-based algorithms, in terms of throughput, resource accounting and latency. We explore a configuration space with $|S| = 2000$, $|T| = \{3200, \ldots, 3500\}$. Data for the LABL algorithm are reported for configurations with threshold latency $\bar{l}$ set to l^{**} and $l^{**} + 1$.

Figure 5a shows the throughput achieved by the three algorithms. The LABL algorithm, in both versions, yields a better throughput, i.e., the task assignment is able to consistently save resources, leaving more server time for other jobs.

Figure 5b reports in a scatter-plot the latency and resource consumption obtained by the three algorithms on the 2000 servers cluster, showing increasing number of tasks in the job by lighter shades. Figure 5b shows that the flow-based algorithm consistently obtains optimal latencies, while the LABL algorithm reduces resource usage. The LABL algorithm and the flow-based algorithm produce solutions that are Pareto-optimal, while the round-robin algorithm produces solutions that are Pareto-dominated by all the others.

On the overall, the flow-based and LABL algorithms produce solutions of interest respectively to optimize latency and resource usage. However, the flow-based algorithm has a higher computational complexity, $\mathcal{O}(|T|^2 \times |S|)$ [7], making the LABL solution more attractive.

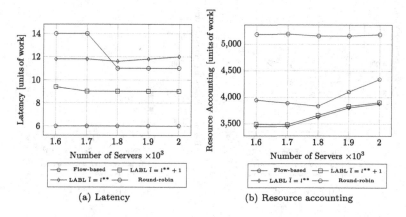

(a) Latency   (b) Resource accounting

Fig. 6. Scalability of the analyzed algorithms

4.2   Scalability

The experiment reported in Fig. 6 evaluates the robustness of the four algorithms
to changes in the availability of servers. Given a set of tasks T, $|T| = 3450$, a
data placement, and an initial workload, we progressively increase the number of
servers that are available for scheduling from a minimum of $|S| = 1600$ to a max-
imum $|S| = 2000$. A desirable property for the scheduling algorithm is that the
number of available servers has only limited impact on the latency — assuming
there are enough servers to actually execute the job. Figure 6a shows that only
the round-robin algorithm is significantly impacted by the change in server availability. This is because the round-robin algorithm makes greedy choices, which
easily prove suboptimal. The other three algorithms behave in a more graceful
way, as their greedy choices are less aggressive — all four algorithms have greedy
components within their heuristics, to limit the complexity, but the greedy component is dominant only in the round-robin algorithm. The LABL algorithm
produces Task Assignments with higher latencies than the flow-based algorithm.
This is expected since, as shown in Sect 4.1, the LABL algorithm trades off
latency to save resources. Figure 6b shows the impact of server availability on
the resource usage. The impact is minimal on the round-robin algorithm, while
the other three algorithms all tend to consume more resources when these are
available, by placing remote tasks on free servers in an attempt to reduce latency.
However, the LABL algorithm, in both versions, always outperforms the flow-
based algorithm, thanks to its greater focus on reducing resource usage.

4.3   Sensitivity Analysis

The experiments reported in Figs. 7 and 8 evaluate the sensitivity of resource
usage to, on one hand, the number of tasks to execute and the number of available
servers, and, on the other hand, the replication factor, i.e., the average number
of copies of the data accessed by a task.

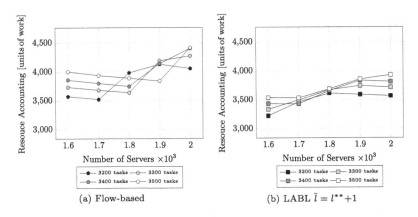

Fig. 7. Resource awareness of analyzed algorithms

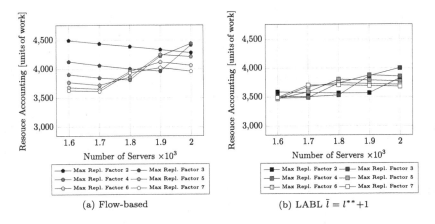

Fig. 8. Replication factor sensitivity of analyzed algorithms

In the first case, only the resource accounting for the flow-based (Fig. 7a) and LABL algorithm with $\bar{l} = l^{**} + 1$ (Fig. 7b) are shown, as these algorithms have proven to be the most effective ones (see Fig. 6). Figure 7 depicts a family of curves representing resource accounting as a function of the number of servers ($|S| = \{1600,\ldots,2000\}$), considering the number of tasks $|T| = \{3200,\ldots,3500\}$ as a parameter. As expected, the LABL algorithm consumes less resources. The results also show that the behavior of the LABL algorithm is much more stable. Moreover, the flow-based algorithm is characterized by a higher resource usage when scheduling more tasks. Focusing on the replication factor, Fig. 8 shows only the resource accounting employed by the flow-based and LABL algorithm (with $\bar{l} = l^{**} + 1$), as a function of the cluster size. The round-robin strategy is not considered since it consistently employs a higher number of resources (see Fig. 6b). We vary the maximum replication factor $\rho_{\max}$ from 2 to 7, so that the average replication factor ranges in $[1.5, 4]$. Thus, the generated data placements have $|\rho(t)|$ uniformly distributed in the range $[1, \rho_{\max}]$ for all tasks. The results show that the LABL algorithm is less sensitive to the replication factor than the flow-based one. The flow-based algorithm takes greater advantage from the increased locality given by the presence of more replicas of each data item, but the LABL algorithm is still able to achieve a lower resource usage. Note that a higher replication factor does impact on the overall costs — keeping up to date copies of the data across the network is bound to have a significant communication cost, so the ability to achieve good resource utilization with a low replication factor is a strong asset of the LABL algorithm.

4.4 Discussion

We will now discuss the interactions of the LABL algorithm with other scheduling goals such as fairness and adaptivity, as well as potential optimizations.

Scheduling for Fairness. The *fairness* property is often desirable in large-scale clusters that are accessed by multiple users. That is, the applications submitted by any user should not be delayed indefinitely. Online scheduling strategies, such as the LABL algorithm, can be integrated into higher level policies aimed at providing such fairness guarantees, that is, at user-application scheduling level rather than at task-scheduling. Indeed, the LABL algorithm could effectively replace the round-robin algorithm that is used as the task assignment component of the *Hadoop fair scheduler* [1,7].

Scheduling Jobs from Multiple Applications. It is possible that, for a given job, some servers of the cluster have no copies of the required data for any of its tasks — or a set of servers $S' \subset S$ has only copies of data needed for a set of tasks $T' \subset T$, but $|T'| < |S'|$, leaving $|S'|-|T'|$ servers idle. In this case, the servers cannot be used to run a local task, either leading to execution delays, if they are used to run a remote task, or to an under-utilization of resources. To further improve resource utilization and throughput, it is possible to schedule jobs from multiple applications at the same time, as these are likely to use different data sets. It is worth noting, however, that scheduling multiple jobs increases the throughput at a cost in latency. The LABL scheduling algorithm, however, can easily handle the schedule of sets of tasks belonging to different jobs coming from independent applications, through simply merging the two sets. The key issue is selecting jobs that map on data held in different servers, so as to allow servers that cannot run tasks locally for one job to be used for another job.

Adaptive Scheduling. A latency-aware scheduling is more attractive when the cluster is under-utilized, as it allows to minimize application latency, providing a better response time to the user. On the other hand, a resource-aware scheduling becomes increasingly important as the cluster utilization grows. Indeed, in a cluster under a heavy workload, a scheduling policy that favors latency may easily lead to low availability for other jobs. A common solution is to artificially limit the amount of resources that a single job can take. The LABL algorithm does that, by construction, optimizing the resource accounting of the scheduled job, while still providing a strong·latency limit. Thus, it adapts better to workload variations, as shown in Sect. 4.3.

5   Related Work

The MapReduce programming model has been formalized in a number of ways. In [9] MapReduce computations have been compared to the PRAM model, focusing on analyzing how PRAM algorithms can be expressed using MapReduce. Among the studies on task assignment, in [11] the authors focus on allocating tasks of multiple jobs in both on-line and off-line scenarios, providing a generalization of the Flexible-Flow Shop problem. However, the authors do not take into account the impact of data placement, which is critical due to the size of the exchanged data. In [7] the Hadoop round-robin based task allocator is compared with a flow-based task allocator, showing that careful consideration of data placement allows to limit job latency. An in-depth comparison with both algorithms is provided in Sect 4. Job latency reduction has been tackled in [16] considering a production-quality scenario, showing how careful job speculation helps on limiting the latency penalty introduced by straggled tasks (i.e., remotely executed tasks on the critical path), at the cost of an increased resource consumption. This technique, while applicable to all tasks, is more effective on *reduce* tasks, since map tasks are much less likely to be straggled. In a typical MapReduce implementation, the set of available resources is equally exposed to all jobs. In [13], on the other hand, a different processing resources are exposed to each job depending on its workload profile in terms of CPU, disk and memory usage. Thus, a task tracker can maximize the use of its resources through executing tasks from jobs with different profiles. This scheme can be easily combined with our own, since in our approach the set of resources is an input parameter, whilst the key aspect of [13] is the definition of the resource set for each job profile. In [14], FLEX, a scheduler for MapReduce systems, is proposed as a replacement for the Hadoop fair scheduling algorithm. With respect to our work, FLEX does not take into account data locality, and works on multiple jobs at the same time in an epoch-based scheme. Similarly, in [15] multiple jobs are managed, aiming at fairness and data locality, but with no latency guarantees. The task assignment problem is common to all DISC schemes. However, the solutions need to be tailored to the specific setup: e.g., [12] deal with *cloud*-based MapReduce services, which rely on a heavy use of virtualization techniques. Virtualization is not attractive for every DISC scenario, due to the need to spawn new virtual machines at high frequency — job completion times follow a long tailed distribution, with 80 % of the successful jobs completing within 6 min, as shown in [10] for a 10-month timeframe on a production Yahoo! Hadoop cluster.

6   Concluding Remarks

We presented an algorithm for assigning the tasks of a job to servers in a MapReduce cluster. The proposed algorithm balances the tradeoff between latency and resource consumption. Simulation results support the insight that a practical implementation would benefit from the proposed approach. Future works include integrating the LABL algorithm within a job-scheduling framework (which will also manage fault tolerance issues) and extending it through taking into account the cluster interconnect topology to model the remote execution time.

References

1. Apache Foundation: Hadoop. http://hadoop.apache.org/mapreduce
2. Bortnikov, E.: Open-source grid technologies for web-scale computing. SIGACT News **40**(2), 87–93 (2009)
3. Chambers, C., Raniwala, A., Perry, F., Adams, S., Henry, R.R., Bradshaw, R., Weizenbaum, N.: FlumeJava: easy, efficient data-parallel pipelines. In: PLDI, pp. 363–375 (2010)
4. Chen, Y., Ganapathi, A., Griffith, R., Katz, R.H.: Evaluating MapReduce performance using workload suites. In: MASCOTS, pp. 390–399 (2011)
5. Dean, J., Ghemawat, S.: MapReduce: simplified data processing on large clusters. In: OSDI, pp. 137–150 (2004)
6. Dean, J., Ghemawat, S.: MapReduce: a flexible data processing tool. Commun. ACM **53**(1), 72–77 (2010)
7. Fischer, M.J., Su, X., Yin, Y.: Assigning tasks for efficiency in hadoop: extended abstract. In: SPAA, pp. 30–39 (2010)
8. Hey, A.J.G., Trefethen, A.: The data deluge: an e-Science perspective. In: Berman, F., Fox, G.C., Hey, A.J.G. (eds.) Grid Computing-Making the Global Infrastructure a Reality, pp. 809–824. J. Wiley & Sons, New York (2003)
9. Karloff, H.J., Suri, S., Vassilvitskii, S.: A model of computation for MapReduce. In: SODA, pp. 938–948 (2010)
10. Kavulya, S., Tan, J., Gandhi, R., Narasimhan, P.: An analysis of traces from a production MapReduce cluster. In: CCGRID, pp. 94–103. IEEE (2010)
11. Moseley, B., Dasgupta, A., Kumar, R., Sarlós, T.: On scheduling in Map-Reduce and Flow-Shops. In: Rajaraman, R., Meyer auf der Heide, F. (eds.) SPAA, pp. 289–298. ACM (2011)
12. Park, J., Lee, D., Kim, B., Huh, J., Maeng, S.: Locality-aware dynamic VM reconfiguration on MapReduce clouds. In: HPDC, pp. 27–36 (2012)
13. Polo, J., Castillo, C., Carrera, D., Becerra, Y., Whalley, I., Steinder, M., Torres, J., Ayguadé, E.: Resource-aware adaptive scheduling for MapReduce clusters. In: Kon, F., Kermarrec, A.-M. (eds.) Middleware 2011. LNCS, vol. 7049, pp. 187–207. Springer, Heidelberg (2011)
14. Wolf, J., Rajan, D., Hildrum, K., Khandekar, R., Kumar, V., Parekh, S., Wu, K.-L., Balmin, A.: FLEX: a slot allocation scheduling optimizer for MapReduce workloads. In: Gupta, I., Mascolo, C. (eds.) Middleware 2010. LNCS, vol. 6452, pp. 1–20. Springer, Heidelberg (2010)
15. Zaharia, M., Borthakur, D., Sarma, J.S., Elmeleegy, K., Shenker, S., Stoica, I.: Delay scheduling: a simple technique for achieving locality and fairness in cluster scheduling. In: EuroSys, pp. 265–278 (2010)
16. Zaharia, M., Konwinski, A., Joseph, A.D., Katz, R.H., Stoica, I.: Improving MapReduce performance in heterogeneous environments. In: Draves, R., van Renesse, R. (eds.) OSDI, pp. 29–42. USENIX Association (2008)

A Periodic Portfolio Scheduler for Scientific Computing in the Data Center

Kefeng Deng[1,2(✉)], Ruben Verboon[2], Kaijun Ren[1], and Alexandru Iosup[2]

[1] National University of Defense Technology, Changsha, China
{dengkefeng,renkaijun}@nudt.edu.cn
[2] Delft University of Technology, Delft, The Netherlands
R.S.Verboon@student.tudelft.nl, A.Iosup@tudelft.nl

Abstract. The popularity of data centers in scientific computing has led to new architectures, new workload structures, and growing customer-bases. As a consequence, the selection of efficient scheduling algorithms for the data center is an increasingly costlier and more difficult challenge. To address this challenge, and contrasting previous work on scheduling for scientific workloads, we focus in this work on portfolio scheduling—here, the dynamic selection and use of a scheduling policy, depending on the current system and workload conditions, from a portfolio of multiple policies. We design a periodic portfolio scheduler for the workload of the entire data center, and equip it with a portfolio of resource provisioning and allocation policies. Through simulation based on real and synthetic workload traces, we show evidence that portfolio scheduling can automatically select the scheduling policy to match both user and data center objectives, and that portfolio scheduling can perform well in the data center, relative to its constituent policies.

Keywords: Portfolio scheduling · Data center · Provisioning and allocation · Scheduling policies · Scientific workloads

1 Introduction

Cluster-based data centers of all sizes are increasingly popular, a result of both increasing demand for efficient computational resources, and of several decades of technological advancement and education of administrators in distributed systems. Especially when servicing the demanding workloads typical of scientific computing [1,2], these data centers need efficient algorithms for scheduling their users' workloads on the data center resources. Many existing scheduling algorithms have already addressed specific workload properties [3,4] and types of applications [5–7], but data centers still rely on (expensive) human system administrators to select a scheduling algorithm and configure it appropriately. Moreover, the selection process is made significantly more difficult by changing workloads due to technology transitions (e.g., the use of virtualization and new networking architectures), and by new customers starting to use data centers as

N. Desai and W. Cirne (Eds.): JSSPP 2013, LNCS 8429, pp. 156–176, 2014.
DOI: 10.1007/978-3-662-43779-7_9, © Springer-Verlag Berlin Heidelberg 2014

Infrastructure-as-a-Service clouds. In contrast to previous approaches, we investigate in this work portfolio scheduling [8]—in this context, the dynamic selection and use of a scheduling policy, depending on the current system and workload conditions, from a portfolio of multiple policies—used to efficiently schedule scientific workloads for the entire data center. Cluster-based data centers have been much employed for scientific computing workloads. For example, small data centers are commonly integrated into multi-cluster grids, such as the World Large Hedron Collider Grid (WLCG), the US Open Science Grid, the French Grid'5000, and the Dutch DAS. However, human administrators have become increasingly rare and more overloaded, as modern data centers rely increasingly on automation and allocate only 5 % of the operational budgets for human administration [9]; this situation is anecdotally supported by our experience with the DAS system over the past decade.

A variety of scheduling and administrative techniques have been developed recently for the data centers, but, simultaneously, data center architectures have evolved quickly. For the former, research has focused on both sharing of networking resources [10] and time-cost-energy optimizations. For the latter, recent work has focused on new layouts of networks [11,12] and new virtualization architectures [13,14]. Our previous scheduling studies [7,15,16], which evaluate a large variety of scheduling policies for various types of scientific computing, indicate that no single policy can accommodate all workload conditions, and all user and system objective functions. Thus, a tension arises in trying to select the appropriate resource scheduling policies for the data center.

Not only the data center architecture, but also the properties of scientific workloads change over time. Long-term arrival patterns can suddenly be interrupted by bursts of arrivals [2]. As systems mature, their users may transition from loosely coupled jobs to more integrated workflows [17] and even tightly coupled parallel jobs. New approaches to computing—MapReduce and its many flavors, the graph-processing model Pregel, etc.—have appeared in the past few years. For months after data centers are launched in production and prior to their decommissioning, reduced yet system-stressful workloads with different operational patterns may appear [18]. Thus, the problem of selecting an appropriate scheduling policy remains open and increasingly in need of a solution.

In this work we investigate if a portfolio scheduler can automatically select the scheduling policy, from the set with which the portfolio is configured, such that the user and the data center's objective functions remain within their target (optimal) range. Among other differences from previous work on portfolio scheduling [8], our context rarely allows an optimal range to be computed; thus, the target range is relative to the performance of individual policies used in the portfolio. A portfolio scheduler should support many types of workload patterns and application types, yet perform similarly to the scheduling policy that has been specifically designed to support the workload pattern and application type. This has an important consequence: portfolio scheduling can then alleviate the need for human expertise in selecting scheduling policies and even configurations, and thus become an important component in the administration of modern data centers.

A full exploration of the concept portfolio scheduling would greatly exceed the scope of this work. Among the challenging questions we do not explore are: Which policies should be selected in the portfolio? How can a portfolio support a mix of application types? Should the portfolio also configure policies, as part of its operational process? Should the portfolio select the scheduling policy periodically or continuously? In this work, we focus on exploring portfolio scheduling, with a twofold contribution:

1. We adapt the notion of periodic portfolio scheduling in the context of data centers (Sect. 3). We propose a periodic portfolio scheduler, and create a comprehensive portfolio for provisioning and allocation of resources.
2. We evaluate our portfolio scheduler experimentally, through synthetic and real trace-based simulation (Sect. 5). We compare the portfolio scheduler against its constituent policies and show evidence that portfolio scheduling can be beneficial in the context of data centers.

2   System Model

In this section we present the system model used throughout this work.

2.1   Workload and Resource Model

The workloads we consider in this work match the cluster-based traces of the Parallel Workloads Archive [19]. We further assume that jobs are CPU-bound and their runtime depends linearly on the speed of the (virtual) processor where they are executed. Because it offers a trade-off between accuracy of simulation and simplicity, this model has been much used by the parallel and grid computing communities for simulation-based work. For example, we have used it in our DGSim simulator [20].

In this work, we consider the functioning of a data center comprised of homogeneous physical resources. This model is common for the multi-cluster grids of the late-1990s up to mid-2000s—many of their clusters and even entire data centers have been initially built with homogeneous resources. This model also matches today's virtualized (homogenized) infrastructure.

Similarly to simulation-based studies in parallel and grid computing, we assume that resources can be benchmarked to quantify their speed for processing typical scientific computing workload, for example with the SPEC CPU2006 benchmark. Although this assumption may fail for other application domains or for scientific applications with irregular operational patterns [21], this approach to benchmarking has been successfully employed in the operation of several multi-cluster grids, such as the Worldwide LHC Computing Grid (WLCG), the French Grid'5000, and the Dutch DAS.

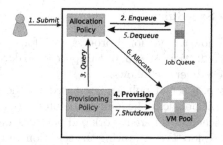

Fig. 1. Operational model of the data-center scheduler.

2.2 Operational Model

In this work, resources are provisioned exclusively from a single data center. We do not consider hybrid computing environments that span multiple data centers, because scientific and especially parallel workloads can rarely withstand co-allocation across geographically-separate data centers without significant loss of performance [6, 22].

In our resource usage model, all resources belong to the data center and are provisioned on-demand for incoming workload as virtual machines (VMs). Besides on-demand resource provisioning, we do not consider in this work advance reservation, consolidation of multiple jobs on the same resources, and other usage models [23]. The use of virtualization allows the data center to service a diverse set of scientific computing users on the same set of physical resources; the performance impact of virtualization for scientific computing has been well studied in the past and shown [24–26] to be small, for non-I/O-bound and small-scale scientific applications.

The data-center scheduling model investigated in this work is adapted from our previous work [15]. As depicted in Fig. 1, users send their workloads to a system-wide scheduler, which uses an *allocation policy* to either allocate these jobs to the VMs already provisioned for the submitting user (the *VM pool*), or to enqueue the jobs in the system-wide *job queue*. VMs are provisioned, that is, leased and released, on behalf of the user by the system-wide scheduler via a *provisioning policy*. To inform proactive provisioning decisions, the provisioning policy can query the state of the allocation. From the perspective of the data center operator, the provisioning policy is in general responsible for the efficient allocation of resources to users.

Inspired by the use of data centers as IaaS cloud infrastructure, we use the billing model of Amazon EC2: VM use is charged in hourly increments.

3   A Periodic Portfolio Scheduler

In this section we adapt traditional portfolio scheduling [8] for use in the data center. We describe, in turn, our periodic portfolio scheduler, an overview of the system including the portfolio scheduler, and the set of policies used by our portfolio scheduler (later used in experimental work, in Sect. 5).

3.1   The Portfolio Scheduler

Portfolio schedulers follow a traditional process with four steps, creation, selection, application, and reflection. We adapt this process to data centers and design a periodic portfolio scheduler, as follows.

In the *creation* step, a set of policies is created for the portfolio scheduler, prior to the actual use of policies. The main trade-off in the creation of this set is between *capability* to schedule different workload patterns and application types, and *time* required to explore the set during the selection and application phases. The selection of policies is usually done by an expert, as we do in Sect. 3.3, but can also be done automatically, for example as the result of an automated comparative study of policies specific to one domain [7,15,16].

During *selection*, the portfolio scheduler has to select one of the scheduling policies, to be used, in the case of *continuous portfolio scheduling*, for the next scheduling decision or, for *periodic portfolio scheduling*, during the next period of taking scheduling decisions. As for the creation step, the selection step can be guided by an expert or be automated, and needs to address a trade-off between time spent in selection and *quality of selection*, which is typically a single-user utility function or a system-wide performance metric. The portfolio scheduler we propose in this work is periodic and automated; we explore various metrics for the quality of selection in Sect. 5. We detail in Sect. 3.2 a practical selection process that can be used in data center scheduling.

In the *application* step, the policy selected in the previous step takes scheduling decisions. Additionally, the portfolio scheduler collects information about the application of scheduling decisions, and may use the collected information to evaluate how the non-selected policies in its portfolio would have performed if selected. Although this step also appears in non-portfolio scheduling, for portfolio scheduling this step can be more complex. If the selected policy is complex, its application may raise non-trivial system stability issues and lead to system inefficiency. For example, the newly selected policy may be undoing some of the advanced reservations or other long-term planning decisions of previously selected policies. We see the exploration of the non-trivial interplay between the selection and application steps, including stabilization of a multi-policy system, as fertile ground for future research.

The *reflection* step analyzes the operation of the last selection and application steps, and may take the decision to change the portfolio or tune the other steps. Changing the portfolio is similar to the creation step. Tuning the other steps may, for example, lead to switching the selection step from a periodic to a continuous process, adapting the selection criterion, and setting different thresholds regarding the overturning of previous scheduling decisions when applying the newly selected policy. We leave the exploration of this step for future work.

Ideally, the portfolio scheduler has the ability to always select, for an arbitrary workload *mode* (i.e., workload pattern or application type), the best scheduling policy in the portfolio. Thus, a portfolio scheduler cannot outperform its constituent policies when confronted with a mono-modal workload. Instead, a portfolio scheduler should become useful when the workload changes modes in

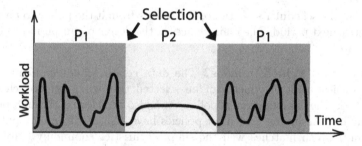

Fig. 2. Selected policy over the lifetime of a system with changing workload modes.

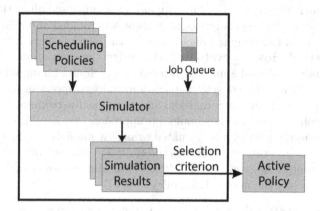

Fig. 3. The policy selection process of our periodic portfolio scheduler.

quick succession. For example, Fig. 2 depicts a synthetic workload that alternates two arrival patterns, to be scheduled by a portfolio scheduler comprised of two policies, each adapted to one of the arrival patterns. In this constructed example, the policy is changed automatically after each selection step, in response to changes in the workload. The result in an alternation between policies P_1 and P_2. Moreover, when the succession is aperiodic or has a long period, the portfolio scheduler should become increasingly more difficult to replace with human decision-making.

3.2 System Using Portfolio Scheduling

We now extend the operational model introduced in Sect. 2.2 to accommodate a periodic portfolio scheduler. The main elements of this model, the system-wide scheduler, the order of operations involving the selected policies, etc., remain unchanged. Because the application of the (selected) scheduling policy remains unchanged from the initial operational model, we focus in this section on the portfolio creation and selection steps of the process introduced in Sect. 3.1.

For our portfolio scheduler, the creation step is executed *once* and the selection step is executed *periodically*. The selection automatically evaluates the set of policies in the scheduler's portfolio, and selects from it the policy to be applied for the entire next period. The main choices in the design of our periodic portfolio scheduler are:

(Creation step) Which policies? The data center scheduler includes various policies, each of which can be selected through portfolio scheduling. Moreover, the combination of policies can also be selected through portfolio scheduling. Assuming that most policies have a similarity in computational demand, which matches well the simple heuristics commonly employed in data center scheduling, the time required for single- and multi-policy selection increases linearly and exponentially, respectively. We design our portfolio scheduler to cover the combination of provisioning and allocation policies, that is, the portfolio is comprised of pairs of provisioning and allocation policies. We detail the specific policies used in this work in Sect. 3.3.

(Selection step) How to evaluate? We design the evaluation of policies to use a *simulation*-based approach; alternatives include running selected workload parts in a reserved system partition and extrapolating results, using historical performance information and periodically risking on previously untried policies, etc. In the simulation approach (see Fig. 3), each scheduling policy in the portfolio is evaluated against a simulated environment that matches the data center, subject to the currently running and queued jobs in the data center. After all the simulations are complete, a *selection criterion* is used to select the next active policy.

The **selection step** also involves several important configuration parameters:

The simulator The choice of a simulator is non-trivial, with the main trade-off in the accuracy of results (the ability to match the real environment) and execution time. Fast and accurate simulators already exist for various data center architectures [20,27]. We select from these simulators and use in our portfolio scheduler DGSim [20], which has been used previously for data center architectures such as independent and multi-cluster system.

The interval between selections (the period of the selection step), τ, is set by the system administrator (e.g., to $\tau = 20s$). If τ is small, the selection may overload the system scheduler and may occur too frequently to allow for meaningful scheduling. It τ is large, delays are unnecessarily incurred on the execution of the workload. We leave for future work the automatic setting and tuning of this system parameter.

The maximal simulation time, T, defined as the maximal duration for each independent simulation. We have selected this single parameter from the broader trade-off between the number of parameters in the system and the ability to configure the maximal runtime for several (classes of) policies.

The selection criterion (or the utility function), U, which is used to select the next active policy after all the simulations are complete. In this work we use a selection criterion that balances the job slowdown as a proxy for user experience, and utilization of the provisioned resources as a proxy for system efficiency and cost; the metric will be detailed in Sect. 4.3.

3.3   Portfolio Policies

In this section, we describe the policies that we select for our portfolio scheduler. We present, in turn, the selected provisioning and allocation policies. We use six provisioning policies from our recent study of IaaS clouds [15] and two allocation policies commonly used in data centers. Our choice of provisioning policies matches the system model requirement of hourly charging per VM (see Sect. 2.2). Among the six provisioning policies, we use the last five policies in our portfolio:

1. (The **baseline provisioning policy**) *StartUp (STU):* This policy leases a new instance whenever there is no idle VM for the current job unless the number of rented VMs reach its maximum. Moreover, the rented VMs will not be released until the end of the workload. The advantage of STU is that it can provide user with good experience by over-provisioning VM instances. However, it cannot deal well with changing workloads such as bursty workload, since it is static and keeps VM instances alive after the flash-crowd even when there are no jobs.
2. *On-Demand Single VM (ODS):* This is a simple dynamic provisioning policy. It leases a new VM instance for each job that is waiting in the queue, whenever available instances can be provisioned in the data center (whenever there are free resources). Since instances are charged hourly, they are released when there is no job for them to run and their run time is reaching integral hours. This policy is naive: although it may lead to good user experience, it also incurs unnecessarily high cost—resources charged for an entire hour may be released after just a few minutes.
3. *On-Demand Geometric (ODG):* Because scientific workloads may include many short jobs that finish before the hourly charging of resources, it is not necessary to rent a new instance for every job. Therefore, The ODG policy is used to rent VMs gradually. ODG leases and releases VM instances in a similar way to TCP's exponential back-off mechanism [28]. A parameter $\alpha \geq 1$ is used to control the growth (shrink) of the number of VMs to be leased (released) at each provisioning step, i.e., this policy leases $\alpha^0, \alpha^1, \alpha2, \ldots, \alpha^n$ instances, successively. We have shown in our previous work [15] evidence that this policy is helpful for bursty workloads.
4. *On-Demand ExecTime (ODE):* Job information may be helpful for taking better scheduling decisions. The ODE policy takes the execution time of the jobs into consideration for leasing VM instances. First, it estimates the run time of the queued jobs as the (historically recorded) average run time of similar jobs, for example jobs submitted by the same user. Then, it computes the number of VMs to be rented by rounding up the total execution time to hours. This policy also uses the VM release strategy of the ODS policy.
5. *On-Demand WaitTime (ODW):* Similarly to the ODE policy, and taken from previous work [15], the ODW policy uses the job wait time to decide how many instances to be rented. First, a threshold is empirically set for the maximal job wait time, to the next 5 min increment that exceeds by 5 times the latency to acquire and boot a VM instance; we set it in this work to 20 min. At every

provisioning point, ODW checks the wait time of each job, then leases VMs for each job having waited longer than the threshold. This policy also releases VMs near integral hours of run time.

6. *On-Demand XFactor (ODX):* This policy tries to give an upper bound for job slowdown. To this end, ODX uses both the (observed) wait time and the (estimated) run time to rent instances. ODX uses the same method as ODE to estimate the job run time. Idle VM instances are reused or, if none exists, leased whenever a job has been delayed longer than its run time (a slowdown of 2). This policy also uses the VM release strategy of the ODS policy.

We also consider two allocation policies for our portfolio, First-Come-First-Served (FCFS) and the second one is Shortest-Job-First (SJF). FCFS is the traditional allocation policy used in many data centers; it is fair but may cause fragmentations in the system. SJF is an aggressive policy: it can reach lower average job slowdown or wait time, but may also cause starvation for long jobs.

4   Experimental Goals and Setup

We evaluate in this section portfolio scheduling for scientific workload executed in the data center using an experimental approach. We compare the performance of the portfolio scheduler and of its constituent policies, when used independently. We conduct this evaluation using simulation (Sect. 4.1). As input to the simulator, we use synthetic and real-world traces corresponding to scientific workloads (Sect. 4.2). Last, as user- and data-center-oriented objective functions we use several metrics (Sect. 4.3).

When presenting results in this section, we use predominantly two-letter terms to denote the policy combinations in our experiments. For the six provisioning policies described in Sect. 3.3 we use the letters **U**, **S**, **G**, **E**, **W**, and **X**, respectively. For the FCFS and SJF allocation policies described in Sect. 3.3 we use the letters **F** and **S**, respectively. Thus, the combination between the provisioning policy OD**X** and the allocation policy **F**CFS is depicted as **XF**. Our portfolio scheduler is indicated through the acronym **PO**.

4.1   Simulator

In this paper, we use simulation[1] to evaluate the effectiveness of our portfolio scheduler, and to compare it with the individual pairs of provisioning and allocation policies that can be formed with the policies introduced in Sect. 3.3.

To this end, we extend our discrete event simulator DGSim [20] with entities such as a cloud-like resource manager and VM instances. The cloud-like resource manager implements Amazon EC2-like APIs for leasing and releasing VM instances, and implements the cost model of on-demand instances leased

---

[1] The simulator used in this section should not be confused with the simulator running as part of the portfolio scheduler. Replacing the simulator used in this section, we have begun experimenting with a real-world prototype of our portfolio scheduler.

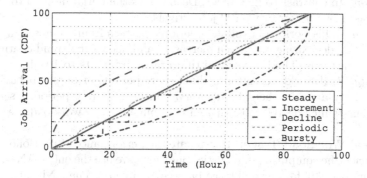

Fig. 4. The arrival of jobs for the five synthetic workloads.

by Amazon EC2. To simulate a virtualized environment, we set realistically a delay for instance acquisition and booting, which is 4 min based on our previous research [15,29]. To enable future comparative experiments between the environment simulated in this work and our real-world system DAS-4, which provides OpenNebula-based and Eucalyptus-based cloud interfaces, the maximum number of VMs that can be rented is set to 64.

Our simulator implements the system model introduced in Sect. 2. We further assume in our simulation that jobs run exclusively on their VMs and cannot be preempted or migrated. Although these assumptions are both common and do not affect the simple allocation policies investigated in this work, we intend to work on relaxing these assumptions, in future work.

4.2 Workloads

We use both synthetic workloads and real workload traces for evaluation. The synthetic workloads are short-term but with significantly different job arrival patterns, allowing us to better characterize the impact of the arrival process on portfolio scheduling. The real workload is a whole trace from the Parallel Workloads Archive [19] and allows us to gain valuable insight into the operation of our portfolio scheduler in realistic conditions.

Synthetic Workloads: In this paper, we generate five types of workloads that have different user behaviors but the same (real) job run times. We take the jobs run times from the first 1000 jobs of the ANL Intrepid 2009 workload from the Parallel Workload Archive [19]. Then, we generate the arrival time of each job such that each synthetic workload exhibits a different arrival patterns. The five arrival patterns, for which the generated workloads are compared in Fig. 4, are:

1. *Steady:* the interval between two consecutive jobs is statically set to 5 min.
2. *Increment:* The initial interval in this workload is set to 10 min. After every 100 job arrivals, the interval is decreased by 70 s.

3. *Decline:* In contrast to Increment, Decline sets the initial interval to 5 s, then increased by 70 s for every 100 job arrivals.
4. *Periodic:* This workload exhibits a periodic pattern from an increasing arrival rate to an decreasing one. Each increasing and decreasing trend continues for 100 job arrivals. The inter-arrival times range from 10 s to 10 min.
5. *Bursty:* Real workloads often include short periods of bursty behavior. For our bursty arrivals, the submit interval during a bursty period is set to 5 s, and bursts include 100 jobs; there are 10 bursts in the workload.

The Real Workload Trace: To evaluate the performance of portfolio scheduling for scientific computing in realistic conditions, we use the entire ANL Intrepid 2009 workload [19] for our real trace-based experiments. The ANL Intrepid 2009 trace has a makespan of 8 months and contains a total number of 68,936 jobs.

4.3 Performance Metrics

We consider in this work various user and data-center objective functions, expressed as traditional and compound metrics. Job slowdown (S) and job wait time (W) are used as common proxies [3] for user objectives. We also measure the total run time of all the jobs (R_J) and the total run time of all rented VM instances (R_V). Because VMs are charged by the hour, the run times are rounded up to the next hour if they are not integer hours; thus, R_V also denotes the *charged cost*. The utilization of the scheduler is defined as the ratio between R_J and R_V, and indicates the efficiency of the policies. Resource utilization is an important metric for both data center administrators and users. For users, it means cost efficiency when using the virtual resources; for system operators, more efficient policies and thus higher market competitiveness.

Although a lower slowdown is to be desired, it may be the result of (much) higher cost, for example when the provisioning policy is STU (StartUp in Sect. 3.3). To balance these considerations, we use an extension of an utility function, which is defined elsewhere [15,16]:

$$U = \kappa \cdot \left(\frac{R_J}{R_V} \right)^{\alpha} \cdot \left(\frac{1}{S} \right)^{\beta}$$

For this metric, κ is a scaling factor for the total score, which we set to 100 in our experiments. The metric parameters α and β are used to express different utility functions: α is used to emphasizes the efficiency of resource usage and β is used to stress the urgency of the jobs. For example, to finish jobs as soon as possible, the utility function is set such that $\beta \gg \alpha$. In this paper, similarly to previous work we set $\alpha = \beta = 1$ to balance system efficiency and user experience.

5 Experimental Results

In this section, we report our experimental results. First, we show the results of using portfolio scheduling for synthetic workloads (Sect. 5.1). Then, we show the

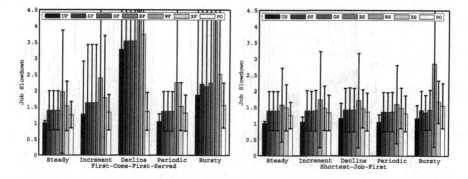

Fig. 5. Job slowdown for different synthetic workloads.

results for a real workload trace (Sect. 5.2). Finally, we analyze the operation of our portfolio scheduler during the experiments (Sect. 5.3). Overall, we find that portfolio scheduling is useful for data centers.

5.1 Results of Synthetic Workloads

We perform this set of experiments to evaluate our portfolio schedule for the five workload arrival patterns described in Sect. 4.2.

We first find that the combined policy US (STU+SJF) delivers the lowest average slowdown, but also that PORTFOLIO delivers consistently better results than the other policies. Supporting this finding, Fig. 5 depicts the average job slowdown for all the policy combinations, for the five synthetic workloads. In general, and consistently with previous studies of slowdown and also job wait time [30], provisioning policies have relatively lower slowdown when combined with the SJF allocation policy, rather than with FCFS. The performance under Steady, Increment, and Periodic workloads is consistent for all the policy combinations. More pronounced variation appears for Decline and, especially, Bursty workloads. Our portfolio scheduler (PO in Fig. 5) performs consistently well in all the cases—PORTFOLIO is the second-best in the first four workloads and very close to the second best in the Bursty workload.

We find that the results for job wait time are much more varied than for job slowdown; as depicted by Fig. 6, PORTFOLIO behaves relatively slightly worse in the ranking of policies than for the job slowdown. For many combined policies, the wait time for Decline and Bursty workloads is larger by a factor of about two than for the other workloads. Bursty workloads introduce very challenging scheduling conditions, in which too many jobs overload the system and wait time accumulates. Decline workloads have a quick arrival of jobs in the beginning, similarly to a Bursty workload. During the rapidly varying conditions of Bursty and Periodic workloads, PORTFOLIO is relatively weaker than several other policies, but still delivers relatively good job wait time.

We now investigate the resource utilization, and depict the results in Fig. 7; we also depict the charged cost in Fig. 8. From these figures, we find that ODW,

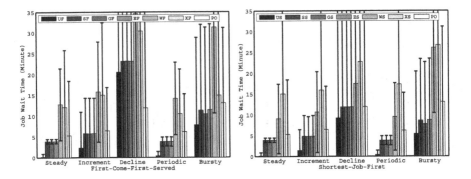

Fig. 6. Job wait time for different synthetic workloads.

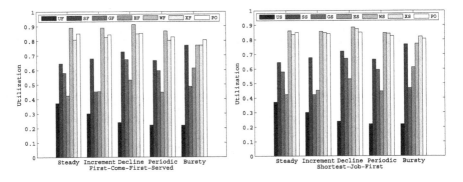

Fig. 7. Utilization for different synthetic workloads.

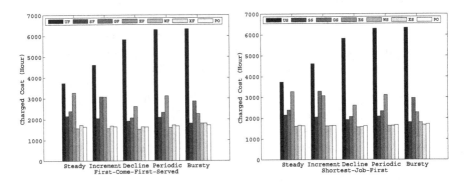

Fig. 8. Charged cost for different synthetic workloads.

ODX, and our PORTFOLIO achieve the highest utilization and the lowest charged cost. As observed in various previous studies [15], the StartUp policy has the lowest utilizations, from 20 % to 30 %–in line to traditional provisioning policies that only look at peak workloads. As in previous studies of

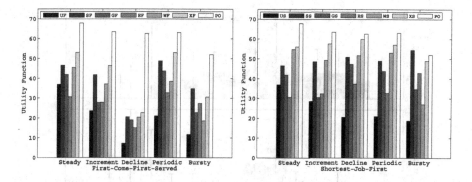

Fig. 9. Value of the utility function for different synthetic workloads.

utilization [31], ODS, the commonly used policy in current data centers, achieves only a moderate utilization of 65 % to 80 %.

Our portfolio scheduler combines consistently low job slowdown and wait time, with low cost (through high utilization). Thus, our portfolio scheduler yields a gain in utility, as depicted in Fig. 9. PORTFOLIO is better than its alternatives for all but the Bursty workload, where the SF (ODS+SJF) policy performs better. For the Bursty workload, jobs are submitted every 5 s, quickly saturating the system. Thus, it is better to provision resources as soon as possible to avoid unnecessary waiting. As our portfolio scheduler does not predict the future workload, it cannot adapt as quickly to sudden workload changes as the SF policy. However, our portfolio scheduler indeed selects the SF policy most of the time during Bursty workloads, as shown in Sect. 5.3.

To conclude the experiments using synthetic workloads, we have shown in this section evidence that, for a variety of workload patterns, our portfolio scheduler *can* automatically select the scheduling policy such that it meets the user and the data center's objective functions at least similarly to, but sometimes even better than, the other scheduling policies investigated here.

5.2 Results of Real Workload Traces

We now turn our attention to the real workload trace collected from ANL Intrepid. We first study the job slowdown and wait time for the real workload trace, and depict the results in Fig. 10. StartUp is the best policy and has a slowdown nearly 1–the jobs do not have to wait for execution. PORTFOLIO is among a group of second-best policies, with a slowdown of around 1.5, but has the lowest standard deviation in the group. This favorable behavior of PORTFOLIO is not repeated for the job wait time metric. We attribute this to the selection criterion used in this work, which is based on slowdown.

We further study the charged cost, utilization, and achieved utility for the various policies, when running the ANL Intrepid trace; the results are depicted in

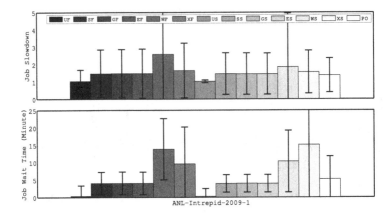

Fig. 10. Job slowdown and wait time for the ANL Intrepid Trace.

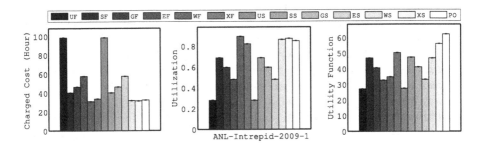

Fig. 11. Charged cost, utilization, and utility for the ANL Intrepid Trace.

Fig. 11. The charged cost of StartUp (the earlier best-performer) is about 3 times higher than the competitive policies such as ODW, ODX, and PORTFOLIO; we attribute this to the workload bursts that ANL and many other production systems exhibit [2]. PORTFOLIO achieves a good combination of utilization and slowdown, leading to overall-best achieved utility.

To conclude the experiments using real workload traces, we have shown in this section evidence that, for the compound metric that characterizes both user and data center objectives, our portfolio scheduler *can* automatically select the scheduling policy achieving better performance than its constituent scheduling policies.

5.3   Analysis of Portfolio Scheduler Operation

To explain the performance obtained in the previous experiments, we analyze the policy selection behavior of our portfolio scheduler. Figure 12 breaks-down the presence of selected policies over entire experiments as relative size (left side) and as absolute counts (right side). Two main conclusions can be made from the

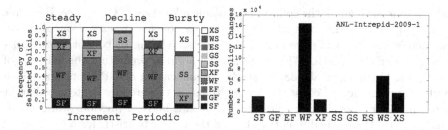

Fig. 12. Ratio and number of policy changes made by the portfolio scheduler.

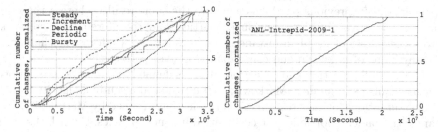

Fig. 13. Cumulative policy changes by the portfolio scheduler, normalized, over time.

figure: (1) although the portfolio scheduler does choose one policy often, several other policies account for a significant fraction of the selections; (2) no single policy is dominant for all the workloads.

We also observe the cumulative number of policy changes over time, and depict this in normalized form in Fig. 13. The policy change patterns match very well with the job arrival patterns, indicating that our portfolio scheduler is adaptive and explaining its good performance.

6   Related Work

In this section we survey a large body of related work, related to the concept of computational portfolio design [8], to the modern portfolio theory in finance [32], and to general scheduling in data centers and IaaS clouds. In contrast to these related studies, ours is the first to apply portfolio scheduling to data centers and scientific workloads. Our adaptations of the seminal idea of Huberman et al. [8] and Markowitz [32] to data centers are non-trivial: designing a portfolio around scheduling policies typical to the data center, selecting of utility functions related to both users and data center operators, and designing an operational process that includes simulation-based scheduling.

Closest to our work, Huberman et al. [8] designs a portfolio of search instruments for hard computational problems. This seminal work has led to the creation of a broad field in satisfiability and algorithm portfolio design [33]. Since then, extensive work has focused on improving the selection by and use of heuristics in the portfolio. Streeter et al. [34] consider the duration of heuristics when selected one of them, in the context of dynamic allocation of CPU time. Bougeret et al. [35] and Goldman et al. [36] study the concurrent execution of different heuristics on parallel resources. Besides scheduling of constituent heuristics, Streeter and Smith [37] simultaneously address predicting the runtime of heuristics. Gagliolo et al. [38,39] study the allocation of CPU time based on performance models of constituent algorithms, in the broader context of bandit problems. Our work differs significantly from this body of previous work: previous use of portfolio scheduling tries to find the fastest heuristic for a given set of problem instances, whereas we seek through our scheduler to find the policy that maximizes the performance objectives given by users and system administrators; the heuristics in previous portfolios generate the same result, whereas those in our portfolio have different solution properties; and the aforementioned work solves a given set of problem instances, whereas our work addresses scheduling of many kinds of unknown and continuous workload patterns.

The portfolio creation and reflection steps, as defined in our work, are important mechanisms in finance. Markowitz [32] introduced a seminal algorithm and set of assumptions for the creation of a portfolio, later refined by Merton [40]. We share with financial portfolios the costs for adding new policies, the risk that the added policy would not perform, the transition costs [41] in changing the portfolio to adapt to expected future conditions in the market or scheduling problem, and the reflection step which is typical in hedging derivatives [42]. Important differences between our work and financial portfolios are that the policies can be infinitely and freely shared among data centers, whereas financial portfolio elements are owned by a single entity at any given time; and that the return of our portfolio is the result of a single, selected policy, whereas in financial portfolios it is the combined return of all the individual assets in the portfolio.

The study of policies for data centers and IaaS clouds has already resulted in a large body of related work. Closest to our work, our own [7,15,16] and related [43–45] studies of multiple scheduling policies have emphasized the inability of any single policy to perform well under a wide yet realistic variety of scientific workloads. The concept of portfolio scheduling may also follow from historical simulation of policies. Historical simulation to adopt the scheduling policy has been done via genetic algorithms in cloud [46] and grid [47] environments. Workloads that have changing properties over time perform better with an adaptive provisioning policy [48], especially one which predicts well the future [49].

7 Conclusion and Future Work

Because data centers around face a growing user base, and an increasingly set of user and data center objectives, the selection of efficient scheduling algorithms is ever costlier and more difficult. Addressing this challenge, we have focused in this work on portfolio scheduling, that is, the dynamic selection and use of a scheduling policy, depending on the current system and workload conditions, from a portfolio of multiple policies.

We have designed in this work a periodic portfolio scheduler for the entire data center. Our portfolio scheduler combines provisioning and allocation policies, and periodically selects from them a pair that optimizes a user-defined or data center-wide utility function. The selection process is simulation-based, that is, our portfolio scheduler simulates at each decision point each of the policies included in its portfolio. Our approach contrasts with previous work on scheduling for scientific workloads, where individual scheduling policies are designed for specific workload patterns and application types but may perform poorly for the dynamic workloads typical of scientific computing. Intuitively, our portfolio scheduling approach holds the promise of exploiting the collective strengths of its constituent policies, and thus alleviate any of their individual weaknesses.

We have evaluated the behavior of our portfolio scheduler through simulations, based on real and synthetic workload traces. By comparing the statistically meaningful results obtained for our scheduler and for each of its individual policies, independently, we have shown evidence that our portfolio scheduler can perform well in the data center, and better than the alternatives we have considered. We have also shown evidence that our portfolio scheduler can automatically select the scheduling policy to match various user and data center objectives that are common in scientific computing, such as low job slowdown, high resource utilization, and a runtime-efficiency-based utility function. Thus, portfolio scheduling can alleviate the need for human expertise in selecting scheduling policies, and become an important component in the administration of modern data centers.

Extending this work, we have explored portfolio scheduling for long-term execution of scientific workloads, and conducted a comprehensive sensitivity analysis that covers all the configuration parameters of our portfolio scheduler, such as the interval between selections and the maximal simulation time [50]. For the future, we will design algorithms for performance reflection and for triggering portfolio selection dynamically. Moreover, we plan to adapt portfolio scheduling for other types of scientific applications such as scientific workflows.

Acknowledgments. Supported by the STW/NWO Veni grant 11881, the Dutch national research program COMMIT, the Commission of the European Union (Project No. 320013, FP7 REGIONS Programme, PEDCA), the National Natural Science Foundation of China (Grant No. 60903042 and 61272483), and the R&D Special Fund for Public Welfare Industry (Meteorology) GYHY201306003.

References

1. Lublin, U., Feitelson, D.G.: The workload on parallel supercomputers: modeling the characteristics of rigid jobs. J. Parallel Distrib. Comput. **63**(11), 1105–1122 (2003)
2. Iosup, A., Dumitrescu, C., Epema, D.H.J., Li, H., Wolters, L.: How are real grids used? the analysis of four grid traces and its implications. In: GRID (2006)
3. Feitelson, D.G., Rudolph, L., Schwiegelshohn, U.: Parallel job scheduling — a status report. In: Feitelson, D.G., Rudolph, L., Schwiegelshohn, U. (eds.) JSSPP 2004. LNCS, vol. 3277, pp. 1–16. Springer, Heidelberg (2005)

4. Klusáček, D., Rudová, H.: Performance and fairness for users in parallel job scheduling. In: Cirne, W., Desai, N., Frachtenberg, E., Schwiegelshohn, U. (eds.) JSSPP 2012. LNCS, vol. 7698, pp. 235–252. Springer, Heidelberg (2013)
5. Sabin, G., Lang, M., Sadayappan, P.: Moldable parallel job scheduling using job efficiency: an iterative approach. In: Frachtenberg, E., Schwiegelshohn, U. (eds.) JSSPP 2006. LNCS, vol. 4376, pp. 94–114. Springer, Heidelberg (2007)
6. Bucur, A.I.D., Epema, D.H.J.: Scheduling policies for processor coallocation in multicluster systems. IEEE Trans. Parallel Distrib. Syst. **18**(7), 958–972 (2007)
7. Iosup, A., Sonmez, O.O., Anoep, S., Epema, D.H.J.: The performance of bags-of-tasks in large-scale distributed systems. In: HPDC, pp. 97–108 (2008)
8. Huberman, B.A., Lukose, R.M., Hogg, T.: An economics approach to hard computational problems. Science **27**(5296), 51–53 (1997)
9. Greenberg, A.G., Hamilton, J.R., Maltz, D.A., Patel, P.: The cost of a cloud: research problems in data center networks. Comp. Comm. Rev. **39**(1), 68–73 (2009)
10. Popa, L., Kumar, G., Chowdhury, M., Krishnamurthy, A., Ratnasamy, S., Stoica, I.: Faircloud: sharing the network in cloud computing. In: SIGCOMM (2012)
11. Greenberg, A.G., Hamilton, J.R., Jain, N., Kandula, S., Kim, C., Lahiri, P., Maltz, D.A., Patel, P., Sengupta, S.: Vl2: a scalable and flexible data center network. Commun. ACM **54**(3), 95–104 (2011)
12. Farrington, N., Porter, G., Sun, P.C., Forencich, A., Ford, J., Fainman, Y., Papen, G., Vahdat, A.: A demonstration of ultra-low-latency data center optical circuit switching. In: SIGCOMM, pp. 95–96 (2012)
13. Gordon, A., Amit, N., Har'El, N., Ben-Yehuda, M., Landau, A., Schuster, A., Tsafrir, D.: ELI: bare-metal performance for I/O virtualization. In: ASPLOS (2012)
14. Ben-Yehuda, M., Day, M.D., Dubitzky, Z., Factor, M., Har'El, N., Gordon, A., Liguori, A., Wasserman, O., Yassour, B.A.: The turtles project: design and implementation of nested virtualization. In: OSDI, pp. 423–436 (2010)
15. Villegas, D., Antoniou, A., Sadjadi, S.M., Iosup, A.: An analysis of provisioning and allocation policies for infrastructure-as-a-service clouds. In: CCGRID, pp. 612–619 (2012)
16. Agmon Ben-Yehuda, O., Schuster, A., Sharov, A., Silberstein, M., Iosup, A.: Expert: pareto-efficient task replication on grids and a cloud. In: IPDPS (2012)
17. Iosup, A., Epema, D.H.J.: Grid computing workloads. IEEE Internet Comput. **15**(2), 19–26 (2011)
18. Iosup, A., Li, H., Jan, M., Anoep, S., Dumitrescu, C., Wolters, L., Epema, D.H.J.: The grid workloads archive. Future Gener. Comp. Syst. **24**(7), 672–686 (2008)
19. Feitelson, D.: Parallel workloads archive, http://www.cs.huji.ac.il/labs/parallel/workload/
20. Iosup, A., Sonmez, O.O., Epema, D.H.J.: DGSim: comparing grid resource management architectures through trace-based simulation. In: Luque, E., Margalef, T., Benítez, D. (eds.) Euro-Par 2008. LNCS, vol. 5168, pp. 13–25. Springer, Heidelberg (2008)
21. Petrini, F., Fossum, G., Fernández, J., Varbanescu, A.L., Kistler, M., Perrone, M.: Multicore surprises: lessons learned from optimizing sweep3d on the cell broadband engine. In: IPDPS, pp. 1–10 (2007)
22. Sonmez, O.O., Mohamed, H.H., Epema, D.H.J.: On the benefit of processor coallocation in multicluster grid systems. IEEE Trans. Parallel Distrib. Syst. **21**(6), 778–789 (2010)
23. Shen, S., Deng, K., Iosup, A., Epema, D.: Scheduling jobs in the cloud using on-demand and reserved instances. In: Wolf, F., Mohr, B., an Mey, D. (eds.) Euro-Par 2013. LNCS, vol. 8097, pp. 242–254. Springer, Heidelberg (2013)

24. Barham, P., Dragovic, B., Fraser, K., Hand, S., Harris, T.L., Ho, A., Neugebauer, R., Pratt, I., Warfield, A.: Xen and the art of virtualization. In: SOSP (2003)
25. Menon, A., Santos, J.R., Turner, Y., Janakiraman, G.J., Zwaenepoel, W.: Diagnosing performance overheads in the Xen virtual machine environment. In: VEE, pp. 13–23 (2005)
26. Youseff, L., Seymour, K., You, H., Dongarra, J., Wolski, R.: The impact of paravirtualized memory hierarchy on linear algebra computational kernels and software. In: HPDC, pp. 141–152. ACM (2008)
27. Donassolo, B., Casanova, H., Legrand, A., Velho, P.: Fast and scalable simulation of volunteer computing systems using simgrid. In: HPDC, pp. 605–612 (2010)
28. Jacobson, V.: Congestion avoidance and control. In: SIGCOMM, pp. 314–329 (1988)
29. Iosup, A., Ostermann, S., Yigitbasi, N., Prodan, R., Fahringer, T., Epema, D.H.J.: Performance analysis of cloud computing services for many-tasks scientific computing. IEEE Trans. Parallel Distrib. Syst. 22(6), 931–945 (2011)
30. Feitelson, D.G.: Experimental analysis of the root causes of performance evaluation results: a backfilling case study. IEEE Trans. Parallel Distrib. Syst. 16(2), 175–182 (2005)
31. Jones, J.P., Nitzberg, B.: Scheduling for parallel supercomputing: a historical perspective of achievable utilization. In: Feitelson, D.G., Rudolph, L. (eds.) JSSPP 1999. LNCS, vol. 1659, pp. 1–16. Springer, Heidelberg (1999)
32. Markowitz, H.: Portfolio selection. J. Finance 7(1), 77–91 (1952)
33. Gomes, C.P., Selman, B.: Algorithm portfolios. Artif. Intell. 126(1–2), 43–62 (2001)
34. Streeter, M.J., Golovin, D., Smith, S.F.: Combining multiple heuristics online. In: AAAI, pp. 1197–1203 (2007)
35. Bougeret, M., Dutot, P.F., Goldman, A., Ngoko, Y., Trystram, D.: Combining multiple heuristics on discrete resources. In: IPDPS, pp. 1–8 (2009)
36. Goldman, A., Ngoko, Y., Trystram, D.: Malleable resource sharing algorithms for cooperative resolution of problems. In: IEEE Congress on Evolutionary Computation, pp. 1–8 (2012)
37. Streeter, M.J., Smith, S.F.: New techniques for algorithm portfolio design. CoRR abs/1206.3286 (2012)
38. Gagliolo, M., Schmidhuber, J.: Learning dynamic algorithm portfolios. Ann. Math. Artif. Intell. 47(3–4), 295–328 (2006)
39. Gagliolo, M., Schmidhuber, J.: Algorithm portfolio selection as a bandit problem with unbounded losses. Ann. Math. Artif. Intell. 61(2), 49–86 (2011)
40. Merton, R.C.: Optimum consumption and portfolio rules in a continuous-time model. MIT, Cambridge (1970)
41. Magill, M.J., Constantinides, G.M.: Portfolio selection with transaction costs. J. Econ. Theory 13(2), 245–263 (1976)
42. Black, F., Scholes, M.: The pricing of options and corporate liabilities. J. Polit. Econ. 18(3), 637–654 (1973)
43. Marshall, P., Keahey, K., Freeman, T.: Elastic site: using clouds to elastically extend site resources. In: CCGRID, pp. 43–52 (2010)
44. den Bossche, R.V., Vanmechelen, K., Broeckhove, J.: Cost-optimal scheduling in hybrid iaas clouds for deadline constrained workloads. In: IEEE CLOUD, pp. 228–235 (2010)
45. Palankar, M.R., Iamnitchi, A., Ripeanu, M., Garfinkel, S.: Amazon s3 for science grids: a viable solution? In: Proceedings of the 2008 International Workshop on Data-Aware Distributed Computing, pp. 55–64. ACM (2008)

46. Hu, J., Gu, J., Sun, G., Zhao, T.: A scheduling strategy on load balancing of virtual machine resources in cloud computing environment. In: PAAP, pp. 89–96 (2010)
47. Gao, Y., Rong, H., Huang, J.Z.: Adaptive grid job scheduling with genetic algorithms. Future Gener. Comp. Syst. **21**(1), 151–161 (2005)
48. Calheiros, R.N., Ranjan, R., Buyya, R.: Virtual machine provisioning based on analytical performance and qos in cloud computing environments. In: ICPP, pp. 295–304 (2011)
49. Ali-Eldin, A., Kihl, M., Tordsson, J., Elmroth, E.: Efficient provisioning of bursty scientific workloads on the cloud using adaptive elasticity control. In: ScienceCloud, pp. 31–40 (2012)
50. Deng, K., Song, J., Ren, K., Iosup, A.: Exploring portfolio scheduling for long-term execution of scientific workloads in iaas clouds. In: SC (2013)

Variations of Conservative Backfilling
to Improve Fairness

Avinab Rajbhandary[1], David P. Bunde[1(✉)], and Vitus J. Leung[2]

[1] Knox College, Galesburg, IL, USA
{arajbhan,dbunde}@knox.edu
[2] Sandia National Laboratories, Albuquerque, NM, USA
vjleung@sandia.gov

Abstract. We apply recent variations of Conservative backfilling in an effort to improve scheduler fairness. These variations modify the compression operation while preserving the key property that jobs never move later in the profile. We assess the variations using two measures of job-level fairness. Each of the variations turns out to be better than Conservative according to one of the metrics.

1 Introduction

This paper looks at scheduling to achieve fairness. From the very beginning of job scheduling research, some notions of fairness have been sought, such as measures to prevent job starvation. Many times, however, fairness has been a secondary consideration behind various performance-oriented metrics such as utilization or response time. Concern for these metrics has led to a variety of different backfilling strategies. We turn this around and look at the use of backfilling to improve measures of fairness.

Our algorithms are variations of the well-known Conservative scheduling algorithm [10]. The specific variations, PC and DC, were developed to exploit some apparent flexibility in the compression operations that Conservative performs when a job finishes before its estimated completion time [8]. These variations perform compression by rescheduling jobs according to a user-specified priority function. By supplying first-come first-served (FCFS) as the priority function, we create two scheduling algorithms that attempt to use backfilling to favor early-arriving jobs, matching an intuitive notion of FCFS as a fair scheduling strategy.

To evaluate these algorithms, we use two previously-formulated notions of job-level fairness [15]. The first of these is that it is unfair for jobs to run out of arrival order, directly incorporating the idea of FCFS. The other notion is that each job deserves an equal share of the system resources. Each of these notions has been formalized, the first in metrics that compare job starting times with their "fair starting time" and the second as metrics that compare the resources jobs receive relative to their "fair share".

N. Desai and W. Cirne (Eds.): JSSPP 2013, LNCS 8429, pp. 177–191, 2014.
DOI: 10.1007/978-3-662-43779-7_10, © Springer-Verlag Berlin Heidelberg 2014

We evaluate the algorithms using trace-based simulations run using traces from the Parallel Workloads Archive [2]. For each job, we take its arrival time, number of processors used, actual processing time, and estimated processing time. The simulated runs are evaluated using the fairness metrics. We find that the two fairness metrics are significantly different and that each of them is favored by one of the scheduling algorithms.

The rest of this paper is organized as follows. We describe the algorithms and fairness metrics in Sects. 2 and 3. Then we describe our simulation results in Sect. 4. We discuss related work in Sect. 5 and conclude in Sect. 6.

2   Algorithms

In this paper, we examine two new scheduling algorithms, both of which are based on Conservative Backfilling [10]. Conservative maintains a profile giving a tentative schedule for all queued jobs. Each job's starting time in this profile serves as a reservation, a time by which the job is guaranteed to start. Newly arriving jobs are placed into this profile at the earliest possible time that does not interfere with any other job. When a job finishes early (i.e. in less than its estimated processing time), this profile must be adjusted. If the jobs are simply rescheduled from scratch in the order they arrived, the resulting profile may cause a job to violate its reservation; the reservation may have required backfilling which is no longer possible in the new profile. Instead, Conservative initiates *compression*, in which each queued job is removed from the profile and rescheduled to the earliest possible time that does not interfere with any other job (including those that arrived after it). Since each job can fit back into its current spot, no job is ever moved to a later time, meaning that Conservative can always give users an upper bound on the starting time of their job.

The order in which jobs are rescheduled during compression is not entirely specified. One effective choice is to use the order that jobs appear in the old profile. This order is attractive because it allows jobs to be rescheduled as they are encountered in a traversal of the profile. Using the as-currently-scheduled order also allows the new profile to be built from scratch since later jobs cannot interfere with a job's ability to reschedule to an earlier time. We use this compression order for the implementation of Conservative that we use as a baseline. The simulator whose results are reported in the original paper to use the name "Conservative" [10] also used the as-currently-scheduled order for compression [3]. Intuition suggests that this compression order tends to preserve the order of jobs in the profile. Since the profile is built as jobs arrive, the initial order has a first-come first-served (FCFS) tendency, making Conservative a logical baseline schedule with respect to fairness.

The idea of performing compression by rescheduling jobs in the order that they originally arrived to enhance fairness was actually suggested in the original paper [10]. Using this order would mean that the rescheduling operations must place jobs into the full profile rather than building a new one from scratch. It turns out that rescheduling in this order can also leave unnecessary gaps in the

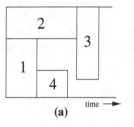
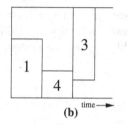
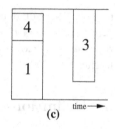

Fig. 1. Instance where compressing in order of job arrival leads to a gap in the profile. Jobs arrive in numerical order. (a) Original profile. (b) Profile after 2 finishes early and 3 is rescheduled. (c) Ending profile after 4 is rescheduled, leaving a gap.

schedule. Figure 1 shows an instance where this occurs. Part (a) shows the profile of 4 jobs which arrived in ascending numeric order; job 4 backfilled to reach the position shown. The displayed width of each job is its estimated running time. When job 2 finishes early, job 3 moves slightly earlier (shown in (b)) and then job 4 moves earlier (shown in (c)), leaving a large gap. Job 3 could move earlier, but it has already been rescheduled.

Lindsay et al. [8] addressed the problem of unnecessary gaps based on an example similar to Fig. 1, but with a different compression order. They proposed two variations of Conservative that are parameterized by a priority function specifying in which compression occurs. Prioritized Compression (PC) attempts to reschedule the jobs in the order specified by this priority function rather than the order they occur in the profile. To resolve the issue of unnecessary gaps, it returns to the highest-priority job whenever a job is successfully rescheduled, potentially rescheduling a job multiple times during a single compression operation. The second variation, conservative with Delayed prioritized Compression (DC), further modifies compression by only rescheduling jobs that can start immediately or if new lower-priority jobs arrive. The goal in delaying rescheduling operations is to allow holes opened by early job completions to grow as much as possible before backfilling. There are some priority functions that are aided by this growth. Both PC and DC preserve the property of Conservative that jobs never start later than the guaranteed start time given when they arrive.

In an effort to improve fairness, we evaluate PC and DC using the FCFS priority function, which orders jobs based on their arrival time. As noted above, Conservative already has a FCFS tendency since it prioritizes jobs in the order of the profile, which is constructed as jobs arrive. Reordering the compression operations by explicitly using the FCFS priority function potentially allows the scheduler to move the profile toward FCFS order even when jobs are initially placed out of this order.

In addition to these algorithms, we also compare our results against EASY [7], a more aggressive backfilling algorithm which will backfill a job unless doing so delays the current first job in the queue. This algorithm is used in practice to promote high system utilization and the restriction that the first job in the queue cannot be harmed by backfilling is sufficient to guarantee that no job starves forever [10], but it has been shown to discriminate against jobs requiring many processors since these jobs have difficulty backfilling (e.g. [18]). Thus, EASY represents a choice that could be used on systems not overly concerned with fairness.

3   Definitions of Fairness

To quantify fairness, we look at two types of metrics, following a classification by Sabin and Sadayappan [15]. The first of these is based on the notion that it is unfair for jobs to "cut" in line and run ahead of jobs that arrived earlier. The second is based on the notion that each job in the queue deserves an equal share of the system resources.

3.1   Fair Start Time

When people are waiting, cutting in line (aka "queue jumping") is viewed as a violation of social justice, with the seriousness dependent on how long one has waited for the resource [9]. If the goal is to avoid cutting, then the gold standard for fairness would be FCFS without backfilling, since it never starts a job before all earlier-arriving jobs. There are two issues with this characterization. The first is performance-related; scheduling without backfilling will reduce system utilization and make all users unhappy. The second is that it assumes that the jobs suffer envy rather than just wanting to minimize their own start time; one job receiving prompt service because it can jump ahead in the queue is not unfair unless other jobs are disadvantaged. Sabin and Sadayappan [15] use the analogy of service in a restaurant to explain this: Restaurant customers typically expect to be served in FCFS order, but do not normally object if someone who just ordered a drink receives it immediately because such an order is quick and does not cause a delay in anyone else's service. In parallel job scheduling, the analogous phenomenon is *benign backfilling*, where jobs arriving later can backfill without delaying the start time of other jobs. Thus, Conservative would be fair under this definition if job lengths were accurately estimated. (The issue of accurate estimates is important because an apparently benign backfill can delay other jobs if their position in the profile is based on an inaccurate estimate.)

Based on the idea that the key to unfairness is delaying a job past its "rightful" start time, Sabin and Sadayappan [15] defined a job's *strict Fair Start Time* (strict FST) as the starting time a job would get if no jobs arrived after it.

One issue with strict FST is that inaccurate estimates can create sets of strict FSTs that are not all together feasible. For example, consider the profile illustrated in Fig. 2. Figure 2(a) shows the Conservative backfilling schedule with two jobs. The shaded portion of job J_1 shows the actual duration of this job, whose length is significantly overestimated. Since job J_2 can start as soon as job J_1 completes, its fair start time is at the end of the shaded region. Now job J_3 arrives and the profile becomes as shown in Fig. 2(b). Job J_3 has backfilled since the reservation for job J_2 is based on the estimated processing time of job

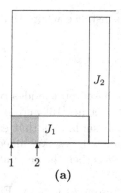 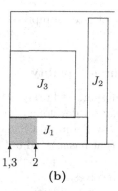

Fig. 2. Instance where strict fair start times are infeasible. Anticipated schedule (a) before and (b) after arrival of job J_3. The shaded region and the block of job J_1 shows its actual length and estimated time respectively. Labels below the figures indicate the strict fair start time of each job.

J_1 rather than its actual processing time. Starting each job at the given fair start times would require running jobs J_2 and J_3 simultaneously, however, and is therefore infeasible.

The recognition that backfilling decisions can make the strict FSTs infeasible justifies a variation. Sabin and Sadayappan [15] define the *relaxed Fair Start Time* (relaxed FST) of a job as its starting time if no jobs arrive after it, but it is not allowed to backfill. In particular, it must start no earlier than the last of the other jobs in the queue when it arrives. This yields generally larger FST values and avoids sets of infeasible fair start times.

To calculate the amount by which a specific job was unfairly treated, we consider the difference between one of the FST values and its actual starting time. To prevent algorithms from benefiting by preferentially treating jobs, we take the maximum of this difference and zero. Averaging this over all jobs gives either the *average strict unfairness* or the *average relaxed unfairness*, depending on which FST value is used. These metrics, proposed by Sabin and Sadayappan [15], are fairness analogs of average waiting time. Other metrics based on FST are discussed in Sect. 5.

As an aside, we note that the FST values require considerable effort to compute. To do so, our simulator copies the current state whenever a job arrives and runs that copy until the job starts, either normally for strict FST or after the last other queued job starts for relaxed FST. This is inconvenient for our experiments, but we note that the calculation is only required for reporting the fairness metrics. As none of the algorithms use the metric values in their operation, this step would not be required for a production scheduler.

We also noted that rarely jobs have higher strict FSTs than relaxed FSTs despite the general tendency for the relaxed FSTs to be larger. This can occur when the last job (whose strict FST is being calculated) affects compression decisions in a way that eventually gives it a later starting time; this last job can move ahead of other jobs in one compression operation and then change the outcome of later compression operations. An instance where this occurs is available in [12].

3.2 Resource Equality

The other measure of fairness that we consider is based on the idea of *resource equality*, a notion developed for serial jobs by Raz et al. [13] and extended to parallel jobs by Sabin and Sadayappan [15]. The basic idea is that each *active* job, i.e. one that has arrived but not yet been completed, deserves an equal share of system resources. A job's perception of unfairness is then the amount less than this that it receives.

There are two subtleties in dividing system resources equally. First of all, no job's fair share of the processors is allowed to exceed the number that it wants to use. For example, in a 30 processor system, if a 10-processor job and a 20-processor job are active, the smaller job is not considered to be unfairly treated for only getting 10 processors rather than the $30/2 = 15$ that would be an equal share. Secondly, fair shares are based on the number of processors in use rather than the total system size. For example, if there are 5 active jobs on a 100-processor system but only 90 processors are being used, each job's fair share is $90/5 = 18$ rather than $100/5 = 20$. This prevents fragmentation from being the cause of unfairness and helps make the scheduler goals of fairness and utilization orthogonal.

We use two ways to calculate the fair share of job J_i. Both are defined in terms of its arrival time a_i, completion time c_i, and number of processors p_i. The first one is its *unweighted fair share*:

$$\int_{a_i}^{c_i} \min\left\{ \frac{\text{util}(t)}{\text{active}(t)}, p_i \right\} dt \tag{1}$$

where $\text{util}(t)$ and $\text{active}(t)$ are the numbers of processors in use at time t and the number of active jobs at time t respectively. For the *weighted fair share*, we replace $\text{active}(t)$ by the proportion of all requested processors that are requested by job J_i:

$$\int_{a_i}^{c_i} \min\left\{ \frac{p_i}{\sum_{J_j \text{ is active}} p_j} \cdot \text{util}(t), p_i \right\} dt \tag{2}$$

This modification increases the fair share allocated to larger jobs, with the idea that they should get a larger portion of the system.

From either of the measures of a job's fair share given in Eqs. 1 and 2, we can calculate the corresponding measure of fairness by subtracting the amount of resources it actually received, which is the product of its processing time and the number of processors used. For a job's *unweighted unfairness*, we subtract the resources received from Eq. 1. Similarly, for its *weighted unfairness*, we subtract from Eq. 2. We report the average of these values over all jobs.

We note that the fairness metrics based on fair share are easier to compute than those based on FST. We compute them as a post-processing step, though it would be possible to keep a running total of each job's fair share as it ran. The only tricky part is that its rate of increase changes each time the system's utilization or set of active jobs changes. Thus, at each job arrival or completion, we increase the fair share values to reflect the contribution since the last arrival or completion event.

4 Results

We evaluated the algorithms with these fairness metrics using an event-based simulator run with traces from the Parallel Workloads Archive [2]. Figure 3 lists the traces used. We largely follow the lead of [8] in selecting traces except that we add the ANL-Intrepid trace. We also removed DAS2-fs0 and HPC2N because the fair start time calculations were taking inordinately long; this deserves closer examination, but the culprit seems to be the queue length, which causes the simulations from each job arrival to complete very slowly.

Even with these omissions, our study uses most of the traces with estimated running times. The exceptions other than the above are LLNL-uBGL (which showed almost no variation between the Conservative, PC, and DC algorithms [8]), Sandia Ross (whose entry in the archive warns about its use because the machine size was changed during the period recorded in the trace), and RICC (excluded for time reasons). Jobs in the traces without user estimates are given accurate estimates. (Simulations by Smith et al. [17] suggest that better estimates reduce average waiting time for Conservative scheduling. The effect of inaccurate estimates on EASY is the subject of many papers; Tsafrir and Feitelson [20] summarize and attempt to settle the issue.)

The trace job counts given in Fig. 3 differ from the values given in the Parallel Workloads Archive [2] because we ignored jobs that were partial executions

Name	Full file name	# jobs
ANL-Intrepid	ANL-Intrepid-2009-1.swf	68,936
CTC-SP2	CTC-SP2-1996-2.1-cln.swf	77,222
DAS2-fs1	DAS2-fs1-2003-1.swf	39,348
DAS2-fs2	DAS2-fs2-2003-1.swf	65,380
DAS2-fs3	DAS2-fs3-2003-1.swf	66,099
DAS2-fs4	DAS2-fs4-2003-1.swf	32,952
KTH-SP2	KTH-SP2-1996-2.swf	28,489
LANL-CM5	LANL-CM5-1994-3.1-cln.swf	122,057
LLNL-Atlas	LLNL-Atlas-2006-1.1-cln.swf	38,143
LLNL-Thunder	LLNL-Thunder-2007-1.1-cln.swf	118,754
LPC-EGEE	LPC-EGEE-2004-1.2-cln.swf	220,679
SDSC-BLUE	SDSC-BLUE-2000-3.1-cln.swf	223,669
SDSC-DS	SDSC-DS-2004-1.swf	85,006
SDSC-SP2	SDSC-SP2-1998-3.1-cln.swf	54,041

Fig. 3. Traces used in simulations

(they were checkpointed and swapped out; status 2, 3, or 4) and jobs that were cancelled before starting (status 5 and running time ≤ 0). We also ignored 8 jobs in the SDSC-DS trace with running time -1 (unknown).

4.1   Fair Start Time: DC

The first thing that jumped out of our results was that DC does very badly for FST-based fairness. Figure 4 shows the percent improvement of DC over Conservative for average strict and relaxed unfairness. (Calculating percent improvement as (Conservative - Other)/Conservative.) The values are nearly always negative, meaning that DC performed substantially worse than Conservative.

The delays before compression operations seem to make DC particularly prone to assigning jobs very low strict FSTs, as in Fig. 2. When this happens, the algorithm is made to seem particularly unfair since the jobs cannot meet the unrealistic fair start times. Consider the following set of jobs:

Job	Arrival time	# processors	Processing time	User estimate
J_1	0	90	100	200
J_2	1	45	100	200
J_3	2	40	95	200
J_4	3	90	100	200
J_5	4	45	100	200

Shortly after all these jobs have arrived, the profile of both Conservative and DC is as shown in Fig. 5. They also generate identical strict FSTs for the first four jobs, as shown in the figure. (We use Conservative here for concreteness, but Conservative, EASY, and PC all generate the same schedule and fair start times

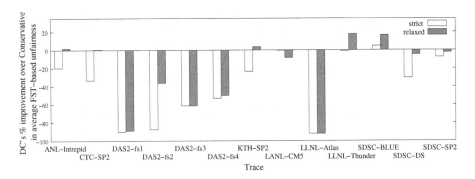

Fig. 4. Improvement in average strict and relaxed unfairness of DC over Conservative. Not shown is LPC-EGEE for which all algorithms except DC produce average unfairness of 0; DC gives unfairness ~ 0.102 for both ($-\infty$ improvement).

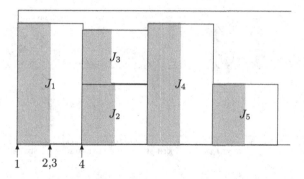

Fig. 5. Profile after all jobs arrive in instance showing DC's potential for unfairness. The shaded region and the block of each job show its actual length and estimated time respectively. Labels below the figures indicate the strict fair start time of each job.

on this instance.) The FST of job J_4 comes from starting jobs J_2 and J_3 immediately after the (early) completion of job J_1 and then starting J_4 immediately after J_2 completes. With Conservative, the FST for job J_5 is then determined by when it can run after job J_4. For DC, however, job J_4 doesn't compress when job J_1 finishes early and jobs J_2 and J_3 start. (Recall that DC only reschedules jobs if they can start immediately or to prevent newly-arrived lower-priority jobs from backfilling.) Thus, job J_5 is able to backfill as soon as job J_3 finishes; job J_4 cannot start at this time because job J_2 is still running. The result is a delay for J_4, making DC significantly unfair.

Note that if job J_5's running time were accurately estimated (and the instance is otherwise unchanged), both Conservative and DC would backfill it. In this case, both would assign identical strict FSTs and they would register as equally unfair. As previously noted, however, job lengths are typically overestimated. This is where DC's hesitation to compress comes in; it doesn't move job J_4 earlier when job J_1 finishes early, allowing it to backfill job J_5 even when its length is overestimated. This tendency to backfill was a design goal of DC, but it seems to be a liability according to the FST metrics even when the FCFS priority function is used.

Note that the example described above only directly explains why DC is so unfair when using the strict FST measure; the instance shown relies on backfilling job J_5. We have a larger example showing that DC can also assign low values to relaxed FST.

4.2   Fair Start Time: PC

PC does much better according to the FST-based fairness measures. Figure 6 shows the percent improvement of PC over Conservative for the FST-based measures. (EASY is also included for comparison.) On the strict measure, PC does as well as Conservative on the DAS2-fs3 and LPC-EGEE traces, but beats it on all the others (admittedly by only 0.16 % on LLNL-Atlas). On the relaxed

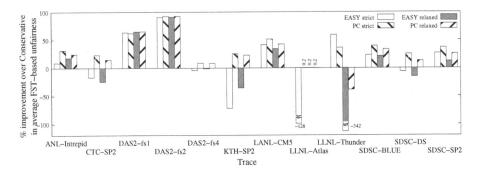

Fig. 6. Improvement in average strict and relaxed unfairness of EASY and PC over Conservative. Not shown are LPC-EGEE (all algorithms except DC produce unfairness of 0) and DAS2-fs3 for which PC gives no improvement and EASY produces "improvements" of −3,010 % and −2,784 % for strict and relaxed unfairness respectively.

measure, the performance is mostly the same: matching Conservative on DAS2-fs3 and LPC-EGEE, beating it by a small amount on LLNL-Atlas, and winning handily on most of the others. The exception is LLNL-Thunder, where it loses to Conservative by nearly 39 %. We are not sure of the cause of this poor performance, but note that this trace gave PC and DC difficulty in previous work [8] as well. LLNL-Thunder is also the trace in which the smallest fraction of the jobs have user estimates supplied in the trace (32.47 %). Since our simulator assigns accurate estimates to jobs without them, this means that only about a third of the jobs in this trace finish early, greatly reducing the opportunities PC has to use its special backfilling operation.

Although it is not targeted at fairness, Fig. 6 also reveals that EASY improves upon Conservative for many of the traces. It is less consistent than PC, however, and performs substantially worse on some of the traces. For strict fairness, PC does at least as well on all but two of the traces, DAS2-fs1 and LLNL-Thunder, and its performance on DAS2-fs1 is comparable (a 61.9 % improvement vs 63.2 % for EASY). For relaxed, PC does at least as well as EASY on all but one of the traces; the exception this time is LLNL-Atlas, on which it gives a 0.16 % improvement vs 0.22 % for EASY.

4.3   Fair Share

While PC clearly outperforms the other algorithms for the FST-based fairness metrics, the situation with fair share metrics is much less clear. Figure 7 shows the percent improvement over Conservative for the other algorithms on the unweighted and weighted measures respectively.

For unweighted fairness, DC seems to be the best algorithm, beating Conservative on all but three of the traces (DAS2-fs1, DAS2-fs3, and LLNL-Thunder) and outperforming all the other algorithms on 11 of the 14 traces. For the weighted measure, both PC and DC do fairly well, each defeating the other

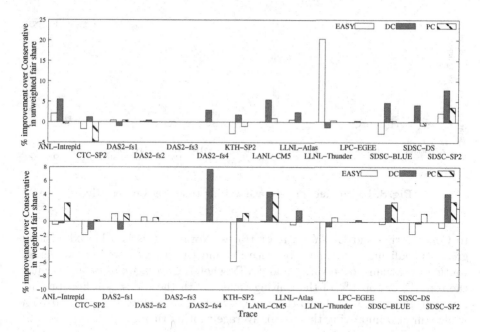

Fig. 7. Improvement in unweighted (top) and weighted (bottom) unfairness (fair share approach) over Conservative.

algorithms on 6 of the traces. With both measures, the improvements are generally by less than 5%, however. The fairness metrics based on fair share seem to be much harder to improve.

4.4 Response Time

We conclude our presentation of the results by showing that our algorithms are not achieving fairness at great cost in terms of traditional performance-oriented measures. Figure 8 shows percentage improvements over Conservative on average waiting time. DC beats Conservative on all but one of the traces (DAS2-fs3), achieving double digit improvements on five of them. PC is worse than Conservative on 9 of the traces, but always by less than 3.5% and by less than 2% on all but two of them.

5 Related Work

There are several types of previous work related to our study.

PC and DC. Lindsay et al. [8] originally proposed PC and DC to improve either overall system responsiveness or the treatment of wide jobs (i.e. those using large numbers of processors). With the shortest job first priority function, PC and DC reduced average waiting time and average bounded slowdown relative

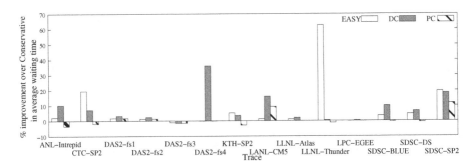

Fig. 8. Improvement in average waiting time over Conservative.

to Conservative and EASY on most traces. Notably, this is achieved without greatly penalizing particular jobs since PC and DC still achieved lower average waiting time than Conservative and EASY when the average was taken over just the top 5 % or top 1 % of the waiting times. With the widest job first priority function, PC and DC reduced the average waiting time of wide jobs by 10–35 % while still also improving the overall average waiting time.

Prioritized Backfilling. Many other scheduling schemes have been proposed that use a priority function in connection with backfilling. A typical approach is to order the jobs by priority and then backfill to improve utilization. Jackson et al. [4] describe a version of this used in the Maui scheduler that provides a reservation to the highest-priority queued job (essentially a prioritized version of EASY). Perković and Keleher [11] add elements of randomization and speculation to this approach. These approaches differ from ours because, like Conservative, PC and DC provide guaranteed starting times to all jobs from the time they are submitted.

Fair Start Time. Srinivasan et al. [18] give a precursor to FST based specifically on Conservative. They define FST as the earliest possible start time a job would have received under FCFS conservative if the scheduling strategy were suddenly changed to strict FCFS without backfill at the instant the job arrived. This version of FST has the advantage of being independent of the scheduler being considered since the FST is always computed using Conservative. The disadvantage is that it partially combines the effects of scheduler throughput and fairness; a scheduler that achieves shorter waiting times will tend to appear more fair since those waiting times also impact where each job finishes relative to its FST. This phenomenon may conflict with user perceptions since increased backfilling could result in both more "cutting" and greater fairness. Sabin and Sadayappan [15] resolved this paradox by generalizing the FST calculation to the definitions we use.

Leung et al. [6] introduce a "hybrid" FST that considers the allocation of specific processors. This is calculated using per-node estimated completion times. Under this scheme, a job's FST is the earliest time that enough nodes will be free; the estimated completion time of these nodes is then updated. The implied schedule is more restrictive than Conservative as holes cannot be used, but it is less restrictive than strict FCFS.

As mentioned above, our average unfairness metric is an analog of average waiting time since it is the difference from when the job "should" start when it does start. Other metrics can be derived from FSTs as well. Sabin et al. [14] use *fair turnaround time*, which adds job running times and is thus an analog to flow time. Sabin and Sadayappan [15] introduce *fair slowdown*, which is the ratio of this to job running time, making it an analog of slowdown or stretch.

Fair Share. The idea of the fair share metric comes out of an effort to quantify fairness in queueing systems; see Avi-Itzhak et al. [1] for a survey. Raz et al. [13] extended this to multi-server and multi-queue systems (but with serial jobs). They used the Resource Allocation Queueing Fairness Measure (RAQFM), which uses the philosophy that all the active users in system deserve an equal share of system resources. This includes the refinement that only the actively used resources should be shared, which becomes our use of only the active processors rather than the total number. Sabin and Sadayappan [15] extended this to the fair share fairness metrics we use, though they did not actually compute the unweighted measure.

Other Approaches. A variety of other scheduling mechanisms have been proposed to achieve various measures of fairness. Schwiegelshohn and Yahyapour [16] introduce a preemptive FCFS (PFCFS) algorithm where a job in the schedule may be preempted by a later arriving job. To prevent starvation, they assign each job a weight equal to its resource consumption and limit the amount of time a job can be delayed by later arriving jobs. Fairness is then measured using a new metric λ *fairness*; a scheduling strategy is λ-fair if no job can have its flow time increased more than a factor of λ by later arriving jobs.

Sabin et al. [14] advocate "dynamic reservations", in which the entire schedule is recomputed from scratch. This lessens the damage caused when later jobs backfill ahead of earlier ones (since these decisions can be revisited until the jobs actually start), but it eliminates the scheduler's ability to give jobs guaranteed starting times when they arrive. Srinivasan et al. [18] propose a scheduler that adds reservations to ameliorate unfairness without rebuilding the schedule. Their strategy does not give reservations to jobs initially, but does once their estimated slowdown (waiting time plus estimated running time over estimated running time) reaches a threshold value. Leung et al. [6] compare the effect of these strategies with several other measures designed to encourage fairness and/or prevent starvation: job runtime limits, job priorities based on the submitter's recent usage, and differential treatment for jobs of heavy users.

Rather than consider fairness on a per-job basis, Klusáček and Rudová [5] consider fairness to each user by considering a measure of the average waiting times for each user's jobs. They combine this with traditional performance-oriented metrics into a multi-objective optimization problem and apply tabu search.

Stoica et al. [19] introduced a scheduling algorithm that uses a market paradigm to achieve user-level fairness and and also provides users with some control over the relative performance of their jobs. In their system, each user has a savings account in which they receive virtual money at a constant rate. To run a job, users create an expense account for it and transfer money to the job. Each job uses its funds to buy the system resources it requires at market rates. The allocation of system resources to each user depends upon the rate at which they receive money and users can control their jobs' relative performance by adjusting the rates at which they are funded.

6   Discussion

The original idea behind PC and DC was to exploit flexibility in the compression operation of Conservative. It was previously shown that this flexibility could be utilized to improve average system response time or to improve the treatment of large jobs. In this study, we have examined whether the same ideas could be used to improve system fairness. We have shown that PC does so for the fairness metrics based on fair start times while DC seems to be better for those based on fair share. Although it would be preferable for a single algorithm to dominate by both metrics, our split result highlights that the different metrics are really measuring different notions of desired behavior. "Fairness" is a somewhat slippery concept, but our results do show that the general approach of modifying Conservative's compression operation has potential to improve it. Notably, both of the algorithms also retain the worst-case predictability of Conservative in that both are able to give arriving jobs a guaranteed start time.

Going forward, we are interested in continuing to explore the fair share metrics to understand how they can be optimized. It is also desirable to develop a modification of DC that avoids its tragic performance on FST-based metrics since it does so well otherwise (in both this study and previous work [8]).

Acknowledgments. We thank the anonymous referees for their helpful comments. A. Rajbhandary and D.P. Bunde were partially supported by contract 899808 from Sandia National Laboratories. Sandia National Laboratories is a multi-program laboratory managed and operated by Sandia Corporation, a wholly owned subsidiary of Lockheed Martin Corporation, for the U.S. Department of Energy's National Nuclear Security Administration under contract DE-AC04-94AL85000. We also thank all those who contributed traces to the Parallel Workloads Archive.

References

1. Avi-Itzhak, B., Levy, H., Raz, D.: Quantifying fairness in queuing systems: principles, approaches, and applicability. Probab. Eng. Inf. Sci. **22**(4), 495–517 (2008)
2. Feitelson, D.: The parallel workloads archive. http://www.cs.huji.ac.il/labs/parallel/workload/index.html
3. Feitelson, D.: Personal communication (2013)

4. Jackson, D.B., Snell, Q.O., Clement, M.J.: Core algorithms of the Maui scheduler. In: Feitelson, D.G., Rudolph, L. (eds.) JSSPP 2001. LNCS, vol. 2221, pp. 87–102. Springer, Heidelberg (2001)

5. Klusáček, D., Rudová, H.: Performance and fairness for users in parallel job scheduling. In: Cirne, W., Desai, N., Frachtenberg, E., Schwiegelshohn, U. (eds.) JSSPP 2012. LNCS, vol. 7698, pp. 235–252. Springer, Heidelberg (2013)

6. Leung, V.J., Sabin, G., Sadayappan, P.: Parallel job scheduling policies to improve fairness: a case study. In: Proceedings of the 6th International Workshop on Scheduling and Resource Management for Parallel and Distributed Systems (2010)

7. Lifka, D.: The ANL/IBM SP scheduling system. In: Feitelson, D.G., Rudolph, L. (eds.) IPPS-WS 1995 and JSSPP 1995. LNCS, vol. 949, pp. 295–303. Springer, Heidelberg (1995)

8. Lindsay, A.M., Galloway-Carson, M., Johnson, C.R., Bunde, D.P., Leung, V.J.: Backfilling with guarantees made as jobs arrive. Concur. Comput. Pract. Exp. **25**(4), 513–523 (2013)

9. Mann, L.: Queue culture: the waiting line as a social system. Am. J. Sociol. **75**, 340–354 (1969)

10. Mu'alem, A.W., Feitelson, D.G.: Utilization, predictability, workloads, and user runtime estimates in scheduling the IBM SP2 with backfilling. IEEE Trans. Parallel Distrib. Syst. **12**(6), 529–543 (2001)

11. Perković, D., Keleher, P.J.: Randomization, speculation, and adaptation in batch schedulers. In: Proceedings of the 2000 ACM/IEEE Conference on Supercomputing (2000)

12. Rajbhandary, A.: Fairness in scheduling algorithms. Honors thesis, Knox College (2013)

13. Raz, D., Avi-Itzhak, B., Levy, H.: Fairness considerations in multi-server and multi-queue systems. In: Proceedings of the 1st International Conference on Performance Evaluation Methodologies and Tools (2006)

14. Sabin, G., Kochhar, G., Sadayappan, G.: Job fairness in non-preeemptive job scheduling. In: Proceedings of the International Conference on Parallel Processing (ICPP) (2004)

15. Sabin, G., Sadayappan, P.: Unfairness metrics for space-sharing parallel job schedulers. In: Feitelson, D.G., Frachtenberg, E., Rudolph, L., Schwiegelshohn, U. (eds.) JSSPP 2005. LNCS, vol. 3834, pp. 238–256. Springer, Heidelberg (2005)

16. Schwiegelshohn, U., Yahyapour, R.: Fairness in parallel job scheduling. J. Sched. **3**, 297–320 (2000)

17. Smith, W., Taylor, V., Foster, I.: Using run-time predictions to estimate queue wait times and improve scheduler performance. In: Feitelson, D.G., Rudolph, L. (eds.) JSSPP 1999. LNCS, vol. 1659, pp. 202–219. Springer, Heidelberg (1999)

18. Srinivasan, S., Kettimuthu, R., Subramani, V., Sadayappan, P.: Selective reservation strategies for backfill job scheduling. In: Feitelson, D.G., Rudolph, L., Schwiegelshohn, U. (eds.) JSSPP 2002. LNCS, vol. 2537, pp. 55–71. Springer, Heidelberg (2002)

19. Stoica, I., Abdel-Wahab, H., Pothen, A.: A microeconomic scheduler for parallel computers. In: Feitelson, D.G., Rudolph, L. (eds.) IPPS-WS 1995 and JSSPP 1995. LNCS, vol. 949, pp. 200–218. Springer, Heidelberg (1995)

20. Tsafrir, D., Feitelson, D.G.: The dynamics of backfilling: solving the mystery of why increased inaccuracy may help. In: Proceedings of the IEEE International Symposium on Workload Characterization, pp. 131–141 (2006)

Author Index

Printed in the United States
By Bookmasters